LEGACIES OF THE DRUNKEN MASTER

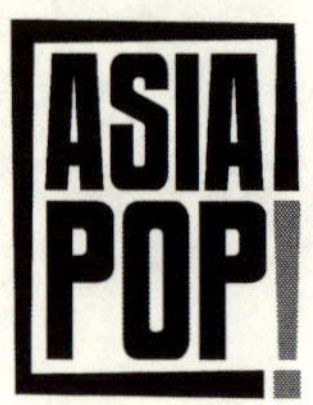

Allison Alexy
Series Editor

Animated Encounters: Transnational Movements of Chinese Animation, 1940s–1970s
Daisy Yan Du

Pop Empires: Transnational and Diasporic Flows of India and Korea
Edited by S. Heijin Lee, Monika Mehta, and Robert Ji-Song Ku

Puppets, Gods, and Brands: Theorizing the Age of Animation from Taiwan
Teri Silvio

Legacies of the Drunken Master: Politics of the Body in Hong Kong Kung Fu Comedy Films
Luke White

LEGACIES OF THE DRUNKEN MASTER

Politics of the Body in Hong Kong Kung Fu Comedy Films

Luke White

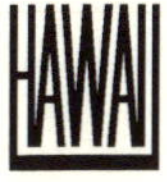

University of Hawai'i Press
Honolulu

Paperback edition 2021

Printed in the United States of America

26 25 24 23 22 21 6 5 4 3 2 1

Library of Congress Cataloging-in-Publication Data

Names: White, Luke, author.
Title: Legacies of the drunken master : politics of the body in Hong Kong kung fu comedy films / Luke White.
Other titles: Asia pop!
Description: Honolulu : University of Hawaiʻi Press, 2020. | Series: Asia pop! | Includes bibliographical references and index.
Identifiers: LCCN 2019052064 | ISBN 9780824881573 (cloth) | ISBN 9780824882983 (pdf) | ISBN 9780824882990 (epub) | ISBN 9780824883003 (kindle edition)
Subjects: LCSH: Martial arts films—China—Hong Kong—History and criticism. | Comedy films—China—Hong Kong—History and criticism. | Human body in motion pictures. | Violence in motion pictures. | Masculinity in motion pictures.
Classification: LCC PN1995.9.H3 W48 2020 | DDC 791.43/65579—dc23
LC record available at https://lccn.loc.gov/2019052064

ISBN 978-0-8248-8971-5 (pbk.)

Cover illustration by Mike O'B

University of Hawaiʻi Press books are printed on acid-free paper and meet the guidelines for permanence and durability of the Council on Library Resources.

Contents

Series editor's preface

It is my pleasure to introduce this dynamic new book in the Asia Pop! series. In *Legacies of the Drunken Master*, Luke White applies serious thought and rich theoretical analysis to an incredibly popular film genre: kung fu comedies. With few exceptions, these movies have received less scholarly attention than more "serious" films, and that gap is much more than just the difference between Bruce Lee and Jackie Chan—to name perhaps two of the most widely recognized names in kung fu cinema. *Legacies of the Drunken Master* goes far to rectify that imbalance by demonstrating the utility of such analysis as well as its value and potential. It shows how much we miss when we fail to take comedy seriously.

White's close examination of this comedic form connects careful attention to the cultural, political, and historical specifics of Hong Kong with deep theoretical engagement. Those less familiar with kung fu comedy cinema will find film theory used as an enticing introduction, pulling readers in with critical readings based in cultural studies and visual studies, but also postcolonial and feminist theory, among other disciplines. Focusing on the kung fu comedic body, White convincingly argues that this genre acts as a field of contestation saturated with politics, ripe for analysis, and full of potent messages. His evocative analysis repositions these films, and the comedy they contain, as required viewing.

Acknowledgments

I would like to thank the Faculty of Arts and Creative Industries at Middlesex University for their ongoing support of my research. I would also like to thank my many colleagues—and students—at the university for the collegiate and comradely discussions that stimulated the development of this work. In particular, the meetings of the Diasporic and Transcultural Practices research cluster (including Anne Burke, Sonia Boyce, Ergin Cavasoglu, Emma Dick, Bharain Mac an Bhreithiún, Keith Piper, and Neelam Raina) were of enormous value to me in thinking about this material. As a result of my involvement with this group, I also embarked on a collaborative project with another colleague, susan pui san lok, around questions of gender in martial arts cinema, which was instrumental for me in developing my thinking about this issue. Some of the insights I gained from this shared work certainly found their way into this book—though I suspect not with the subtlety of understanding that susan brings to the topic. I would also like to thank my other colleagues in the Fine Art department, in particular Alexandra Kokoli, Katy Deepwell, John Timberlake, and Alberto Duman, who have all offered at various points both practical advice and intellectual input.

Also important in the development of this book was the appearance of the Martial Arts Studies Research Network (MASRN, funded by the UK's Arts and Humanities Research Council) and the growth of an international community of academics interested in the serious and interdisciplinary investigation of the martial arts. It was at MASRN events that I first presented and tested out some of this material, and I am grateful for the illuminating feedback I received. The level of enthusiasm in "martial arts studies" for discussion across very different disciplinary boundaries and methodological investments is an inspiring thing to behold. Paul Bowman and Ben Judkins have been the dynamo that has made this happen, but aside from them I am also grateful in particular to ongoing exchanges about the filmic and visual cultures of the martial arts with Meaghan Morris, Kyle Barrowman, Wayne Wong, and Eric Pellerin—and others too numerous to mention. Some of the material in Chapter 1 is included in *The Martial Arts Studies Reader,* edited by Paul Bowman and published by Rowman and Littlefield.

Part of my research on the "bratty" heroes of the kung fu comedies was first presented at the World Youth Martial Arts Mastership International Academic Conference at Cheongju University in 2017, and I would like to thank Gwang Ok for my invitation to do so and to the conference's organizers for funding my trip there.

I would also like to thank the Asia Pop! series editor, Allison Alexy, and University of Hawai'i Press editor Stephanie Chun for their supportive editorial help, and the press's anonymous reviewers for their generous feedback on my manuscript. I am also grateful to Jennifer McIntyre for her close attention in copyediting the manuscript.

Beyond academia, I owe a huge debt of gratitude to the teachers and students at the Mei Quan Academy of Taiji, where my interest in the cultures of the martial arts, taken as a serious and rich practice not only of the body but also the mind, has been nurtured.

My biggest thanks, however, are reserved for my wonderful family, who have always put up with my obsessions and supported my endeavors. I very much hope that this book makes them proud.

LEGACIES OF THE DRUNKEN MASTER

INTRODUCTION

> Laughter and its forms represent, as we have said, the least scrutinized sphere of the people's creation.
>
> —*Mikhail Bakhtin*

In 1978 two films, *Snake in the Eagle's Shadow* and *Drunken Master,* both directed by Yuen Woo-ping and starring Jackie Chan, shook the Hong Kong box offices and changed the landscape of the colony's martial arts cinema. They bucked the trend—already flagging in its appeal to audiences—that had dominated the genre over the previous decade for tragic and heroic stories, offering instead a formula based on comedy. Redefining the recipe for success, they kick-started a spate of imitations, many of which were spearheaded by the extended cast and crew of the original productions, but soon also by a host of new players.

The "drunken master" comedies that ensued in the following years were usually set in an indefinite part of rural southern China, at some time vaguely around the transition between the end of the Qing Dynasty and the start of the Chinese Republic, at the start of the twentieth century. The righteous and invincible heroes of previous kung fu films were replaced by bratty, impish, and anarchic young protagonists. These were often paired up with elderly, disreputable, vagabond masters to fight truly evil villains. The world they inhabited—rather like the hyper-capitalist Hong Kong of the 1970s and 1980s in which they were produced—often seems a dog-eat-dog, materialistic, and amoral one, but these films were primarily lighthearted, even cynical in tone, in stark contrast, again, to the often-somber martial arts cinema that preceded it. Their comedy was decidedly "lowbrow," often revolving around basic bodily functions. When it came to action, they mixed kung fu with slapstick clowning, Beijing opera acrobatics, and a fantastically ingenious manipulation of props.

Frequently, an extended sequence depicting physically grueling kung fu training would stand at the core of the film's narrative as the protagonists turned themselves from lazy and cynical "brats," lacking all "humility and respect,"[1] into skilled and heroic fighters capable of exacting revenge and defeating evil.

This, along with the master–student relationship that was so often foregrounded, placed the learning of kung fu—conceived in particular, I shall be arguing in this book, as a problem of "legacy"—at the thematic center of the films.

By the early 1980s, the genre had started to mutate and to produce new forms of kung fu comedy. Often created by the same stars and crew who had made their names in the original "drunken master" comedies, these films often drew on, varied, and reworked the formula of their earlier successes, hybridizing it with other genres and tracking the changing tastes and sensibilities of the times. In 1983 Jackie Chan's *Project A* cast him not as a rebellious youth but rather as a dutiful, if rather hapless, policeman, and it would be in such comic kung-fu-cop roles that Chan's career would be primarily defined in the following decades. Some of these films, like *Project A*, were set in the past; most, like the Police Story series, which started in 1985 and lasted throughout the 1990s, were set in the present and increasingly revolved around spectacular chases and stunts, rather than more straightforward martial artistry.

As we shall see later in the book, alongside its hybridization with the crime genre, the kung fu comedy was also mixed with the supernatural and magical in the fantastical Miracle Fighters films that Yuen Woo-ping (director of *Drunken Master*) and his brothers went on to make between 1982 and 1984, and this was extended in the kung-fu-comedy-horror genre pioneered by Sammo Hung's *Encounter of the Spooky Kind* (1980) or the Mr. Vampire franchise that ran between 1985 and 1992, which in their turn created an explosion of "hopping corpse" (*geongsi*) movies. Kung fu comedy was also spliced into contemporary "caper" or spy films, such as in the Aces Go Places series (which ran from 1982–1989), or the ensemble Lucky Stars films (1983–1996), in which kung fu comedians were cast alongside veteran comic actors such as Eric Tsang and Richard Ng.

By the 1990s, the "classic" era of the kung fu comedy in Hong Kong cinema was over, as martial arts filmmaking focused increasingly on wirework-enhanced swordplay films rather than the kung fu styles of the 1970s and 1980s. Nonetheless, comedy—often drawing on the motifs, thematics, and devices of the earlier films—remained a key ingredient of the overwrought film style of these swordplays.[2] Stephen Chow, to take just one prominent example from the time—not himself a kung fu acrobat like the stars of the generation before him, but a comedian with an obsession with the history of Hong Kong's martial arts cinema—updated the combination of kung fu and comedy to suit not only his own absurdist performance style, but also the new swordplay aesthetic. Jackie Chan—still a megastar across Asia and a constant presence at the top of the Hong Kong box-office charts—revisited his *Drunken Master* persona with a sequel in 1994 that also reworked familiar characters and motifs from the original within the film conventions of the time. The following year, Chan would eventually get his big break in America in *Rumble in the Bronx* (dir. Stanley Tong, 1995), internationalizing his comic kung fu cop persona and laying the ground for his Hollywood success in *Rush Hour* (dir. Brett Ratner, 1998) and a host of other films since.

Overall, the kung fu comedy, as pioneered in *Drunken Master* and *Snake in the Eagle's Shadow,* took sheer physical performance to new acrobatic and inventive heights, with extended scenes of combat that brought fight choreography squarely into the realm of the marvelous. Such scenes were interleaved—at a breathless pace that often left little room for redundant plotting—with bravura performances of slapstick clowning, sight gags, banter, and Cantonese wordplay. The "drunken master" comedy also brought to the fore a new array of colorful stars, including the rotund but rubbery Sammo Hung Kam-bo (nicknamed "the Fat Dragon"), the unfeasibly agile Yuen Biao ("Little Tiger"), the hyperkinetic Leung Kar-yan ("Beardy"), or the impish "Mad Monkey" Hsiao Ho. Phenomenal martial artists such as the Korean superkickers Hwang Jang-lee and Hwang In-sik provided fearsome and iconic villains against whom the genre's heroes were pitted, and character actors such as the ever-present Dean Shek, with his grotesque face-pulling, offered light comic relief in contrast to melodramatic plot developments.

Should We Be Serious about the Kung Fu Comedy?

All this would seem to point us toward not only a historically significant phenomenon, but also a rich cinema that potentially offers its audience no small amount of pleasure, and the significance of the kung fu comedy is only amplified when we remember that the genre's lovable everyman and global megastar, Jackie Chan, for many years regularly topped box offices not only in Hong Kong but across Asia before making the jump in the 1990s to a level of Hollywood superstardom not even achieved by Bruce Lee.[3] By the time of *Forbes*' 2015 rich list, Chan had become the second highest-paid actor in the world, signaling, perhaps, not only the rising Chinese market for cinema at the start of the twenty-first century, but also the role martial arts comedy has taken in bridging Eastern and Western film cultures, presaging a global market within which films can be made. In 2016, furthermore, Chan became the first Chinese actor to receive an Academy Award when he received an Oscar for lifetime achievement.

Chan's global impact is mirrored by that of the director and choreographer of his breakthrough films, Yuen Woo-ping. Rising to prominence and developing his visual style within the kung fu comedy genre, Yuen would go on to choreograph action in a number of Hollywood films as well as productions from greater China, with his credits including, for example, *Crouching Tiger Hidden Dragon* (dir. Ang Lee, 2000), *The Matrix* and its sequels (dir. Wachowski Bros., 1999–2003), *Kill Bill I & II* (dir. Quentin Tarantino, 2003–2004), *Cradle 2 the Grave* (dir. Andrzej Bartkowiak, 2003), and *The Grandmaster* (dir. Wong Kar-wai, 2013). Both Chan and Yuen have also more recently been involved with Indian cinemas, with Yuen choreographing the Tamil language *I* (dir. Shankar, 2014) and Chan starring alongside Aamir Khan, Amyra Dastur, and Sonu Sood in the Sino-Indian production *Kung Fu Yoga* (dir. Stanley Tong, 2017).

Chan and Yuen were in fact among the first Hong Kong talents to be taken up in Hollywood in the 1990s. The success of *Rumble in the Bronx* in the US market not only paved the way for Chan's own American-produced films such as *Rush Hour* and *Shanghai Noon* (dir. Tom Dey, 2000) but also arguably proved a resurgent audience demand for images of Chinese martial arts, paving the way for the release in the West of (more "serious" and "artistic") swordplay movies such as *Crouching Tiger* or *Hero* (dir. Zhang Yimou, 2002). Chan's success as a martial arts comedian has, of course, also been echoed in the global popularity of Stephen Chow's martial-arts-themed comedies *Shaolin Soccer* (2001) and *Kung Fu Hustle* (2004), suggesting an enduring appeal of the genre beyond Chan's own persona.

Emerging in Hong Kong in the 1970s and 1980s, then, the kung fu comedy, in addition to being a rich and dynamic genre, has not only enjoyed the kind of success on the local Hong Kong market that would in itself seem to mark it as a legitimate—even important—object for study, but was also significant in the growing acceptance of Hong Kong cinema in the West and as a global rather than a local or regional phenomenon. All this might be considered a part of the significance—both aesthetic and historical—of a cinematic "legacy" of the drunken master films.

Nonetheless, as Mikhail Bakhtin has noted, it has often been the fate of comic genres to remain underexamined and undervalued—especially by the intellectual elites who write cultural history. After all, comedy simply isn't *serious*, is it? The kung fu comedy genre, certainly, remains critically ignored and often denigrated, especially with relative regard to the more "serious," "heroic," "epic," or "tragic" Hong Kong kung fu and swordplay films that preceded its emergence.

A first indication of this is that up to now, no book-length academic exploration of kung fu comedy in the English language has been published. Something similar is evident if we take a comparison of the status of particular star performers within Anglophone publications. Aside from an avalanche of how-to books, biographies, quotation compilations, and fan-oriented literature, Bruce Lee's ("serious") films have inspired full-length scholarly monographs such as Paul Bowman's *Theorizing Bruce Lee* and *Beyond Bruce Lee;* M. T. Kato's *From Kung Fu to Hip Hop,* which in spite of its fairly broad title is organized almost exclusively around analyses of Bruce Lee films; and Charles Russo's *Striking Distance,* which examines Lee's impact on the development of American martial arts.[4] Jackie Chan—though his films are far more numerous, and ultimately his stardom, at least in box-office terms, has outstripped Lee's by orders of magnitude—has provoked no equivalent academic publications.[5]

This book, then, seeks to redress the critical neglect of the kung fu comedy, offering a detailed exploration of its aesthetic properties and pleasures, contextualizing it and making sense of its social and political significance. My fundamental gambit is to take the kung fu comedy seriously.

Popular Culture and the Neglect of the Kung Fu Comedy

A first task in doing so, however, is to establish, trace, and further understand the reasons for the genre's critical neglect. Understanding what it is that makes the kung fu comedy sit at the blind spot of the histories of Hong Kong martial arts cinema is, after all, central in opening up "other" approaches to it that may begin to illuminate it further as an object of study. Bakhtin's comment about the wider neglect of laughter by cultural historians, with which this introduction started, already signals a fundamental reason for this: it may well be the very nature of laughter as "people's creation"—as a low rather than a high pleasure, and as associated with dangerous plebeian energies—that brands it historically as an illegitimate object of study.[6]

The irony of this with regards to the kung fu comedy is that the same neglect and critical denigration of the "popular" has motivated a longer-term suspicion of the wider phenomenon of Hong Kong and Chinese martial arts cinema, from its very beginnings—a suspicion from which the "serious" martial arts film has now largely disentangled itself, even if the comedy has not.

As Stephen Teo has described in his history of Chinese martial arts film genres, even with the rise of the first swordplay films in the era of Shanghai's silent screen in the 1920s, Chinese intellectuals, though to some degree excited about the links between martial arts and a strong nationalist spirit, bemoaned the folkish superstition inherent in the spectacle of magical effects and superhuman powers, and the emotional excitement with which a popular audience enjoyed it.[7] All this smacked far too much of the disastrous Boxer Rebellion of 1899–1900, in which an army of peasant rebels, under the sway of a mystical martial arts sect that promised them physical invulnerability in battle, had sought to eject the Western powers from Chinese soil and reverse the semicolonial status to which China had sunk. Easily overcome by Western firearms, the "Boxers" were still remembered vividly in the coming decades by intellectual elites concerned with national strengthening as a humiliating emblem of China's weakness, backwardness, and inability to compete in the "modern" world of international politics, war, and trade.[8] Worried about martial arts cinema's potential to encourage violence, superstition, and political subversion, the Republican government went as far as banning it from Chinese screens from 1931 onwards.

When the "kung fu craze" hit Western screens in 1973, with the release of films such as *King Boxer / Five Fingers of Death* (dir. Jeong Chang-hwa, 1972) and the arrival of Bruce Lee, American critics were hardly more sanguine. *Variety* magazine, reporting on the arrival of such films within its charts, discussed them in epidemiological language as a "rash of Kung Fu–karate imports." Lacking redeeming features, the success of such films was put down to the fact that "sheer violence remains as potent at the b.o. [box office] as . . . sheer sex."[9] Critics—even academics—associated such violence primarily with the delinquency of youth from the lower classes. Stuart Kaminsky, in one of the earliest Anglophone essays to seriously examine the kung fu genre, reads it as addressed to the "ghetto viewer" and as establishing a "mythic relationship" to their (putative) system of values. Kung fu films for him are lacking in redemptive morality, progressive values, or a concern with society beyond the individual, and they remain lodged in the depiction of "dirty, graceful fighting" through which the "ghetto kid" can imagine himself (*sic*) compelling "respect" from others.[10] Aside from its stereotyped portrayal of young men from the underclass, Kaminsky's evocation of the specter of the "ghetto viewer," to contemporary eyes, strays at the very least close to racism, making the common association of the genre with African American culture, and even going as far as commenting that "the number of black youths who practice pseudo-Kung Fu is strikingly evident on urban streetcorners."[11]

Such assumptions about the nature of the American audience in terms of race, class, and gender would seem to extend not only to critics but also to the distributors themselves, who, as David Desser has documented, often pitched their releases in particular to theaters in black inner-city areas and in the rural South and double-billed them alongside "Blaxploitation" films, advertising them in the same sensationalist manner established more generally for "exploitation" genres.[12] Thus, for example, the robust, tough, and always modestly dressed Angela Mao Ying was marketed as a "Deadly China Doll," and her film *Tiezhang xuanfengtui* (dir. Wong Fung, 1972)—literally "Iron Palm,

Whirlwind Kick"—was released in the States under the rather sexualized title *Deep Thrust,* a name that carried with it a pun on the title of the film *Deep Throat* (dir. Jerry Gerard, 1972), which had become infamous the previous year when it stirred controversy by taking pornography into the mainstream. Posters for it, furthermore, promised, in a suggestive language of double-entendres, "the deadly stroke of bare-handed combat" and urged audiences to "SEE . . . The naked finger vs. the knife! The naked fist vs. the club! The naked hand vs. the sword!" They depicted, in a hand-illustrated image, a Chinese woman—presumably it is supposed to be Mao—launching a bare-legged kick in a revealing outfit that is a far stretch from the demure apparel she wears throughout the film.

The kung fu film then, within a public discourse dominated by the middle classes, fell foul of a larger suspicion of popular culture in its very relation to the proletarian and subproletarian other—an other that has long been stigmatized by elite discourse as related to the body and its dangerous, disruptive, irrational, and potentially antisocial forces or desires (for sex and violence among other things). Such a popular body is conceived—certainly within a Western metaphysics going back to Plato and Aristotle—in opposition to the "mind," with which the ruling class associates itself.

Critical Redemptions

For the more "heroic" kung fu genres—as typified, perhaps, by Bruce Lee in films such as *Fist of Fury* (dir. Lo Wei, 1972)—this stigma of the popular has slowly fallen away. The kung fu craze itself coincided closely with the establishment of disciplines such as cultural studies and film studies in universities, which challenged older cultural hierarchies and valorized popular culture by treating it as meaningful and even as politically significant. The arrival of kung fu films in the West, in fact, may well be understood as a part of the wider countercultural wave to which cultural studies belonged. This global wave of social unrest had challenged traditional racial, gender, colonial, and class privileges during the 1960s and 1970s, and had opened culture up to a new and international pluralism, as well as to a rebelliousness that certainly some later critics would associate with the kung fu film itself.[13]

Cultural studies approached popular culture from a New Left perspective and, drawing on the ideas of Gramscian Marxism and psychoanalysis, it rejected older ideas of mass culture as an ideology beamed into the heads of the poor by the rich, seeking instead to find in it a complex "compromise formation" between the interests of the elite who owned the means of cultural mass production and the counterposed interests of the "subordinated" groups who consumed it.

For cultural studies, these consumers, though they are denied access to the means of production and so are condemned to create their culture from the products made available for them, nonetheless through the very act of consumption retain the power to choose to buy or not to buy. Popular culture must therefore address their desires and experiences. In a free market of cultural products, not to address these experiences and desires would be to lose out to one's competitors who did, so some degree of "relevance" to the audience is ensured in the very structure of the commodity form of culture.[14] After all, the cultural artifact, in Marx's terms, has to instantiate both an exchange-value for the capitalist to create profit and a use-value for the consumer, who requires it to mean something in some way to them. Cultural studies thus sought to disentangle the ideological force of popular culture, inasmuch as it imposed the conservative worldview of the dominant class who produced it, from the purportedly emancipatory urges, desires, and needs of its mass of consumers that were coexistent in it. At times, cultural studies took the expression of such desires all too directly as necessarily radical or progressive, perhaps reading desire as a much more rational thing than it is.[15] Nonetheless, this understanding of popular culture as crisscrossed with both emancipatory and conservative forces, and as a battleground through which a culture's values and vision of the world are constituted, has provided a lasting impetus in the recognition of popular culture as meaningful and worthy of study—an intellectual project with which this book would align itself strongly.

It is thus to a large degree with the influence of cultural studies that kung fu cinema has increasingly been valorized, and it is unsurprising that attempts to read it as significant have often revolved around the key coordinates and themes of cultural studies. Kung fu cinema has been investigated in terms of its expression of national and ethnic identity, the reclamation of pride in "Chinese masculinity" (or its destabilization of such a category), or of colonial and postcolonial experience—complex as some of these issues are in Hong Kong.[16] This is to say, it has been understood to be valuable to a large degree because it can be interpreted as significant with regards to social issues and especially inasmuch as it can be understood to express a resistant "political" content with regard to them. For Stephen Teo, for example, Bruce Lee is important inasmuch as he expresses an "abstract nationalism" felt by Chinese people in diaspora with regard to an absent homeland, but one drawn apart from its political instantiations in the regimes of the People's Republic of China (PRC) in the Communist mainland, the nationalist Guomindang (GMD) in Taiwan, or the British colonial management of Hong Kong itself.[17] For M. T. Kato, Lee's films exemplify the countercultural revolt against globalization in popular culture, while Vijay Prashad recounts how his films resonated with the Indian Maoist and anticolonial struggles of the early

1970s, and with a wider experience of the transcultural struggle of oppressed minority and Third World groups.[18] Frances Gateward similarly explores—in a reversal of Kaminsky's negative judgments on this—the investments of African American audiences in kung fu cinema, which offered liberating images of a world and history just for once not organized around white people, and which even articulated alternative moral frameworks.[19]

Within this project of critical reclamation there have certainly been some interesting attempts to discuss kung fu comedies, which I shall be drawing on as the book continues, and I am far from claiming complete novelty as an academic recognizing their merit.[20] As my observations on the comparative body of literature on Bruce Lee and Jackie Chan suggest, however, kung fu comedies have nonetheless been relatively marginalized within the project of revalorization, and there may be a number of reasons for this. Most centrally, I would argue, this entails a continuing prejudice against the popular, and against the body, with which it is associated. The comedy film, after all, is at the opposite end of a high-to-low cultural spectrum from martial-art-house movies such as the swordplay films of Ang Lee, Wong Kar-wai, and Zhang Yimou, mentioned above, or, even more recently, Hou Hsiao-Hsien's *The Assassin,* which won the Best Director award in Cannes in 2015. In this simple regard, it may be one of the hardest genres to reclaim.

In his study of Hong Kong cinema, David Bordwell, for example, has little to say about kung fu comedy itself. He tends to conflate it into the more general category of the kung fu film and to express an aesthetic preference for high-art swordplay films such as King Hu's *Touch of Zen* (1971), which he discusses at length. However, with his astute eye for film form and phenomenological detail, he does have a lot to say about the popular in Hong Kong cinema more generally, contrasting it to Hollywood's more staid and bourgeois productions, and his comments are useful for understanding how the kung fu comedy may end up marginalized through the very categories and procedures through which film is hegemonically interpreted.[21] Bordwell notes the tendency of popular cinema and literature in general to stray from (bourgeois) forms of narrative unity and character development around which film criticism (in spite of many critical revisions over recent years) still tends to be fundamentally organized. Popular cinema inclines instead to episodic construction and to "set pieces" in which sensory immediacy, performance, and sheer spectacle are foregrounded. It often aims to stimulate as many emotions as possible. It is frequently "vulgar," prefers strong effects to subtlety, and foregrounds the body—especially the lower body functions and what Bordwell terms the "base constants of human life."[22] In terms of a Western metaphysics, while "high" art addresses the critical, rational, and intellectual subject, "popular culture" is sunk into the bodies of its audiences. All this the kung fu comedy does in spades, causing it to clash fundamentally with the ground-in aesthetic preferences of critics from the educated classes, as well as with any critical tools of analysis and approbation that remain tied to these. In a film-historical project such as Bordwell's where "film form" is paramount, the kung fu comedy's folk-materialist disregard for the idealism of good form perhaps makes it one of the hardest genres to absorb, in spite of Bordwell's interest in thinking form more openly in order to valorize popular cinemas. Though I am perhaps leaping ahead of myself to say so here, intellectual culture's denigration of laughter itself more generally, certainly in the way that Bakhtin understood the issue, may well be connected to its link to such a materialist, rather than an idealist or formalist worldview, and to its address to the pleasures of the body rather than the mind.

The Social Context of the Rise of the Kung Fu Comedy

However, I would not like to reduce the marginalization of kung fu comedy films by critics with a broader interest in discovering martial arts cinema as carrying radical or progressive material to such a single cause. Humor may well be somewhat culturally specific, and it is not only "elite" audiences in the West who have found the comic elements of the kung fu comedy difficult to enjoy. Meaghan Morris has, for example, noted the prevalence of dissatisfaction with "annoying comedy" or "unfunny hijinks" in internet fan literature, too.[23] This may to an extent simply evidence the untranslatability of comedy—physical as well as verbal. It may of course also evidence the extent to which in the West a "high" version of taste has permeated cultural consumption, creating a "popular" audience who nonetheless rely on the terms of elite discourse for their judgments, creating a "sense of aesthetic propriety [that] no longer tolerates even the melodramatic and vaudevillian traditions of Western popular theatre."[24] It might also—even more significantly—relate to the Orientalist investments of Western audiences, for whom the Asian martial arts are fantasied as vehicles of transcendent Eastern wisdom rather than toilet humor.

A further reason, however, for the critical marginalization of the kung fu comedy, is that it is simply much harder to read across from them to other "radical" currents in their social and political context than it was for other martial arts subgenres. In the late 1960s and early 1970s, during which Hong Kong's heroic martial arts cinema grew to new prominence with first a wave of bloody "new swordplay" films and then the arrival of the kung fu genre, the world was caught in a moment of global tumult, and Hong Kong was hardly an exception.

The Cultural Revolution was happening just over the border in mainland China, and large-scale rioting—and even left-wing terrorist bombing campaigns—occurred in the colony itself in 1966 and 1967.[25] Hong Kong was a deeply unequal society, and though it had a small elite of fabulously wealthy businessmen, a significant proportion of the population lived in shantytown slums, on or below the poverty line. It was still ruled by colonial decree and without democratic representation. Systemic institutional racism marked the native Chinese population as inferior. Little was offered in the way of social welfare, public housing, or even labor-protection legislation. Many people worked long hours for low pay, with little or no job security.[26]

By the late 1970s, when the kung fu comedy made its mark, much of this was changing. Economically, Hong Kong remained a deeply divided society, with poverty still pervasive. However, shocked by the anticolonial and procommunist riots of the 1960s, the British authorities had put in place expanded schemes of housing and welfare, in an attempt to ensure that citizens had a stake in the colony's social contract. They also enacted stringent measures against leftist groups, all but annihilating any organized opposition and instituting a strict regime of political censorship.[27] The excesses of the Cultural Revolution across the border had in any case delegitimated political dissent, which was marked with the taint of the worst aspects of the Maoism from which many inhabitants of the colonial enclave, or their parents, had fled in the first place. The choice for many would not have seemed to be between colonialism and liberty, but rather between London and Beijing. This ushered in a period of political conformism, in which not rocking the boat seemed a priority in public discourse. Ackbar Abbas has understood the developing culture of Hong Kong in this time as characterized by the "disappearance" of politics, which became substituted instead by an excess of interest in material accumulation and conspicuous consumption. As he puts it, this was a mentality in which, "if you cannot choose your own political leaders, you can at least choose your own clothes."[28]

As the 1970s progressed, Hong Kong, furthermore, became very much the poster boy for the globalized neoliberalism that was emerging at the other end of the unrest of the 1960s. As the economist and right-wing ideologue Milton Friedman put it, "If you want to see capitalism at work, go to Hong Kong."[29] The colony's lack of democratic representation meant that "free market" reforms could be implemented and businesses run with little regulation or taxation, enjoying the benefits of a cheap workforce with few labor rights. As it grew to become an "Asian Tiger" economy, the enclave became both a center of banking and manufacture, in an era in which "made in Hong Kong" became a familiar mark on plastic and electronic goods across the world.

Film as Reflection or Dialogue?

Certainly to the extent that the readings of kung fu comedies have relied on understanding them as "reflections" of social and political realities, then, they have found it hard to discover in them the same "radical" power as the earlier Hong Kong martial arts genres, and while the violence and rebelliousness of the heroic films of the late 1960s and early 1970s can be seen as echoing the unrest of the moment (and often, from what their directors have said, deliberately so)[30] or playing to the resentments of their audiences both at home and abroad, these kinds of readings are much harder to make with the kung fu comedy.

We find such attitudes in some of the earliest discussions of the kung fu comedy genre, in for example the essays of Chan Ting-ching and Ng Ho in two collections published by the Hong Kong International Film Festival in the early 1980s on the history of martial arts cinema.[31] Chan reads the kung fu comedy as a "reflection of a modern competitive society in which only the fittest survive and the younger are generally fitter."[32] Similarly, for Ng the "emphasis on individual achievement and an outdoing of one's own master parallels the ethos of capitalism."[33] In an article from the late 1990s, Lau Tai-muk has made similar judgments, arguing that Jackie Chan's "slick and playful" performances express and endorse "the 'virtues' of 'adaptability' and 'using the brain' in capitalist societies."[34] Drawing on such readings of comedy kung fu as "embracing Hong Kong's hypercapitalist ethos," Leon Hunt suggests that the genre emerges from the collective culture and the values of stuntmen working in a deregulated, highly competitive, individualistic (and ultramacho) industry, who came to the fore as its auteurs and stars.[35] Man-Fung Yip, even more recently, has argued that the "lighter, more playful" tone of the kung fu comedy "paralleled" Hong Kong's recovery after the 1973 economic crisis.[36] For writers such as Chan, Ng, Lau, Hunt, and Yip, the upbeat character of the kung fu comedy thus marks a retreat from the stormy idealism and sociopolitical engagement of the heroic kung fu film and an accommodation with the new globalized, neoliberal order and its values. Similarly, when Yuan Shu compares and contrasts the impact of the star personas of Bruce Lee and Jackie Chan in the Asian American context, he reads Chan as reversing Lee's threateningly militant pose to offer a vision of multiculturalism that "has nothing to do with racial politics or cultural diversity but points to the fact that Kung Fu cinema now aims to accommodate the tastes and needs of the middle class on a global scale for profits and entertainment."[37]

Though these narratives of "authentic" nationalist rebellion lapsing into inauthentic and accommodated commodification may mirror the global-historical transformations of the 1970s, they also follow, in their trajectory from truth to simulacra, the familiar narrative format that Rey Chow has traced around the figure she calls the "protestant ethnic"—a notion I will return to at a number of places in this book.[38] Punning on Weber's famous book title to rethink its themes for the postcolonial era, Chow highlights the ways that the "ethnic" individual is defined through "protest" and through the confessional act of speaking one's difference that this entails. (Chow also plays on Descartes: "I protest therefore I am.")[39] Within the global-capitalist-postcolonial cultural system it is through such protestations that ethnic others achieve visibility and claim "authenticity." However, Chow also highlights the ways this serves to discipline the ethnic, who is always, in any case, found wanting in terms of a lost "authenticity" and "purity"—they can never protest their ethnicity enough.[40] Such a quest for authenticity also turns out—just as with Lee in his guise as the archetypal rebel with an ethnonationalist cause—to involve the ethnic subject within the processes of the commodification and spectacularization of identity. In this regard the contemporary, postcolonial "protestant ethnic"—just like Luther's gesture of defiance in Weber's book—ends up as a prop for the "spirit of capitalism." Chow's incisive analysis raises questions about the kinds of valorization of Bruce Lee and the "heroic" mode of the kung fu film we have just described, and the negative judgments that they entail with regard to the later comedic films.[41] It suggests that an account is needed that moves beyond such a framework and that understands the negotiations of identity and politics involved in postcolonial culture outside demands for purity, authenticity, or "protest." A move beyond the eth(n)ics of protest may thus offer a far more productive framework for the revaluation of the kung fu comedy.

Such accounts as Chan, Ng, Lau, and Hunt offer also often come close to reading film as a passive reflection of its social context, and the danger is that it thus forgets the agency of film and its involvement in what Bordwell terms an "open-ended dialogue with its culture."[42] The question I would like to address in this book, then, is how the Hong Kong kung fu comedy film responds or reacts to its moment in time. Drawing on the insights of cultural studies into popular culture, and approaching the films from a fundamentally left-wing perspective, I am interested in investigating the extent to which, alongside forces within them that seem to reinforce the dominant ideologies of the moment in which they were made, they might also harbor moments of rebellion or resistance—if, perhaps, not of downright "protest" or revolution.

Such an investigation will need to offer different kinds of reading to those often proffered of the heroic kung fu film. Such readings frequently rely on the existence of a "militant" context and explore the ways in which films become political through their engagement with such social movements. The striking and interesting thing about the kung fu comedy, however, is the relative lack of such activist groups or discourses within its context, both within the famously hyperconformist and depoliticized context of the Hong Kong public discourse of the time of their production, but also in terms of wider global audiences at a moment when the utopian ferment of the 1960s had given way to the "postmodern" resignation of the 1970s and 1980s, and to the swing to the conservative right exemplified by the rise of politicians such as Margaret Thatcher and Ronald Reagan.

In this regard, kung fu comedies offer us a case that may be indicative for understanding our own position within still-neoliberal societies. While we are often used to thinking of change as starting in a Western "center" and moving toward a "Third World" periphery, it is striking that in many respects the transformations of the 1960s and 1970s seem to have run the other way, with Hong Kong, as well as many other supposedly "marginal" places, functioning as a laboratory for testing conditions that have been since been rolled out across the planet: media saturation, intensive consumerism, deregulation of finance capital, a "thin" welfare state, "flexible," unprotected, precarious working conditions, and an ever-widening gap between the rich and the poor . . . In many respects, Hong Kong in the 1970s served as a vanguard of the world we now all live in, and the study of the fate of "politics" within its popular culture can thus be instructive in thinking about the possibilities of our own. If Hong Kong culture in the late 1970s seemed to lack a strong activist context, today's society, globally, seems also to be marked with increasing ideological conformity and a lack of viable social movements presenting an alternative to the status quo. The Hong Kong kung fu comedy film offers us a place to examine whether and how the rebellion and resistance I alluded to above might continue without such a contextualizing movement, at a moment not of political strength and optimism, but of weakness and disillusion.

The Kung Fu Comedic Body

Central within my attempt to identify an ongoing "politics" within the kung fu comedy is a concern with the body. In my discussions of the denigration of the popular above, I have already noted the persistent association of the body with the poor, and the prominence that Bordwell has noted of the low and corporeal within popular cinemas across the world, Hong Kong movies being a case in point.

The broader martial arts genres extend this focus on the body and its powers of performance to an extraordinary degree; and in fact, as a number of commentators have noted, our "kinesthetic" response to action cinema—functioning through a body-to-body recognition or identification between audiences and the stars on the screen—is its defining pleasure and its fundamental aesthetic fact. David Bordwell describes the effect beautifully:

> As you walk out of the best Hong Kong action movies you are charged up, you feel like you can do anything. . . . [Such films] infect even film professors, heavy with middle age and polemics . . . with the delusion that they can vault, grave and unflappable, over the cars parked outside the theater.[43]

Leon Hunt has argued that the centrality of such Bordwellian "motion emotion" within the kung fu genre and its mimetic effects on the spectator's body mark it out as belonging to what Linda Williams and Steven Shaviro have discussed as the "body genres."[44] Such genres—classically including the musical, "weepies," and horror films—are usually located squarely within a "low" rather than "high" culture and perched at the edge of critical respectability. They address themselves not to the intellect but more directly to the viewer's body and its "capacity for being affected,"[45] drawing on its desires, pleasures, sensations, and emotions.

The kung fu comedy, of course, only adds further elements of the concern with the corporeal to the kung fu film's display of perfected and spectacular martial skills. Such displays are supplemented with acrobatics incorporated primarily from the opera stage, which amplified to a new degree the physical mobility of the performing star's body and the "motion emotion" it expresses. Physical clowning and slapstick were also incorporated into the mix, along with a humor that often revolved around "base" biological functions, so sinking the films thematically into the material of the body even beyond questions of performance.

However, although Bordwell himself does not pursue this line of investigation, the kinesthetic effect he discusses is notable inasmuch as it seems to involve a certain utopian wish-image. Inasmuch as it offers an image of astonishing physical freedom, self-determination, and expressivity—a freedom seemingly at points from the laws of physics themselves—it carries with it a critical charge within a world where the body is disciplined and constrained as a site (*the* site) of the social and political management of the individual.[46]

Elsewhere, in the context of an analysis of the epic-heroic films of the late 1960s and early 1970s, I have thus proposed that there is a significant echo between Bordwell's fantasies of grave, unflappable car-vaulting and certain passages in the classic account by the pioneering critic of colonialism Frantz Fanon, written at the start of the 1960s, of the often-violent fantasies inhabited by the colonized subject as a response to their oppression and the "narrow world, strewn with prohibitions" in which they live.[47] Fanon writes of the "dreams" of such a colonial subject:

> The dreams of the native are always of muscular prowess; his dreams are of action and aggression. I dream I am jumping, swimming, running, climbing; I dream that I burst out laughing, that I span a river in one stride, or that I am followed by a flood of motor-cars which never catch up with me.[48]

Fanon's description of such fantasies of muscular prowess, action, and aggression, I argued, describe closely the content of the heroic kung fu film and root it in a psychology of anticolonial resentment. Such utopian wish-images, however, are surely open to rearticulation in a number of different ways—if they weren't, martial arts cinema would surely not have the enduring appeal it has outside such a colonial context. For it to remain so popular a genre, they must speak to ongoing desires and hopes within the globalized world, appealing not only to Fanon's "wretched of the earth," but also first-world "film professors, heavy with middle age and polemics" and others besides. Retaining such an appeal, conventions developed in Hong Kong martial arts cinema provide what are still today key aesthetic elements within transnational action cinemas. Hong Kong action cinema, itself, has offered a whole series of differently nuanced versions of such a wish-image, from the blood-drenched swordplays of the 1960s, through the kung fu bodies of the 1970s and their comic variants, to the weightless flying bodies of wirework in the 1990s and beyond.[49]

The kung fu comedy, then, plays such a fantasy out in very particular ways and in a rather different mode to the politically charged anticolonialism and ethnic nationalism that permeated much of the kung fu cinema of the previous period. The kung fu comedy offers us the paradox of a set of violent images that, in relation to the earlier martial arts cinema, have become increasingly stylized and dance-like, and less earnestly bloody, but where the body has become all the more mobile, acrobatic and expressive, and in this regard all the more utopian. Starting to investigate such paradoxical images and to think through whether and in what ways comic kung fu bodies continue or reverse the anticolonial wishes of the heroic kung fu era will thus become a key task this book will pursue.

Organizing the Book, Theorizing the Kung Fu Comedic Body

With this task in mind—an investigation of the political valence of the kung fu comedic body, taken up in the context of a relative paucity of serious literature on this genre—the book is not organized as a simple linear history, although a brief skeleton of this was given at the very start of this introduction, and a further examination of the emergence of the genre and the establishment of its key aesthetic characteristics is introduced at further length in Chapter 1. I take it, in any case, that answers to more broadly empirical questions are easy enough to find nowadays, either in other more broad academic works on Hong Kong or action cinema, in books addressed to a wider "fan" audience, or simply through the wealth of basic factual information now available on the internet.[50] This is not to say that a reader will not find out a lot about the histories of kung fu comedies through reading this book (or that they will need beforehand to know these histories intimately to understand it), but this certainly is not its primary reason for being.

I thus understand the kung fu comedy not as inaccessible or undocumented, but rather as under-analyzed and under-understood, and so the book is primarily structured thematically rather than chronologically, in order to pursue the deepening of an understanding of my object of study. This thematic organization also allows an exploration of the question of "legacy" and of the relations between films from different moments in time, in order to explore common and recurrent forms or contents, as well as moments of change and transformation. This said, the work does start (in Chapter 1) primarily by exploring the initial explosion of kung fu comedy in the "drunken master" cycle itself; as the book progresses, the center of gravity of each chapter—even though comparison and contrast to older and newer films often takes place—edges increasingly toward the present.

Concerned as this book is with analysis rather than description, each chapter takes the form of a theoretical "foray" into the territory of the kung fu comedy, each investigating a particular issue I take as key to such a deeper understanding; each applying a particular cluster of concepts and theoretical approaches. The inquiry is also held together with an organizing concern with the significations of the body, which I have identified above as being so central to the pleasures and meanings of these films. An appropriate metaphor for what I hope to achieve with this mode of organization might be a three-dimensional object, shown in two-dimensional images from a range of different perspectives, each showing a different aspect of its form, and together amounting to a greater sense of the whole than any single viewpoint might allow. Though each chapter develops a different insight, then, the book aims to develop a picture of the kung fu comedy as a rich, multi-dimensional genre, crisscrossed and overdetermined by a complex of often contradictory forces and existing ambivalently within the cultural battleground of a series of local, regional, and global sociopolitical contexts, and there are also a series of echoes and links between concerns of the different analyses offered.

The text—in its investigation of this body—is insistently interdisciplinary, drawing on ideas, approaches, and authors from cultural studies, film and literary theory, visual culture, philosophy, postcolonial theory, gender studies, feminism, Marxism, and psychoanalysis, among other fields. The focus on the body, furthermore, shifts us away from more purely "film studies" approaches to the genre. Rather than an analysis at the level of the film as text or as formal object, the focus on the body involves both a shift toward the particular ("profilmic") aspect within the films of performance, but also a shift beyond the film toward a consideration of these performances as legible within a wider culture of the body itself. In this regard, one of the key intellectual contexts on which this current book draws—and to which it would hope to contribute—is the emerging field of "martial arts studies."[51] This discourse has opened up an understanding of the martial arts as forms of embodied practice and knowledge taking on significance through their mediation within the global flow of cultural representations. Conversely, what a cinematic image of a "kung fu" body (comedic or otherwise) signifies is also formed by the complex cultural and social histories of the martial arts in China and their transformation in the modern era, implicated as these were with questions of class, ethnicity, nation building, gender, and identity, among other concerns, and by the globalization of the martial arts phenomenon.

This book, then, is unashamedly "theoretical": I take the critical encounter between "theory" and film analysis as a generative, illuminating moment. Such an investment in "theory" remains controversial within film studies, in the wake of what are often called the "theory wars" of the late 1980s and early 1990s. During this, writers such as David Bordwell and Noël Carroll challenged the orthodoxy, primarily developed around the journal *Screen* during the 1970s and 1980s, of film studies' methodological and theoretical investments in French poststructuralism and psychoanalysis. Bordwell humorously termed this "SLAB" theory: the acronym stood for Saussure-Lacan-Althusser-Barthes, but the resulting word also evoked "film theory" as a dense, monolithic, blunt, gray, and homogenous mass.[52] In the wake of these attacks, many in film studies turned away from "theory"—and certainly from the mixture of psychoanalysis and poststructuralism that had previously characterized the discipline and that the term "theory" had come to name—toward more empiricist, formalist, and phenomenological accounts of film, with investments (where theory was admitted) in analytic rather than "continental" philosophy and in cognitive psychology rather than psychoanalysis. Bordwell and Carroll's attack was valuable in challenging what had become an orthodoxy with a certain aspiration to a totalizing vision. "Post-theory" opened the study of film to new and productive ways of understanding it. The danger, however, has been that "post-theory" itself may ossify into a reduced set of legitimated practices and approaches.

If the "post-theory" position has now become established—perhaps even dominant—in film studies as a discipline, film is also an object of analysis by scholars with broader, more interdisciplinary investments in popular culture, emerging primarily from the fields of cultural studies and visual culture, where theory and theoretical work remain highly important, as well as by specialist film scholars who remain in dialogue with these broader currents of cultural analysis. In contemporary academic writing on Hong Kong martial arts cinema, there are film scholars with more neoformalist or historicist approaches, prominent examples being David Bordwell himself or Stephen Teo, but also writers such as Kwai-Cheung Lo, Paul Bowman, or Meaghan Morris with closer ties to an interdisciplinary cultural studies, for whom "theory" (if not quite in its classic "SLAB" form) is an important part of their analytical method. It is squarely within this latter tradition that I would locate this book. Although the reader will find almost nothing of Saussure, Lacan, Althusser, or Barthes here (I focus instead on European cultural Marxism, Frankfurt School critical theory, gender studies, and postcolonial theory), nonetheless, traditions of twentieth-century continental philosophy and psychoanalysis remain at the heart of what I bring to the kung fu comedy.

I aim, furthermore, to engage the theorists on whom I draw critically, and some significant space within the book is given over to this consideration. This seems especially important given that an essentially European canon is being applied to cultural production from a postcolonial, East Asian context. Since the writing I examine is produced in a somewhat different historical context to the films I discuss, the implications of such cultural transplantation require examination in order to understand why and how they may be of use in understanding the kung fu comedy, where the limits of their interpretative power may lie, and how they may need to be modified to be of use. I aim, in critically examining my conceptual and theoretical choices, to ensure that the Hong Kong context does not get "emptied out" by my analysis and that "theory" does not get hypostatized or universalized.

The Drunken Master's Legacies

The abandonment of a chronological mode of organization has also made the delimitation of the field of my inquiry more complicated. Where do the temporal (or even geographic) boundaries of such a study begin and end? What should or should not be included?

My solution to this problem has been to identify the 1978 release of *Snake in the Eagle's Shadow* and *Drunken Master* as the core moment in which the genre was defined, and from the standpoint of which its histories make their best sense.

It is these films, and what they introduce, that form the organizational focus of the current work. This is not to claim a position for them as the "first" kung fu comedies. They have, as I shall discuss at further length in Chapter 1, a number of precursors, and a comedic tradition around kung fu performance in Hong Kong cinema can certainly be traced back into the 1950s—and also beyond this back into the much longer histories of the operatic stage.[53] However, the phenomenal box-office success of these two films starring Jackie Chan and directed by Yuen Woo-ping marked the closest thing to what we might term, loosely in the sense of philosopher Alain Badiou, the "event" of the kung fu comedy.[54] For Badiou an event is something unpredictable within the terms of the world that precedes it, which nonetheless erupts into it, and which radically and permanently changes the field into which it enters. Within the world of Hong Kong martial arts cinema—admittedly a somewhat limited field compared with the grand and all-encompassing scale that Badiou tends to mean with his use of the term—the sudden success of the "drunken master" formula might entail such a transformative phenomenon, initiating a torrent of imitations and kick-starting a new series of genre transformations. *Drunken Master* and *Snake in the Eagle's Shadow* (the former in particular) seem to be the films to which later martial arts comedies inevitably refer and from the material of which they so often form themselves.

The organizing metaphor through which this book defines its field of investigation, then, is one of "legacy"—a notion that, in any case, as we shall see especially in Chapter 5, is an organizing trope of the Hong Kong martial arts movie itself.[55] The most immediate way I use the notion of "legacy" as a way to think about the history of the kung fu comedy film (rather than as just a theme within it) is by exploring the development of the genre in the immediate aftermath of *Drunken Master,* and the focus of the book is certainly on a period of the "classical" kung fu comedy, which Leon Hunt, for example, has defined as stretching from its inception in the late 1970s until around 1982.[56] For my own purposes, however, I expand this timeframe further, encompassing the period of vibrant transformation and hybridization that mixed kung fu comedy with other genres throughout the 1980s. As I have noted above, primary among these hybridized genres are those that include the supernatural—for example, in films such as *Mr. Vampire* (dir. Ricky Lau, 1985)—and those that mix comedy and kung fu with police action-drama, as exemplified in some of Jackie Chan's most prominent movies of this decade.

The question of "legacy" also allows me to stretch this analysis further toward the present, thinking about the afterlife of the drunken master genre in the globalization of Jackie Chan's success in the 1990s and 2000s, in films made not only in Hong Kong, but also the USA, or Stephen Chow's films such as *Kung Fu Hustle* and *Shaolin Soccer.* In many ways, though Chow's work is structured quite differently to the classic kung fu comedy, and though, as a comedian primarily rather than a stuntman, his mode of physical performance diverges from the acrobatic virtuosity of, say Jackie Chan, Sammo Hung, or Yuen Biao, his films nonetheless remain replete with references to the older genre (alongside a host of other Hong Kong movie tropes) and in many ways are unthinkable without it. Veteran kung fu comedy directors Yuen Woo-ping and Sammo Hung even choreographed the action for *Fung Fu Hustle,* and among its star performers are Yuen Wah and Yuen Qiu as the landlord and landlady, respectively, of its fictional setting, the slum tenement "Pig Sty Alley." Their matching surnames mark the fact that they were classmates at the same Beijing Opera school as Jackie Chan, Sammo Hung, and Yuen Biao, perhaps the three most prominent comedic kung fu performers of the 1970s and 1980s.

This organization around "legacy" also helps us lift the kung fu comedy out of the narrow moment and social history that provide the context for its production (though this is certainly a concern throughout the work) and think about the continued relevance of the kung fu comedy within our contemporary world—a world which, I have intimated above, has grown from and lies in continuity with the 1970s Hong Kong within which the drunken master cycle of films was created. Given that my question is also one of the politics of the genre, such a way of understanding ourselves as in receipt of a part of the "legacy" of the kung fu comedy opens up questions of whether, if there are indeed "utopian," "radical," "progressive," or even "resistant" elements within them, these might be a part of what the kung fu film has passed into our culture—or whether it has alternatively burdened us with ideologies that we would rather be free from. Through its insistent thematization of filial duties and of the relationship between master and student, the kung fu movie itself tells us that "legacy" involves not only what we have, but who we are, encompassing our relation to the past—and our very identity. Such a way of thinking might hold a key to the problem of what the legacy of the kung fu comedy means today as part of our global cultural heritage.

Opening the historical kung fu comedy into the present in this way aims to stop it ossifying as a historical product of a past moment, and, in the terms of Walter Benjamin—a writer who will be prominent in a number of the analyses offered in this book—it presents us with images from the past as filled with a *Jetztzeit:* the time of the "now."[57] Benjamin wrote of the past flashing up as an image in a moment of danger, taking on its meaning with regards to the crises of the present, and being filled with their urgency. I seek to grasp the "legacy" of the kung fu comedy in the present in something of this manner. Benjamin also wrote of stories from the past entering the present like dormant seeds, locked in an ancient jar, discovered by archaeologists thousands of years after their burial, yet able to sprout.[58] Could the kung fu comedy also harbor seeds of a better world within it?

Legacy and Genealogy

Michel Foucault's essay "Nietzsche, Genealogy, History" highlights a number of further methodological implications of such a decision to organize my treatment around the notion of legacy.[59] Certainly as Foucault articulates Nietzsche's schema for thinking historically in his *Genealogy of Morals,* the notion of "genealogy"—an idea, of course, closely linked to problems of inheritance—is intended to offer an alternative to attempts to discuss the past in which "origins" become fetishized and in which such origins are expected to offer frozen images of an eternal "essence" or truth.[60] Foucault suggests that instead the conception of genealogy reveals behind phenomena "not a timeless and essential secret, but the secret that they have no essence or that their essence was fabricated in a piecemeal fashion from alien forms."[61] Genealogy opens out into plurality and heterogeneity rather than closing on a single point of "truth." Such, then, would be my hope in taking *Drunken Master* as the point around which this book revolves. Genealogically—or in other words, in terms of legacy—this film opens out both into its multiple (and unfinished) inheritors, but it also presents a point in which a series of what Foucault terms "numberless beginnings"[62] manifest themselves: the prior development of the martial arts and comedy films during the 1960s and 1970s, the political and social transformations of Hong Kong, the histories of the Chinese martial arts, opera, regional politics, and the emergence of new forms of globalized capitalism and global countercultures, to note just a few of these. In Foucault's terms, what presents itself as an origin is in fact a moment of "emergence"—a "leap from the wings to center stage."[63] This moment of emergence into view is congruent with my proposition above that *Drunken Master* and *Snake in the Eagle's Shadow* are important not as "firsts" but as marking a defining "event" in the history of the kung fu comedy. This "genealogical" approach is also useful in the extent to which, rather than presenting us with a fixed object ("*the* kung fu comedy"), it presents us instead, inevitably, with a historical flux in which the object of study is in transformation, and it is as such a changing object that we will meet the "kung fu comedy" in its developing forms.

What's In and What's Out?

On a more practical level, there are, nonetheless, implications, with regards to what has been selected, of my choice to organize the book around the "legacies" of *Drunken Master.* With its theoretical, thematic, and analytical rather than chronological organization, "coverage" is, of course, not the priority of the book, as it might be with a more straightforward historical survey. The films I discuss have been chosen more for their representative usefulness in opening up understandings than as a fully comprehensive selection.

The choice of *Drunken Master* as the book's focal point inevitably tends to place this film's auteurs and performers center stage. Given the towering influence of Jackie Chan and Yuen Woo-ping, this is perhaps not too bad a thing; it's hard to overestimate their importance. Other filmmakers, however, do start to appear more marginal. In particular, the works of Sammo Hung and Lau Kar-leung—though certainly discussed and acknowledged in the following chapters—take something of a relative backseat.

Hung's martial arts performance, choreography, and direction have not only been enormously prolific but also influential. While Jackie Chan is known affectionately in the Hong Kong film industry as *Da Ge* (Big Brother), a title usually offered to the oldest of brothers and marking seniority, Hung is jokingly referred to as *Da Ge Da* (literally "Big Brother Big," or "Biggest Big Brother") to hint at his even greater influence. Though discussed here both as a performer and a choreographer/director, the extent and range of Hung's work is thus not fully explored.

Lau Kar-leung's oeuvre might have offered a different starting point for this book. Lau's debut film as director, *Spiritual Boxer* (1975), in many ways anticipated the drunken master films. Lau would go on to produce a series of highly successful films incorporating comedy to lesser and greater degrees, parallel in timeframe to the drunken master cycle, and they often resonate with the wider themes and motifs from this. Wonderful as they are, however, Lau's films were probably less influential than Chan's and Yuen's in defining the field of the kung fu comedy. This is primarily, I would argue, because of the shifting commercial landscape of film production within which they were made. Lau was a contract director for Shaw Brothers, the studio that had dominated the Hong Kong industry throughout the 1960s and early 1970s, largely pioneering and defining the martial arts film in these decades. Shaw had set up a production-line filmmaking system, funded by its vertical integration with a network of cinemas across East and Southeast Asia. Sheer scale enabled production values that made other studios look shabby and ensured Shaw's increasing monopoly.[64] As the 1970s pushed on, however, increasing competition emerged from smaller, more mobile studios that could offer innovation for which Shaw, locked into its formulae, was poorly equipped. The fact of Lau's very promotion from choreographer to director in 1975 and his freedom to experiment with the comic format is in itself evidence of Shaw's loss of confidence in its previously dominant heroic-epic martial arts formulae and the increasing drain of audiences from these.

Lau, however, continued to make his comedies in the Shaws' crisp, lushly colorful and aesthetically dense house style. With their epic scale and formal beauty, reliant on lavish sets and costumes as well as high-end film equipment, the films were hard to imitate for the smaller independent companies who flooded the market with kung fu comedies in the wake of *Drunken Master.* Stylistically Lau's films often looked back to Shaw's golden era as much as forward to the new conventions that were emerging, often hybridizing comedy with heroic drama. In contrast, *Snake in the Eagle's Shadow* and *Drunken Master,* produced by Ng See-yuen's Seasonal Film Company on shoestring budgets, offered much more meaningful models for independent film producers and for the pleasures that they could offer.[65] Lau's comedies, including *Mad Monkey Kung Fu* (1979), *Dirty Ho* (1979), *Return to the 36th Chamber* (1980), *My Young Auntie* (1981) and *Legendary Weapons of China* (1982), could be judged as some of the great artistic achievements of the golden age of the kung fu comedy. However, perhaps it is their sheer "artistic" quality and Lau's status as a self-conscious auteur that differentiate them from contemporaneous "genre" offerings, making them somewhat atypical.

Drunken Master, in fact, launched such a profusion of imitations—of variable quality—that it would be impossible to set out to map the whole field of these within a single book. With Jackie Chan's rising fame, a whole generation of comic kung fu clowns emerged, including, for example, Cliff Lok, Elton Chong, Dragon Lee, Casanova Wong, Conan Lee, and Lee I-Min. Again, their work is less explored here than that of Chan, Hung, Yuen, and their various collaborators, who form the backbone of my account.

Organization of the Book

In Chapter 1, I begin the book's attempt to theorize the kung fu comedy by setting out to distinguish the aesthetic of the kung fu comedy and its vision of the body from that of the more "serious" (non-comedic) martial arts films of the preceding decade. To do this, I locate martial arts cinema within the context of the wider twentieth-century histories of the Chinese martial arts and their reform movements, and their entanglement with nationalism and ethnic identity.

I argue, however, that the kung fu comedy cannot be located as simply within such a context as a non-comedic film such as Bruce Lee's *Fist of Fury* (dir. Lo Wei, 1972). The latter is not only set within an iconic moment of Chinese nationalist martial arts culture in 1910s Shanghai, but also, in its vision of an ideal, honed (male) physical body that Lee comes to signify, reflects the concerns of this moment. I argue that, in contrast, the kung fu comedy—as exemplified not only by *Snake in the Eagle's Shadow* and *Drunken Master*, but also by the more recent cinema of Stephen Chow—articulates an alternative aesthetic of the body, which emerges at a moment when in Hong Kong the nationalist narratives of the martial arts were becoming less powerful and Hongkongers increasingly defined their identity as much against "Chineseness" as in its terms. This kung fu comedic body articulates "postcoloniality" rather differently, and somewhat outside of the framework of the "protestant ethnic" that Lee takes on in *Fist of Fury*.

I propose that the kung fu comedic body is radically open and passes repeatedly beyond its "proper" boundaries. It is emphatically nonideal ("freakish," even), always in transformation. Insistently material and connected to the "lower" functions of the body, it is frequently abject or revolting. Following Leon Hunt's account of the genre, I propose that such a body strongly parallels what literary theorist Mikhail Bakhtin, in his work on medieval European carnival, terms the "grotesque body." However, transferring an aesthetic category from a study of Medieval and Renaissance Europe to the context of twentieth-century Hong Kong is, of course, problematic, and so the chapter examines the viability of rethinking the Bakhtinian "carnivalesque" as a postcolonial aesthetic that helps understand the changing nature of identity and politics in 1970s Hong Kong. Doing so, I argue, helps us move on from the kinds of "reflectionist" judgments discussed earlier in this introduction, which read the kung fu comedy simply in terms of depoliticization and accommodation to the growing capitalist globalization of the moment, and of the waning of resistance to colonial rule. This is not, however, to argue that the kung fu comedy is unproblematically progressive; rather, as with the chapters that follow, I set out to explore some of the complexities, tensions, and contradictions in the genre. The point is, instead, to think about the ways that a politics of the kung fu comedic body might be thought "beyond" the militancy of the figure of the "protestant ethnic." Although it has too often been used in naively affirmative terms, I argue that Bakhtin's account of carnival offers us useful methods for grasping the ways that politics, ambivalent as they are, may continue within the kung fu comedy.

Chapter 2 builds on Chapter 1's recognition of the kung fu comedic body as open and in constant transformation. However, I move on from Bakhtin's theorization of this to examine the qualities of such a body through the lens of

Walter Benjamin's comments on early cinematic comedy from America. Benjamin was—initially at least—fascinated and enthusiastic about both physical slapstick (Keaton and Chaplin in particular) and the anarchic world of the early Mickey Mouse cartoons. Kung fu comedies, of course, are frequently compared to the products of this historical moment, with Jackie Chan himself, for example, not only frequently talking in interviews about his debt to silent-era stars such as Buster Keaton, but directly adapting and replaying their stunts.

Benjamin recognized in cinema the potential to create surrealistic counter-images to the everyday order of capitalist life, envisioning both the world and the body itself as taking on something of the uncanny transformative power of capitalist technology. Benjamin sees in—or projects onto—such films what he terms a "utopia of the body": powerful wish-images in which the alienating forces of capitalist modernity are appropriated into the embodied self for purposes not of exploitation and domination but of freedom. Such, I argue, is echoed in particular in the training montages so common in the kung fu comedy. As with Bakhtin, however, the lifting of Benjamin's insights from their original context requires—and so receives—reflection, allowing an analysis in particular of Jackie Chan's manipulation of his body and his environment in *Project A* as a negotiation of a modernity that is now (post-)colonial and globalized.

However, Benjamin's early enthusiasm for slapstick and Disney cartoons—even in and because of their "positive barbarism"—became increasingly counterbalanced by an anxiety that at their core lay an acceptance of the brutality of capitalism (exemplified most strikingly in the rise of fascism). Such an anxiety was taken up by Benjamin's friend and interlocutor, Theodor Adorno, who saw the hapless Donald Duck as a figure in whom the cinemagoer might recognize and come to casually accept as inevitable their own brutalized conditions. Worse, however, such an acceptance, Adorno thought, could lead audiences to complicity in dishing out the same brutality to others.

Starting with an examination of Benjamin and Adorno's correspondence over the nature of cartoonesque film violence, Chapter 3 therefore examines violence in kung fu comedies. The potential of the human body both to inflict and to suffer violence is, of course, not only a core thematic of the martial arts genres, but also a fundament of its spectatorial pleasures. It would, in this respect, be foolish to let things finish, as Chapter 2 does, with an image of the kung fu body only as a figure of freedom and transcendence; it is also one inscribed by drives to domination and destruction. Not all depictions of violence, however, represent it in the same way, or with the same effect. My work here, therefore, takes on an examination of the kung fu comedy's particular mode of representing the violent potential of the human body. This includes a constant shifting between grace and slapstick; between acrobatics and martial artistry; between sadism and masochism; and between light, comic, stylized, and de-emphasized violence and more "earnest," even melodramatic depictions. Drawing on Leo Bersani's deconstructionist Freudian analysis of violence in both ancient Assyrian friezes of ceremonial royal lion hunts and Pier Paolo Pasolini's notorious film *Salò, or the 120 Days of Sodom* (1975), I mount an analysis of the complex ethics of violence in the kung fu comedy, discussing examples including, especially, three films made at the cusp of the 1980s: *The Young Master* (dir. Jackie Chan, 1980), *Knockabout* (dir. Sammo Hung, 1979), and *Thundering Mantis* (Teddy Yip, 1980).

Chapter 4 draws the question of carnival and its mode of politics, with which the book started, in a different direction. It takes its cue from Allon White, who has remarked on the close connection between the imagery of carnival and the fantasies and symptoms of the nineteenth-century patients of Sigmund Freud and Jean-Martin Charcot, who were diagnosed as suffering from hysteria. Hysteria has in fact been another term used to describe the qualities of Hong Kong martial arts cinema (by, for example, Bhaskar Sarkar and Mark Gallagher). It also sparks my interest with regards to the kung fu comedic body in that it is an illness where "symptoms" express themselves corporeally and, of course, often precisely through laughter. The famous images of hysterics that emerged from Charcot's clinic, especially those undergoing what Charcot termed the phase of "clownism" in the hysterical attack, often look uncannily like they are stills from a kung fu comedy training or fight scene in the muscularity and gymnastic athleticism of their poses. Can hysteria, then—outmoded as it is as a diagnostic term, and loaded with problematic conceptions of gender—help us think about the politics of the kung fu comedic body?

Drawing on feminist reappropriations of the term since the 1970s (in particular that of Hélène Cixous), I argue that it can, precisely *because* it is a term that, in its entanglement with gender, articulates itself around patriarchy, power, and forms of exclusion and "othering." Feminist analyses of the position of the ("female") hysteric with regards to access to ("male") language within patriarchy seem in many ways useful in thinking about the relation of the colonized to the discourse of paternalistic colonialism. Similarly, feminist accounts often highlighted the complex forms of simultaneous complicity and resistance exhibited by "hysterical" patients. In this regard, they further highlight mechanisms of the "carnival" politics of the kung fu comedy, and the ambivalent relationships to authority that are registered in them, helping develop this beyond a vision of the militancy of the "protestant ethnic."

This analysis allows me to reconsider the ambiguous forms of compliance and resistance registered in *Project A*, and the construction within this of the character of the dutiful policeman that Jackie Chan would go on to reprise repeatedly within his films of the remainder of the 1980s and 1990s—and that would become prominent within Chan's "crossover" to the American market in *Rumble in the Bronx* and the Rush Hour films, for example. Hysteria as an analytical category also raises important questions about gender, and considering Chan's American films through this concept allows me—drawing on Mark Gallagher's analysis of these—to think about the ways that Chan negotiated and positioned himself through the comedic mode with regards to the norms of masculinity in Hollywood action cinema and the places that are available for an "Asian other" within these.

However, though it is a concern throughout, it is in Chapter 5 that I primarily place questions of gender and masculinity to the fore as a theme of the kung fu comedy. Though masculinity seems a core concern of much kung fu cinema, it seems notable that while the non-comedic swordplay and kung fu genres of the late 1960s and early 1970s gave us, alongside their male stars, a panoply of action heroines, the comedic kung fu genre did not do this, suggesting that masculinity is all the more at the core of its concerns. Building on the arguments of Chapter 4, I explore the gender hysteria that we might discover in these films, as they are invaded by anxieties regarding the stability of masculinity. I trace these instabilities—and the threat posed in these films by both the "feminine" and a series of increasingly terrifying castrating father figures—from the drunken master cycle of the late 1970s through into the hybrid genres that combined kung fu comedy with the supernatural and horror in the late 1980s and 1990s, as exemplified in the Miracle Fighters and Mr. Vampire series.

I develop this analysis through an exploration of the questions of "legacy" that are inscribed in patriarchal notions of identity common to both the Western capitalist culture and the more traditional "Confucian" forms of Chinese culture between which Hong Kong culture is suspended. Within these, it is in and through the father's name that identity—as well as masculinity, wealth, power, and cultural location—is constructed and passed down. Within the kung fu film, "kung fu" itself (passed from master to student or father to son) becomes a cipher for such phallic inheritance of masculinity. Within the Hong Kong context, in particular as the 1997 handover of control of the colony loomed closer, these questions about legacy are reinflected with regards to questions of ethnicity and culture, with anxieties with regards to broken and continued relations to an "ancestral land," and with regards to the traumatic histories of Hong Kong and Chinese modernity. These explorations allow an account of the cinematic legacies of the Drunken Master in terms of the thematics that Elisabeth Bronfen proposed underpin the classic fantasies of the hysteric—themes of the mortality of the body, its desire, and its origin—in terms of historical questions of Hong Kong identity.

The final chapter returns us emphatically to the present, exploring what the "legacy of the Drunken Master" might be within today's transformations of both Hong Kong and its film industry. Questions of the political have rearisen as pressing concerns in Hong Kong after the handover to China, where the ambivalence toward mainland China and Chineseness explored in previous chapters have only become amplified, especially in the wake of Scholarism, the 2014 Occupy Central protests, and the development of "Localist" and independence movements. At the same time, the Hong Kong film industry has increasingly shifted away from a concern with local specificity and integrated into a larger national cinema, following the opening of mainland markets. Simultaneously, Hong Kong stars and filmmakers have been increasingly finding a presence in transnational cinemas and markets. Such a context allows a consideration of more recent work by Jackie Chan, Yuen Woo-ping, and Stephen Chow.

The book's conclusion turns away from the field of film production to think about the questions of "legacies" and "inheritance" for global audiences, rather than producers. Weighing up the balance of emancipatory and reactionary elements in the kung fu comedy, I finish the book considering the kung fu comedy's address to the present and to the future, asking if they do have some aspect of the utopian, "messianic" force that Benjamin hoped for in popular culture.

Thinking of "legacy," however, also binds us into what I understand to be complex questions of historical temporality in which the present is folded into the past and the future in complex ways. This allows further consideration of the ways that films from the 1970s might travel beyond their original moment to take on new (and old) senses in the present; but precisely in doing this, I argue, the contemporary encounter with the kung fu comedy—in particular with its roots in operatic practices and aesthetics—entwines us in a popular cultural history that stretches back beyond modernity into the folk past and forward toward both utopian and dystopian possibilities.

CHAPTER 1

Carnival

> From one body a new body always emerges in some form or another.
>
> —*Mikhail Bakhtin*

In my introduction, I have established something of the context for the rise of the kung fu comedy. There I proposed that it departed in significant ways from the aesthetic of the Hong Kong martial arts cinema of the late 1960s and early 1970s, which had been primarily epic, heroic, and tragic in tone. The blood-drenched "new swordplay" genre had emerged in the shadow of the Cultural Revolution and of the explosion of anticolonial riots in Hong Kong in 1966/7; this paved the way for the rise of the "kung fu" film at the start of the following decade. These genres, I suggested, can be interpreted as redolent with the social violence and the mood of grand historical change that swept not only Hong Kong and China but also the wider world in the late 1960s. The kung fu comedy, however, emerged at a time when this turmoil was subsiding, when the forces of neoliberal or globalized capitalism were establishing themselves, and when a new climate of social and political conformism was being instituted, in part by the force of the colonial administration of Hong Kong and in part due to anxieties about the excesses of Maoism on the mainland.

This chapter, then, will turn to an initial investigation of the changing representations of the body as we find it in the comic films of the late 1970s—in the immediate wake of the genre-establishing *Snake in the Eagle's Shadow* and *Drunken Master* (both dir. Yuen Woo-ping, 1978). The kung fu body as we meet it in these films, I will be arguing, is very different from that which we meet in their heroic, epic, or tragic counterparts and provides a first blueprint for the mutating martial arts comedies of the following decades. To make sense of these differences between comic and tragic kung fu cinema—and of their political significance—I will be situating them not only within the more immediate contexts of Hong Kong's social, economic, cultural, and cinematic history, but within the larger context of the history of the discourses around the body of the martial artist in twentieth-century Chinese culture and the projects of nation building within which these played a part. This will afford a reading of the comedic kung fu body with regard to the shifting attitudes to nationality and nationalism in Hong Kong in the late twentieth century as the enclave was transformed by new forms of capitalism and colonial administration.

The central theoretical resource I will draw on here to describe and understand the kung fu comedic body and its relation to nation and identity will be Mikhail Bakhtin's account of the "grotesque body," which he reads as typical of a medieval European carnival tradition. The striking "fit" between Bakhtin's description of carnival bodies and those we find in kung fu comedy has not escaped critics in the past, and I respond here in particular to the use of the concept by Leon Hunt and Mark Gallagher.[1] However, as we shall see, application of Bakhtin's notion of the grotesque body to the globalizing and postcolonial Hong Kong context needs careful critical consideration. My argument is that when we do this it is a useful tool in understanding both the emancipatory and conservative aspects of the kung fu comedy, and of registering the ways that politics continued to be at stake within it. Though later chapters pursue different angles on the kung fu comedy, the understanding opened up through this analysis forms the basis upon which they largely stand.

Exit the Dragon: Bruce Lee, the Heroic Body, and the Legacy of Early Twentieth-Century Martial Arts Movements

Before thinking about the kung fu comedy as offering change, however, we first need to consider the genre from which it broke: the "heroic" kung fu film of the early 1970s. For a paradigmatic example of this I take Bruce Lee's performance in *Fist of Fury* (dir. Lo Wei, 1972). Lee, of course, is a complex figure whose meaning has been much contested.[2] However, the reading that I would primarily like to draw on here is that of Stephen Teo, who—among others—has proposed Lee as a nationalist icon.[3]

Fist of Fury is the film that most supports such a reading and that best helps us think about the politics of the heroic kung fu body. In it, Lee was cast in an explicitly anticolonial story, as a Chinese hero fighting back against European and Japanese occupiers in the Republican-era Shanghai International Settlement of the 1910s, which was conceded for occupation by a consortium of foreign powers (initially led by Britain) in the Treaty of Nanking at the end of the First Opium War (1839–1842). The iconic freeze-frame of Lee's flying kick into a hail of gunfire at the end of the film vividly illustrates its overall tone of melodramatic heroism in the face of foreign occupation. Though perhaps atypical within the genre in the explicitness of its political allegory (Hong Kong itself was still at this point a British colony, as well as one that had suffered badly under Japanese occupation during the Second World War), *Fist of Fury* not only spawned a flurry of imitations, but also brought to the surface what may be the deeper ideological stakes of the kung fu body Lee exemplified through his performance in it.

Lee's body was muscular and sculpted in a way that anticipates the bodies of the Hollywood bodybuilder stars of the 1980s (see fig. 1.1).[4] His construction of his image has been understood—for example by Teo—as a riposte to narratives of China as the "sick man of East Asia" and as reclaiming Chinese "masculinity" as strong, muscular, and active in the face of feminizing Orientalist stereotypes.[5] This, in its turn, inscribes Lee's body within a longer and broader history of discourses in modern China about the relation between individual bodies and a national/racial body politic, within the particular context of China's humiliation, weakness, and reduction to semicolonial status during the nineteenth century and the demand to modernize in order to compete with other nations. Through the practices of "body cultivation" or "physical culture" (in Mandarin: *tiyu*), Nationalist and Communist governments alike took seriously the task of strengthening the nation through the cultivation of the individual body, whether this involved taking up Western forms of sport and calisthenics or a turn back to (a modernized form of) "traditional" and "indigenous" martial arts.[6]

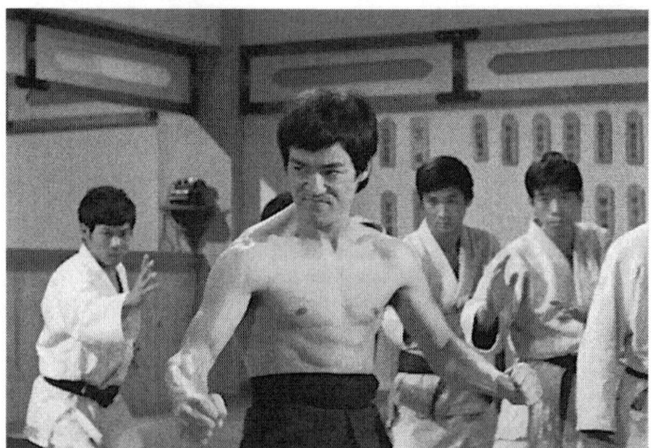

Fig. 1.1. Bruce Lee's idealized, muscular body, mobilized within a plot of Fanonian anticolonial resentment, as Chen Zhen prepares to dismantle a Japanese dojo in *Fist of Fury*. Video still. © Star TV Filmed Entertainment 2004.

The plot of *Fist of Fury,* in fact, inscribes Lee's body into an iconic moment within this history, with his character Chen Zhen depicted as a fictional student of the real-life martial artist Huo Yuanjia, the founder of the Jingwu Athletic Association, a pioneer organization within early twentieth-century debates around martial arts, modernity, and patriotism. Jingwu sought to promote traditional martial arts as offering a path to strength and modernity that drew on and reinforced China's unique culture and identity, avoiding its reduction to a mere imitation of the West.[7]

Andrew Morris contextualizes this moment as one in which the practice of physical culture was being taken up not only in China but around the globe as a response to the imperatives of the emerging modern nation-state as the universal form of political organization.[8] Morris's argument locates sport and fitness movements as linked to the nation-state's "biopolitical" foundation in the custodianship of the health and life of its people and its management of these as economic and military assets.[9] The urgency of nation building, however, was added a further twist in the colonized world, where the muscular body arguably also took on the burden of carrying the fantasies of violent physical action diagnosed by Frantz Fanon as endemic to the resentful, confined, and dominated colonial subject, as discussed in this book's introduction. If we read Lee's muscular body (as seen in fig. 1.1) biopolitically, then, it seems to waver—with all the ambiguity of anticolonial nationalism—between the fascist-imperialist regimentation of the self and dreams of liberation from oppression.[10]

Changing Hong Kong Identity and the Rise of Cinematic Comedy in the 1970s

As the 1970s drew on, however, it was increasingly comedy rather than epic heroism that came to dominate the tone of Hong Kong kung fu cinema—suggesting, perhaps, that the fantasies of the body exemplified in Lee's *Fist of Fury* were a decreasing draw for audiences. The origins of this shift toward comedy are complex and cannot be pinned to a single moment or cause—especially because there is no clear line between primarily "serious" films laced with comic episodes and films where comedy has become the primary tone of the film, or between films with an increasing predominance of comic elements and the existence of a "genre" of the kung fu comedy as such, with all this implies about an established set of conventions. Other critics, such as for example David Bordwell, have certainly remarked on Hong Kong cinema's broader and longer tradition of mixing the comic and serious.[11] In turn, this tendency has its deeper roots in the comic interludes that pervade even heroic operas in the traditional popular theaters of China. Discussing these, Colin Mackerras and Elizabeth Wichman explain that "the Chinese audience has little patience with unrelieved solemnity."[12] Perhaps the thing in this context that needs to be explained is not the "appearance" of comedy in the late 1970s, but rather the existence of films with a surprising *lack* of comedy in the late 1960s and early 1970s—the humorlessness of a film such as Chang Cheh's *Assassin* (1967), for example, or Lee's *Fist of Fury* itself.[13] My own argument, pursued elsewhere, has been that the tenor of these films derives from the violence of the ideological struggles that surrounded their production and first consumption.[14] For example, in interviews Chang Cheh, a pioneer of the new violent martial arts genres of this moment, has stated that he consciously sought to create a cinema that addressed and was appropriate to such "troubled times."[15]

However, as the 1970s progressed, comedy was becoming increasingly important in Hong Kong's popular culture. Already in 1973, Bruce Lee's *Enter the Dragon*—in spite of its star's shocking death and the outpouring of emotion that this caused—was kept from the number one spot at the box offices not by another action movie, but by Chor Yuen's *House of 72 Tenants,* a comedy celebrating the struggles—and mutual aid—of the impoverished residents of a Hong Kong slum tenement block. The popularity of *House of 72 Tenants* seems to point to a series of factors that help us understand the new potency of comedy at this moment, and that will thus help us understand the rise of the kung fu comedy as a genre. One aspect of this is Hong Kong's increasing cultural distance from the mainland and its increasing development of an identity separate from—and even opposed to—China. As Man-Fung Yip has argued, this was a moment in which Hongkongers' identity and sense of their "modernity" was being "shaped more by capitalist subjectivity than by nationalist ideology" and in which "belonging to a nation was far from a natural thing."[16]

A key catalyst in Hong Kong culture's articulation of this changing consciousness was the emergence in 1967 of TVB's Cantonese-language channel, Jade, the first such channel broadcasting out of the enclave with a program of material produced specifically for its population. Discussing the construction of national identity more generally, Benedict Anderson has noted how media promote identification with an "imagined community" of viewers, brought together by a common language and cultural reference points.[17] *House of 72 Tenants* drew its star appeal from an ensemble cast of faces familiar from TVB Jade.[18] The extent of its popularity was a double shock to studio executives, inasmuch as it was not only a comedy rather than an action film, but was also released in Cantonese, the "local" language of Hong Kong, bucking the prior trend towards a Mandarin cinema that positioned Hong Kong audiences within a larger imagined community of diasporic Chinese, defined in relation to the lost homeland and its "official" national language. While *Fist of Fury*, then, addressed its audience as outraged patriotic Chinese people not only through its Shanghai setting but also through the very language in which it was released, *House of 72 Tenants* was set in Hong Kong, with familiar local actors speaking the dialect of everyday local life in the enclave.[19]

Within such a context, comedy in its spoken dimension takes on a special role, foregrounding the particularities of language itself, offering its spectators the pleasure of play within this shared medium, and, through this pleasure, affirming the bonds of a linguistic community. Wordplay—and in particular play not just with the Cantonese language but with the specificities of Hong Kong slang—remains a significant element in Hong Kong comedies to the present day; the fast-talking *mo lei tau* (nonsense humor) of Stephen Chow is a prominent example.[20]

However, the comedy that came to typify Hong Kong cinema in the wake of *House of 72 Tenants* was not purely linguistic, but mixed physical slapstick with witty verbiage—often drawing on and lampooning the martial arts genre as a part of this (as Stephen Chow so famously still does). One question that this opens up—and which will be pursued later in this chapter—is whether the performing comedic body, alongside linguistic particularity, plays a role in defining local identity.

Further popularizing the comic in cinema in the mid-1970s were the films written, produced, and directed by Michael Hui, in which he starred alongside his brothers, Sam and Ricky. These topped the box offices for 1974 (*Games Gamblers Play*), 1975 (*The Last Message*), 1976 (*Private Eyes*), and 1978 (*The Contract*).[21] Just as with *House of 72 Tenants*, the Hui Brothers were already stars from their own show on TVB.[22] Their comedy films—a mixture of farce, Cantonese wordplay, and physical knockabout (sometimes choreographed by martial arts action directors such as Sammo Hung)[23]—were, in contrast to the typically historical kung fu and swordplay genres, distinctly contemporary and local, defining the Hong Kong inhabitants in terms of their quick-witted survival strategies in the fast-moving cut and thrust of the colony's ballooning, entrepreneurial economy.[24] For Jenny Lau, in spite of their comic form, Michael Hui's films developed a social realism that both looked back to the "issues"-based films of the 1950s and forward to the Hong Kong New Wave of the 1980s.[25]

Kung Fu Comedy: Enter the Drunken Master

Since comedy was so evidently successful at the box office, it is hardly surprising that producers and directors of martial arts films sought increasingly to integrate comic elements into their work. Already in 1973, Lo Wei, who had directed Lee's *Fist of Fury*, was turning away from the formula of that film. In *Back Alley Princess* he cast martial arts heroines Polly Shangguan Lingfeng and Angela Mao Ying alongside comedian Sam Hui, hybridizing the comic vision of the landscape of present-day Hong Kong familiar from the Hui Brothers films with a plot revolving around martial arts action and conflict. By this time, Bruce Lee's *Way of the Dragon* (1972) had already injected a self-deprecating humor into his own repertoire. Alexander Fu Sheng, throughout the early and mid-1970s, developed an impish persona across a series of film performances, in contrast to the stoic masculinity of the genre's stars alongside whom he was often cast, offering an element of light relief and anticipating the unruly kung fu "punks" (*xiaozi*) who would typify the young and lawless heroes of kung fu comedies later in the decade. Lau Kar-leung's *The Spiritual Boxer* (1975) offered something much closer to a full-blown kung fu comedy, not only discovering an acrobatic and anarchistic hero in its star Wong Yue, but even looking forward to genre conventions in its depictions of an inebriated master (who is nonetheless absent through much of the film) and its injection of knockabout tricksterism into fight sequences.[26] Sammo Hung's *Iron Fisted Monk* (1977) also grafted comic scenes into an otherwise conventional patriotic kung fu plot and setting, revolving around the Qing-era resistance by disciples of the Shaolin Temple against the ("foreign") Manchurian occupation of China. In it, light moments of slapstick sit alongside graphic bloodshed in the heroic mold of Bruce Lee.

These attempts to combine kung fu and humor were also undertaken in a context in which comedians, too, were incorporating martial arts action into their comedies, staging tongue-in-cheek kung fu combat scenes that often competed well in terms of entertainment value with their "straight" counterparts. *Private Eyes* included a much-imitated scene in which Michael Hui fought off an opponent with a nunchaku made of a string of sausages. Sam Hui, though not a trained martial artist, often played a character with a love of kung fu (also in, for example, *Private Eyes*). John Woo's *Pilferer's Progress* (1977), which starred the third Hui Brother, Ricky, alongside comedian Richard Ng, came to its climax with a spectacular, exhilarating, and extended battle of the heroes against the villain's Shaolin-trained henchman, played by veteran stuntman and kung fu performer Lee Hoi-sang. The sequence was choreographed by Fung Hak On, a ubiquitous villain in Shaw Brothers kung fu films and a fine stunt performer, who had studied Beijing opera alongside a number of other prominent martial arts performers and choreographers, including Lee Hoi-sang, Lam Ching-ying (who would become famous in his role as a Daoist magician in the Mr Vampire films and their many spin-offs), and Mars (a stalwart action director, performer and even costar in Jackie Chan's films).[27] The fight pitted Lee Hoi-sang's martial arts skills against the heroes' tricky wits and ability to take a slapstick fall. In the fight, Lee parodically performs a series of established kung fu villain tropes—such as when he falls into a vat of golden dye and his invulnerable body takes on the image of the Shaolin "bronzemen" of numerous films—not only satirizing overfamiliar motifs but also replaying their pleasures.

A number of experiments had already been made, then, in combining martial arts and comedy by the time of the release in 1978 of *Snake in the Eagle's Shadow* and *Drunken Master* (both directed by Yuen Woo-ping and starring Jackie Chan and Simon Yuen). It is nonetheless these films that, through their commercial success, cemented the genre as a viable one,[28] establishing a winning formula of stock characters, settings, plot devices, cinematography, narrative structure, action style, and comedic devices. Doing so, they not only initiated a cycle of comic films by the expanded cast and crew involved in their making but also sparked off an innumerable multitude of imitations.

Snake in the Eagle's Shadow and *Drunken Master* also, of course, marked the career breakthrough of Jackie Chan. After earlier false starts, in which producers had attempted to cast him in the heroic "Bruce Lee" mold, it was in these two films that Chan established the onscreen everyman-clown persona and comic performance style that he would go on to develop to become the most globally successful martial arts star.[29] The films, however, emerged from a broader milieu and also define the breakthrough moment for a wider group of filmmakers, both in front of and behind the camera.

Like Chan, many of the auteurs (whether this term be understood in terms of stars engaged in creating their own performance style, directors developing cinematic form, or choreographers envisioning new forms of action) who came to define this moment rose to prominence through experience as stuntmen in the Hong Kong film industry during the kung fu boom. Many of the most prominent also had training, before this, in Beijing opera performance. Involved in *Snake in the Eagle's Shadow* and *Drunken Master* (which shared a core cast, playing very similar roles) were figures, in particular, from two operatic "clans."

Chan himself was one of a group of performers who had trained together as children in the China Drama Academy, a prominent Beijing opera school, in the 1960s, and who went on to develop careers in the film industry as stuntmen and choreographers—most prominent amongst whom were Sammo Hung, Yuen Biao, Yuen Wah, and Corey Yuen. The surname that many adopted for their performance careers echoes the "Yuen" in the forename of their teacher, Yu Jim-yuen, as a mark of their debt to his training.

Snake in the Eagle's Shadow and *Drunken Master,* however, also cast Chan alongside and under the direction of members of another operatic dynasty that has played a prominent part in the development of onscreen martial arts. Confusingly for an English-speaking audience, this clan also uses the surname Yuen, though in fact in Chinese the two names are written with quite different characters. Playing Chan's teacher in both films is Simon Yuen Siu-tien. Yuen was a prominent opera performer and choreographer who made a shift into cinema in the 1940s and 1950s.[30] The director of both *Snake in the Eagle's Shadow* and *Drunken Master* was his son, Yuen Woo-ping, most famous today in the West as choreographer for the *Matrix* films (dir. Wachowski Bros., 1999–2003), *Kill Bill I* & *II* (dir. Quentin Tarantino, 2003–2004), and *Crouching Tiger Hidden Dragon* (dir. Ang Lee, 2000). Having apprenticed under his father, Yuen, alongside his brothers, had been working as a stuntman and choreographer throughout the 1960s and 1970s, and *Snake in the Eagle's Shadow* was his directorial debut. The Yuen Brothers, alongside Chan and his classmates, would go on to be key voices within the development of the kung fu comedy genre, and it is in many ways from their shared background in the acrobatics and physical clowning of Beijing opera performance, with its roots in folk culture, as well as in the physical rigor of stunt work, that the distinct aesthetics of the kung fu comedy genre emerged.

The Corporeal Aesthetic of Kung Fu Comedy

This aesthetic involved a very different vision of the martial arts body to the hyperidealized, sculpted, muscular—and ultimately nationalist—body presented in films such as Bruce Lee's *Fist of Fury.* Instead, the bodies we find in kung fu films are insistently imperfect, disorderly, abnormal, and excessive. In its idealizations a body like Bruce Lee's becomes immaterial—or, in Kwai-Cheung Lo's terms, even "sublime." Lo writes of a "hollow space punched out by Lee's muscular body," marking in its perfection an absent locus of transcendent desire through which postcolonial identity can form, a "fetish" marking the impossibility in Hong Kong identity produced by the absence of the motherland.[31] In contrast, the kung fu comedic body plunges us into the basely material, into everything that refuses sublimation. Action often revolves around the locations of the gambling den, the market, the restaurant, or even the brothel—locations that signify the appetitive rather than the disciplined body. We are presented with a cast of cripples, drunkards, beggars, fools, and drifters, effete scholars, scabrous (or often wine-guzzling and lecherous) monks, fat or elderly women, and white-haired eunuchs, all endowed nonetheless with fantastical agility, speed, and strength. Characters sport sprouts of excessive (or inadequate) facial hair, or moles and warts, or we find medicinal plasters attached to their temples. Freckles or red noses are painted on their faces, evoking, perhaps, the made-up face of an opera clown. Their eyes cross, or they squint through thick glasses. When they are hit on the head, absurdly oversized lumps appear.

The appetites of the body and its transgressions of its own limits in eating, puking, farting, and shitting come to the fore. As a mark of this, tableware items frequently become props in training or even weapons in fighting. For example, in almost the very first scene of *Snake in the Eagle's Shadow,* Simon Yuen's drunken beggar fights off a group of armed attackers using just a pair of chopsticks and a bowl. Later on, he demonstrates his fantastical physical skill to the film's protagonist, Chien Fu, by juggling with a bowl, and initiates Chien Fu's martial arts training by challenging him to snatch it from him, performing a series of acrobatic tricks with it balanced on his head. Food also plays a prominent role in *Drunken Master,* in a scene where the hero cheats a huge free meal from a restaurant. We see him manically guzzling down the gargantuan feast he orders, finally loosening his trousers and lifting up his shirt to display a swollen belly. Caught in the act, however, he is then beaten by the restaurant staff until he vomits it all back up.

Food even becomes a weapon in many kung fu comedy films. In *Drunken Master,* Jackie Chan attempts to fight a sword-wielding opponent with a pair of cucumbers, one in each hand, and later on spits wine in an opponent's face to blind and disorient them. For the "drunken boxer" in this film, wine itself becomes a source of power and inner strength (rather like Popeye's spinach). In *The Odd Couple,* Sammo Hung's character forces a series of raw eggs into Dean Shek's mouth and then beats him until, one by one, they are made to re-emerge, yolks unbroken, running down his face. In *Project A II* (dir. Jackie Chan, 1987), the hero, Dragon Ma (Jackie Chan) chews up handfuls of chili peppers, spitting the juice onto his hands to smear in the eyes of his opponents.

Toilet humor is prevalent, too, and the stink of body odor, farts, and bad breath are even used as an offensive/defensive strategy by characters, for example by Beggar So in the *Magnificent Butcher* (dir. Yuen Woo-ping, 1979). In *Drunken Master,* Jackie Chan's Wong Fei-hung descends even further into the scatological, not only farting in his opponent's face—calling it, in a parody of the poetic names of martial arts postures, "A Fart for the King of Sticks"—but also humiliating him by pressing his face into a cowpat, christening this move "Dog Eating Shit."[32] In *The Prodigal Son* (dir. Sammo Hung, 1981), Wong Wah-bo (Hung) teaches Leung Chan (Yuen Biao) a martial arts form—called, in the English dub, "Great Relief"—which mimes sitting on the toilet, straining, wiping, and flushing, complete with sound effects.

Perhaps, however, it's the figure of the "drunken master" himself (in some films named Beggar So / Sam Seed and played repeatedly until his death by Simon Yuen)[33] who most clearly epitomizes this shift. While, as Lau Tai-muk argues, it is from their youth, health, and physique that Bruce Lee's characters seem to derive their prodigal martial arts powers,[34] casting Yuen in a major fighting role, frequently beating multiple, skilled opponents, problematizes any such link between bodily perfection and kung fu ability. Yuen was an actor approaching his seventies, and, with the growing portliness that age produces, brings a certain stiffness and immobility to the role, one that he clearly "hams up" in certain scenes. This is undercut by the physical deftness Yuen had developed through a lifetime of opera performance (the aforementioned scene where he juggles a bowl is breathtaking, for example) and by the use of stunt doubles (usually Yuen's own sons) who facilitate the character's sudden manifestations of a dazzling physical agility unexpected from his shabby and ambling frame. While the *tiyu* (physical culture) movement of the twentieth century sought to use martial arts to promote youthfulness, fitness, health, and hygiene as the path to an empowered Chinese modernity, the "Drunken Master"—even in his very name—seems to transgress such an equation (fig. 1.2). Aged, alcoholic, and slovenly, as a wandering beggar the iconic figure of the drunken master lives outside both the respectable Confucian family and the world of work, defying both the productivity of the modern body and its reproductive powers. Unwashed and dressed in filthy, stinking rags, he refuses the disciplinary forces that twentieth-century martial calisthenics sought to embed in its practitioners, and the films seem to refuse the processes of political subjectification that "kung fu" might thus have offered.

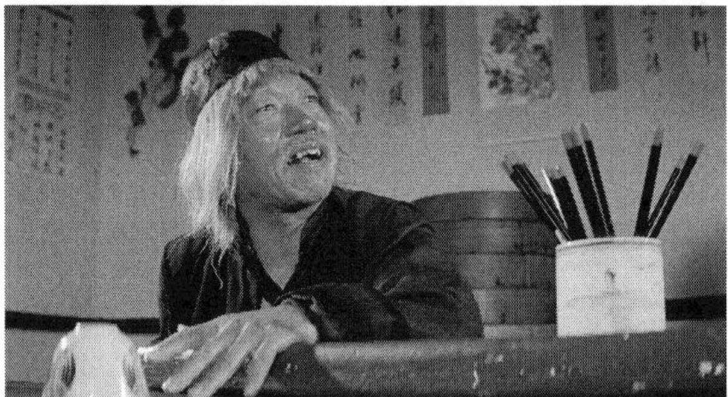

Fig. 1.2. A striking contrast to Bruce Lee – Simon Yuen as Beggar So in *Drunken Master*. Video still. © 1978/1985 Seasonal Film Corporation / 2017 Sony Pictures Home Entertainment / Eureka! Entertainment.

A further example of the comedic kung fu body's disregard for the norms and values of earlier martial arts culture is given in the rise of the portly figure of star, action coordinator, and director Sammo Hung. Christened "The Fat Dragon" in the eponymous title of one his films,[35] Hung's famously rotund frame belies the prodigal physical strength, agility, and flexibility evidenced in his performances. Lacking the looks to take on heroic roles during the early 1970s, Hung (like Simon Yuen) came into his own as a star with the rise of the kung fu comedy. In *Magnificent Butcher* (dir. Yuen Woo-ping, 1979), he was written into the drunken master cycle as Butcher Wing, one of the students of a now mature Wong Fei-hung (the character who Jackie Chan plays as a youth in *Drunken Master*) who, like Wong in the earlier film, turns to Beggar So for martial training. In *Knockabout* (dir. Sammo Hung, 1979), however, rather than playing the heroic lead, Hung takes on the role of Fat Beggar, a wily drunken-master-like character who teaches the film's protagonist (Yuen Biao) a style of "Garbage Kung Fu" to defeat his enemy. Despite Hung's obese frame and his character's disheveled and lazy appearance, the final scenes of this film—an extended fight in and outside a teahouse—his and Yuen Biao's acrobatic performances in the "monkey style," leaping and rolling over and under furniture and even swinging from the ceiling, have rarely been surpassed in terms of sheer, manic physical exuberance. Hung's very ability to move between "ageing master" and "young hero" roles perhaps says something about the erasure of a hierarchy of physical differences that might have been expected to structure these different narrative positions, performance styles, and star images.

Comedy Kung Fu and the Changing Economic, Political, and Social Context of Hong Kong

But what, then, are we to make of the "politics" of this new body? One set of responses has been to see the transition from the dominance of epic, historic, and heroic kung fu to its comedic counterpart as a simple process of depoliticization or of accommodation to the new conditions and demands of globalizing capitalism that characterized the rise of Hong Kong in the 1970s. This, after all, is the era Ackbar Abbas writes about as that of the "disappearance" in Hong Kong of the political under the combined forces of Cold War and post–Cultural Revolution paranoia, colonial censorship, and economic growth. Describing the culture of the 1970s and 1980s, he proposes that

> One of the effects of an efficient colonial administration is that it offers almost no outlet for political idealism. . . . As a result, most of the energy

> is directed toward the economic sphere. Historical imagination, the citizens' belief that they might have a hand in shaping their own history, gets replaced by speculation on property or the stock markets, or by an obsession with fashion or consumerism. If you cannot choose your own political leaders, you can at least choose your own clothes.[36]

As we saw in the introduction, this reading of the emergence of kung fu comedy as entailing a retreat from the political and an accommodation to the new forces of neoliberal capitalism and consumerism has been propounded by Leon Hunt, Chan Ting-ching, Ng Ho, Lau Tai-muk, and Yuan Shu, amongst others.

Chan, for example, has proposed that the films' historical settings are paper thin (they are usually located in a vague past, sometime around the end of the Qing or the early Republican era in an indeterminate backwater countryside presumably in Southern China, but well away from direct contact with historical events) and that they serve to offer us a "reflection of a modern competitive society in which only the fittest survive."[37] Such an argument might seem all the more emphatic if we consider the knockabout humor of these films and their cast of lower-class characters attempting to survive in a dog-eat-dog, materialistic world as derivative of the stories of modern Hong Kong told in the Hui Brothers' comedies. By projecting these conditions into the past, a satirical edge is removed from the films and they serve, perhaps, to naturalize and dehistoricize—and hence depoliticize—them.

Such a perspective offers one persuasive—though I will be arguing only partial—understanding of a number of characteristics of the body in such films, as noted above. If the body here seems to be thematized around excess, incompleteness, and transgression of boundaries, this could be read—in a rather "reflectionist" manner—as analogous to (or as expressing ideologically the new ontology of) the hyperliquid postmodern capitalism of the globalizing era. Such a consumer-oriented capitalism might be focused around the appetites of the body, which resurface repeatedly in these films. This consumer appetitiveness can be contrasted to the productive and disciplined body as required by earlier forms of capitalism and celebrated by the martial calisthenics movements of the earlier twentieth century—and in the heroic body celebrated in the films of the late 1960s and early 1970s.

My argument here, however, will be that rather than simply an abandonment of politics, what we see with the rise of the kung fu comedy is its transformation into a form that is less easy to read in the familiar terms of the modernist politics of the heroic body. As we will meet it in this book, the kung fu comedy remains a complicated and ambivalent site of ideological contestation, crisscrossed by opposing currents of accommodation and rebellion, progress and regress, left and right, modernity and tradition—just as, in fact, the patriotic body of the early twentieth-century *tiyu* movement and the heroic kung fu film are, too. Politics is not abandoned but displaced. As a result of this displacement we need somewhat different conceptual tools.

The suggestion that such films mark a retreat from politics, to begin with, assumes a form that the embodiment of "politics" takes. Within such a perspective, the politics of the body are imagined to involve its militarization/militantization through the kinds of corporeal technologies mobilized by techniques such as those of the martial calisthenics movement of the early twentieth century. In order to resist, the body is made strong and healthy—not to mention properly "masculine"—through the discipline that makes it conducive to political co-optation, whether this be leftist or rightist, imperialist or anticolonial. Such a version of the kung fu body exemplified the logic that, as discussed in my introduction, Rey Chow has critiqued through the notion of the "protestant ethnic." Here, "ethnic" identity is defined and valorized (only) in terms of the authenticity of resistance ("protest"). For Chow, however, this forms a mode not of emancipation, but of the management and commodification of ethnic identity. With an eye on Chow's critical schema, the narratives of heroic (authentic) resistance followed by (inauthentic) commodification and depoliticization that are so often woven around the kung fu comedy start to appear problematic. Perhaps, instead, what we see in the emergence of the kung fu comedy is precisely the waning of the very mode of politics we still see in Bruce Lee—and its bodily form—with "kung fu" taking on new and different valences. But how, then, are we to think about the politics of the kung fu comedic body?

Comedy Kung Fu and the Carnivalesque

The beginning of an answer to such a question has already been suggested in the analyses I have posed above of the figure of the drunken master. Rather than kung fu's traditional politics of discipline, the politics here would have to be one focused on *indiscipline.*

When dealing with such revolting and indisciplined bodies and their politics, one theorist it seems very hard not to introduce is Mikhail Bakhtin. As noted at the start of this chapter, this is something that both Leon Hunt and Mark Gallagher have already done in their accounts of kung fu comedies. However, such a move also requires critical scrutiny. Transposing Bakhtin's descriptions of medieval European culture to the context of modern Hong Kong raises significant questions. Furthermore, as supposedly "subversive," Bakhtin's category of the carnivalesque has also received somewhat breathless application to a range of contemporary cultural practices, making it at its worst a theoretically vapid and catchall valorizing term. There are nonetheless such close matches, at the very least in terms of surface characteristics, between the comedic kung fu body I have described here and Bakhtin's famous account of carnival that such a reference seems impossible to avoid.

Bakhtin argues that during the European Middle Ages, on carnival or feast days the normal, tightly enforced order of society was overturned: its morality, its rigid social hierarchies, the regimentation of life, and the denial of the flesh under conditions both of religious abstinence and drab poverty were all put aside. Instead, a world of celebration, laughter, freedom, and transgression was enacted. As Bakhtin puts it, "carnival celebrated temporary liberation from the prevailing truth and from the established order; it marked the suspension of all hierarchical rank, privileges, norms, and prohibitions,"[38] and it provided a "second life of the people, who for a time entered the utopian realm of community, freedom, equality, and abundance."[39] Significantly enough for our argument here, carnival was not a matter of "protest" and negation, but more of affirmation and celebration.

At the core of the riotous laughter of carnival was an experience of what Bakhtin terms the "grotesque body." Carnival and the folk culture within which it was embedded, rather than mortifying or transcending the flesh, plunged headlong into corporeality, celebrating in particular the body's "lower stratum."[40] The eating, shitting, and farting and the potbellies, lumps, and strong smells that are also so prominent in Hong Kong's kung fu comedies were also prominent amongst medieval carnival's characteristic tropes.[41] This grotesque body is posed in Bakhtin in contrast to the regimented, ideal body of Renaissance classicism, which asserts reason and order over the chaos and base materiality of the flesh. The "debasing" features of the grotesque body, however, are represented in a mode of celebration, rather than abjection and disgust, affirming rather than denying its anarchic appetites. The grotesque body, Bakhtin argues, is on the side of the *id* and of the return of all that the official order would otherwise repress.[42]

Bakhtin's ideas were taken up enthusiastically by late twentieth-century cultural theorists, and applied to any number of contemporary cultural phenomena, in order to propose ways that they offer "transgressive" pleasures that subvert forms of authority and order.[43] Such uses of Bakhtin were, however, often criticized, too: how transgressive are the actual "transgressions" at stake here? Peter Stallybrass and Allon White, for example, highlight the ambivalence of carnival, which on the one hand offered a break from the repressive order of everyday life in the middle ages, but on the other kept this within the strict temporal bounds of the carnival days. Carnival might then be understood as a "safety valve" for the frustrations of the poor, ultimately ensuring the continuation of the power of the elite for the rest of the calendar.[44] Would we ultimately have to say much the same with regard to the transgressions of contemporary cultural products? Read in this way, although the anarchic, "low," and bodily pleasures of the kung fu comedies of the 1970s could be understood as offering a realm of freedom and laughter, these are nonetheless contained within the ritual of the cinema visit and thus banished from the world of the everyday, where domination and poverty could thus be maintained.

Such misgivings might be amplified by another key difference between carnival and modern popular cinema: Bakhtin stresses that carnival is a lived, participatory mode of practice and experience, rather than a spectacle to be viewed.[45] As Bakhtin puts it, "carnival knows no footlights, in that it does not acknowledge any distinction between actors and spectators. . . . Carnival is not a spectacle seen by the people; they live in it."[46] It would seem a wild exaggeration to suggest the same for kung fu cinema, even if its modes of viewing—both by Hong Kong and Western audiences—seem to suggest something far more raucous and popular than properly bourgeois forms of cinema consumption.[47] Bakhtin admittedly suggests that mediation, too, can have a positive aspect—in, for example, the transformation of carnival into the "carnivalesque" literature of Rabelais—where the immediacy of the "lived" is sacrificed to allow a level of "self-awareness" that returns its energies to the realm of politics proper.[48] However, as a primarily commercial and generic rather than auteurial mode of cinema, the political intentionality of these kung fu comedies, too, remains weak.

Robert Stam thus argues that carnival, in fact, is neither intrinsically conservative nor radical, but has always been a zone of "complex crisscrossings of ideological manipulation and utopian desire."[49] As a result, we often have to *situate* individual manifestations of the carnivalesque within the particularity of their context to make more sense of how the tension between subversive and recuperative tendencies plays out. Similarly, Stallybrass and White warn against "false essentializing": while carnival could in many contexts provide a "stable and cyclical ritual" over long periods, perhaps even supporting that stability, in others it suddenly exploded politically, providing both a catalyst for and locus of struggle.[50] Similarly, although the debasing images of carnival could overturn the hierarchies that served the privileged elites, they were also—in a way that Bakhtin often ignores—frequently turned against the marginalized, weak, or different within society in ways that only served to reinforce rather than challenge dominant structures of power and exclusion.[51]

All this means that any serious attempt to think about comedy kung fu cinema through the carnivalesque will have to pay close attention to the particular politics within which it is entwined, and my account here introduces the notion of carnival not to suggest in it an inherent radicalism that replaces some other mode of revolt in the heroic martial arts film (or that it is radical simply because it negates something ultimately authoritarian in the latter), but to offer a way of thinking about them as complex, contradictory, and contested cultural products. Carnival does not so much name a political value of the films in itself, but rather helps us think about the form that politics takes in them.

Furthermore, Bakhtin's account of the carnivalesque has a very particular cultural reference in the popular cultures of medieval Europe, and this raises questions about what it might mean to map Bakhtin's figures onto late twentieth-century Hong Kong. One danger here is that we impose a blanket universalism that denies the existence of history, imagining the "popular" as an unchanging transhistorical and transcultural phenomenon, rather than a (shifting) product of relations of power and subjection. We may also project onto contemporary Hong Kong the image of a "premodern" European past, imagining Hongkongers as living primitives. The account offered here, which (drawing on Stam and Stallybrass and White) resists the abstracting tendency of Bakhtin in order to think about historical particularity, aims to avoid these core pitfalls.

Relocating Carnival

There are also, however, a number of arguments that support the applicability of Bakhtin's observations on the medieval European carnival. The first argument that may suggest Bakhtin's account may not be entirely specific to the European Middle Ages is that Bakhtin himself often slides from a historical description into the realm of an ideal prescription.[52] Because of this, Bakhtin has often been taken up as offering a broader "epistemological category."[53] In this regard there may be something useful in Bakhtin's tendency to universalize, at least when this is placed in dialectical tension with the need to rehistoricize.

Furthermore, written during Stalin's repressive rule in the Soviet Union,[54] Bakhtin's book has a clear allegorical intent. The absolute and tyrannical authority of the medieval church or monarch was meant, from the get-go, to intimate the nature of more modern forms of state power.[55] Researched and written during the 1940s, Bakhtin's text offers a critique of a wider totalitarian logic and its incorporation in the individual body that underpinned, amongst other things, the ideal bodies of the Olympian and mass calisthenics movements of the era, to which, we have already seen, the modern culture of martial arts was co-opted. The "carnivalesque" qualities of the comedic kung fu body appear—or reappear—at the moment when that regime is waning in power and offer an alternative to the drilled and perfected political body we still find in *Fist of Fury*.

Bakhtin's book itself was only able to find a publisher during the post-Stalinist thaw and the heady global tumult of the mid-1960s. It quickly received an English translation in 1968 and, as Stallybrass and White note, had already become a fashionable theoretical resource by the end of the 1970s.[56] In this regard, Bakhtin's book belongs to the same cultural developments that surrounded the rise of martial arts cinema, and its concerns also permeate the politics of the body of that era. We can thus see the comedic kung fu body as displaying something of the impetus of the 1968 generation, and so as a progressive force, certainly with regard to the body cultures that preceded it. The anarchistic ethos of the kung fu comedy seems to take the side of the forces of libertarian and hedonistic revolt of that era, even if such a revolt against a repressive, disciplinary society and its forms of incorporation was all the less urgent in the moment it found cultural expression in a comedic martial arts cinema some years later. The carnivalesque body of kung fu in this regard may be subject to the kinds of criticism levelled at the 1968 rebellions themselves, which some argue only paved the way for (and were only enabled to exist by) the emergent order of a rising socioeconomic constellation—neoliberalism—that had been held in check by the already-redundant conservatism of older forms of capitalism.

An understanding of the ultimate political valence of the grotesque body of kung fu comedies with regards to the subversion of such a form of discipline might, then, depend on how we understand the nature of globalized capitalism and its regime of flexible accumulation. For those who think that a society of regimented "mass" production was at this very moment being replaced by one of undisciplined consumption and regulated not through Foucauldian "disciplinary" mechanisms, but by those which Deleuze identified as typifying a newer "society of control,"[57] the kind of reading made by Hunt, Chan, and Ng, discussed above, will seem to make a certain kind of sense. However, one might also argue that though consumption and forms of "indiscipline" have become increasingly important, we still live in a society powerfully determined by production and the social relations inherent in this—and that to overstress consumption as determinate may be to mistake capitalism's ideological self-image for its underlying reality, which still in many ways requires repression and discipline from us. From a Marxian perspective, labor remains the "real" of such a society. Perhaps this marks a key contradiction within the regime of flexible accumulation—which ultimately requires its subjects to be both undisciplined, desiring consumers and disciplined, repressed workers.[58] Such a split might be understood as passing through the individual and their consciousness; through the temporal order of society (split into work hours and those of—quasi-carnivalesque—leisure); and also as marking geopolitical boundaries, dividing the "rich north" from the "poor south." Hong Kong in the 1970s, as a trading and manufacture hub on the boundary between East and West, and as a rapidly developing "Third World" zone, lies very much on this fault line. It was a place not just of rising consumption, but also, as Man-Fung Yip has stressed in his analysis of the kung fu film, of sweated and poorly paid labor.[59] Just as it was becoming a liberalized, Westernized city, it was also nonetheless characterized by still-colonial forms of authority, not to mention enduring "traditional" or "Confucian" hierarchies. Formed within this complex interplay of contradictory forces, the political function of the kung fu comedy seems to me to be a complex compromise formation comprising both "progressive" aspects and also others that accommodate themselves with the new social and economic forms of the regime of "flexible accumulation."

Grotesque and Acrobatic Bodies in the Kung Fu Comedy: Excess and Becoming

These contradictory forces and valences within Hong Kong's post- (or neo-) colonial situation can be further pursued into a Bakhtinian account of the way that the body is represented in these films, in order to begin to articulate the precise ways in which the films do offer resistance or recuperation.

Bakhtin proposes that at the core of the imagery of the grotesque body lies a principle of excess in which the body constantly transgresses its own limits and boundaries, as well as those of the society that imposed on it a proper order and form. This constant overflowing of boundaries and perpetual transgression of form is, for Bakhtin, a matter of the grotesque body always being in a process of metamorphosis—just like the fragments of ornament in Titus's baths after which the "grotesque" was named, where animal, vegetable, and human forms are constantly transforming one into the other.[60] This perhaps marks the root of the dangerous power of the grotesque, which contravenes the necessity, in the perspective of systems of order and control, of imposing stability, order, and permanence and fixing the identities and forms that might be a part of that. Rather than providing an ontology of things and their proper places, the grotesque proposed that "the inner movement of being itself was expressed in the passing of one form into the other, in the ever incompleted character of being."[61]

Certainly at a descriptive level, this principle seems to offer a powerful key to the nature of the body in kung fu comedy. This, too, is a body in flux and in constant transgression of its own limits, as well as in transgression of stable norms and ideals. Bakhtin frequently sets his "grotesque body" against a "classical" body, which is ideal, unified, and "finished," where the protuberances and openings to the world and its processes are denied or smoothed out, and around which an "aesthetics of the beautiful" was articulated—much like the sculpted body of the *tiyu* movement or Bruce Lee's "perfected" physique.[62] For Stam, the grotesque body resists the kind of "body fascism" that such idealized physiques might entail—an idealism that we might associate, again, with the totalitarian and nationalist projects of Stalin, the GMD, and the CCP alike.[63]

From a Bakhtinian perspective, in the kung fu comedy even the hyperflexibility and superathleticism of many of the stars—whose gymnastics outpace those of the heroic films made just a few years before by a qualitative leap rather than just a quantitative degree—seem paradoxically to fold back into the images of the abject and (seemingly) dysfunctional, "imperfect" body of the genre's cripples, drunks, and geriatrics. Rather than presenting us with a norm or ideal, the comic kung fu gymnast adheres to a logic of excess, and acrobatic performance is raised to the freakish or marvelous rather than standing for normalizable corporeal perfection. The device finds its apotheosis in the films where "drunken boxing," "crippled fist," or even "sickness kung fu" paradoxically become the ultimate (and most physically demanding) martial arts.[64]

In action, the acrobatic power of the kung fu comedian's body is also used to upend the hierarchy of the body. While the heroic martial arts star holds their body upright (and while their heroism is linked to their "upright" character), the comedian rather literally inverts the body, repeatedly turning upside down to fight, standing on their hands to kick or to evade, or rolling and tumbling around their opponent (fig. 1.3). The order of the body is scrambled by its very versatility as not only fists become weapons, but also every imaginable part of the anatomy.

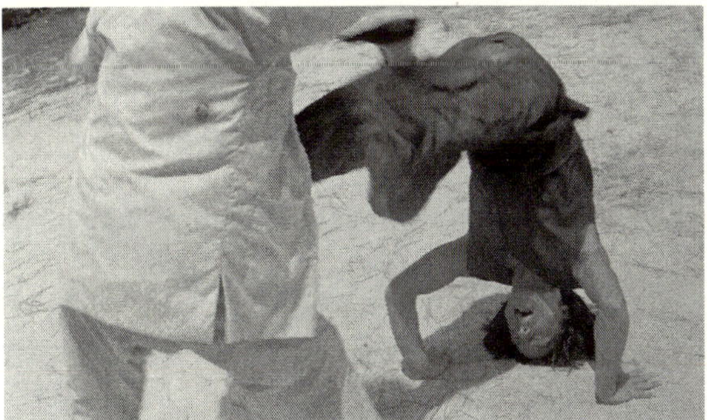

Fig. 1.3. The world turned upside down, acrobatically. Jackie Chan inverts his body to kick an opponent in *Drunken Master*. Video still. © 1978/1985 Seasonal Film Corporation / 2017 Sony Pictures Home Entertainment / Eureka! Entertainment.

In the Miracle Fighters series of films (discussed at further length in Chapter 5), clothing, prosthetic limbs, and disguise are often used to further scramble the order of the body, turning its back into its front, reversing gender, or even making arms function as legs. For example, in one of these films, *Shaolin Drunkard* (dir. Yuen Woo-ping, 1983), two characters attempt one night to lure out and confront a child kidnapper by dressing up as children—attaching masks to their buttocks and walking backward, bent in half to create diminutive beings. The fight choreography in their confrontation with the villain is cut to oscillate rapidly between shots of the performers' bodies dressed as their characters in the film are ("back to front") and then recostumed according to the "normal" orientation of the body to allow the actors full physical movement, creating for the viewer an uneasy sense of an unstable human anatomy in constant flux.

This logic of excess and incompletion overflows from the grotesque body into film form itself, where the attention to physical performance becomes superfluous to—and even corrosive of—the proper shape of narrative. The films tend—much to the dismay of many Western viewers—to "disintegrate" into a series of episodic set pieces that overwhelm the Aristotelian unity of the storyline.[65] Just as with the architectural decorations after which the grotesque was named, ornamentation outruns form or function and visual pleasure outweighs sense and "meaning." An enthusiastic Bakhtinian might read here the potential for resistance to the terms of ideological capture that the "closed" narrative might entail. Similarly, in terms of composition of shot, kung fu comedies generally seem to lack the interest in formal beauty that characterized, for example, the early films of Chang Cheh.

What is foregrounded in the kung fu comedy, then, is not only corporeal excess, but what Stephen Heath has dubbed "cinematic excess." Discussing Heath's idea, Kristin Thompson has read cinema as "a struggle between opposing forces": those which "strive to unify the work," making structure manifest, versus "those aspects of the work which are not contained by its unifying forces—the 'excess.'"[66] For Heath it is narrative in particular that provides a structuring force, while the "material practice" of a film's production inevitably returns to "haunt" the structure imposed by narrative.[67] In the kung fu comedy it is, above all, the physicality of performance—and of a performance tradition older than cinema—that returns to disturb the closure of narrative or of the film's "ideological" message. This often leaves the film "text" in a state of structural disunity and incoherence—an incoherence that will be taken up later in this book when I discus the hysterical nature of the kung fu comedy. This refusal (or failure) of closure or signification leaves the spectator—somewhat like the viewer of the avant-garde experiments Thompson celebrates—in a position where they are no longer "imprisoned," passively following a narrative, but where there is an openness to their active meaning-making from the film experience. This takes on a further significance in a colonial context and in a culture where censorship is in force and where the meanings made by the text and the ideological structures that it supports are inevitably organized for someone else's benefit. The poor and ethnically or otherwise marginalized groups who take such a prominent place within the global fan-base that emerged around kung fu cinema are similarly positioned.

The extent to which perpetual flux in such films is at the root of this openness and excess is also thematized within the extended training sequences that became characteristic of the genre. I will discuss these at further length in Chapter 2, where Bakhtin's insights find a cross reference in Walter Benjamin's discussion of early comic cinema. As will be further discussed there, these training sequences center on a transformability of the body and its capacities, and on its often bizarre, even surreal forms of becoming-other.[68] These are imagined through what Hunt has recognized as the increasingly outlandish martial art styles to be found in the genre.[69] In the kung fu comedy, we are treated to elaborate processes of becoming snake, cat, monkey, mantis, crab, or any number of other creatures. In *Drunken Master,* this also entails becoming-drunken-god (and not just one but eight different divinities) and even, finally, becoming-woman. (This will be discussed at further length in Chapter 5, where gender and masculinity become the focus.)

Again, we can remark something antiauthoritarian, which resists not only a set of traditional roles and norms—the conventionality of "Confucian" culture and the regimentation of the factory alike—but also resists the kind of co-optation to a "fascizing" nationalist project that was involved in the *tiyu* movement. On the other hand, however, we might again also see in all this restless transformation an image of the liquidity of neoliberal capital itself, in which, more than ever, Marx's famous description of capitalism as a system under which "all fixed, fast-frozen relations . . . are swept away" and "all that is solid melts into air" seems apt.[70] The gymnastic body in this regard accommodates itself to flexible accumulation's demand for its workers' malleability—and perhaps even literalizes this.

Globalization, Diasporic Consciousness, Parody, and the Carnivalesque Body

Having established the "carnival" characteristics of the kung fu comedic body, we can now return to the questions of Hong Kong identity raised earlier in the chapter, in order to think about the ways in which the grotesque might signify with regards to (post-)colonial and diasporic experience. That the carnivalesque may be a fertile concept through which to pursue such a question is suggested by the fact that, as Stallybrass and White note, the most successful attempts to apply ideas of carnival to contemporary culture often focus on "literatures produced in a colonial or neocolonial context where the political difference between dominant and subordinate culture is particularly charged"—perhaps most famously Roberto DaMatta's account of carnival as a key to Brazilian identity.[71] Discussing DaMatta, Stam notes that Bakhtin's theory itself is especially predisposed to the analysis of such postcolonial contexts because it was developed in a Russia that stood in a somewhat marginal or "liminal" relation to a European, metropolitan "mainstream." For Stam, late twentieth-century Brazil and early twentieth-century Russia share "insecure or tremulous nationalism in societies dominated by foreign-influenced elites," as well as an awareness of censorship and possible repression—all of which might also apply well to Hong Kong in the 1970s, and to many of the Southeast Asian countries that constituted its expanded regional market.[72]

In Stam's analysis, the appropriateness of carnival to the understanding of postcolonial (or neocolonial) popular cultures thus lies in the "double" nature of consciousness that such societies foster. Carnival itself provided a "double" life for its participants in contrast to the official culture with its pieties and proscriptions. In carnival, the world and the words of the official culture were rearticulated differently. Carnival participants lived in a world where their lives were both already spoken by the alien, oppressive discourse of power, but also re-spoken and re-appropriated in the ironized parodies of that discourse which carnival allowed. For Stam, this doubleness that comes from being the subject of both an official and a folk consciousness is echoed in the liminality of the colonial subject, who belongs simultaneously to the culture of the foreign or metropolitan elite and also to their "own" culture. Such might be a description of the hybridity of 1970s Hong Kong identity. That we see an assumption of the parodic forms of carnival in Hong Kong culture may bespeak the forms of irony that its subjects inhabited.

Such parody is evident in the character of the "drunken master" himself. Such a "drunken master" is something of an oxymoron in traditional Chinese terms, the "martial arts master" (or teacher of any sort) being expected to embody staunch, upright, noble, patrician values. Such values were associated in particular with the character of Wong Fei-hung, who above all others provided the archetype for the martial master in Chinese cinema during the 1950s and 1960s, serving as the hero of nearly a hundred films over those two decades.[73] The irreverent, parodic register of the kung fu comedy is signaled by the transgressive gesture made in *Drunken Master* of recasting Jackie Chan as a young Wong Fei-hung, "before" he became an upright master, imagining him as a rebellious, kung fu "punk" kid, causing trouble by mouthing off to senior students in his martial arts class, getting into fights seemingly for the thrill of it, and even molesting a young woman in the marketplace. Here, the "noble" figure of Wong is brought down to earth in a gesture of carnivalesque inversion. Wong's teacher in the film—and his model for moral behavior—is then figured as Beggar So, another Cantonese folk hero and one of the famous "Ten Tigers of Canton," usually imagined as patriotic and chivalrous defenders of the weak. In this film, So becomes a wandering alcoholic, unwashed, unkempt, ragged, and living on his wits.

It's not just the sacred cows of martial arts mythology and its cinematic representation that get this treatment: kung fu comedy films subject their world in its entirety to a parodic cannibalization that extends even to the soundtracks, which feature music famously appropriated from Hollywood (*Ironside* and *Star Wars* were favorites.) It is perhaps this pervasive ironic debasement of the high and mighty that leads commentators such as Hunt to read the genre as amoral and its heroes as cynical and self-interested.[74] Instead, this "amorality" might also be read as involving a parody of the modernity of the laissez-faire competitiveness of the capitalist culture of contemporary Hong Kong, also lampooned in the Hui Brothers movies, but now projected back into the backwardness of small-town provincialism of turn-of-the-century rural Guangdong. (This question of the supposed amorality of the genre will be taken up again in Chapter 3.)

The question of identity in Hong Kong, which Stam's location of carnival as a postcolonial aesthetic raises, is something that has already been discussed here as having been important in the more general rise of the comedy genre in the 1970s, with films such as *House of 72 Tenants* and those directed by Michael Hui. These, I have suggested, instituted a genre whose success seems to have paved the way for the formula of the kung fu comedy. I proposed that with these films, language was important in articulating a shift of identification from greater China toward more emphatically local identities, sometimes defined precisely in opposition to the mainland. It is perhaps suggestive that the rise of the kung fu comedy, too, largely coincided with a shift from the Mandarin production of martial arts films to Cantonese. The question, then, might be whether the comedy of the carnivalesque body—as opposed to linguistic humor—plays a part in such identity formation.

A film such as *Fist of Fury,* I have noted, offers us an image of longing for the lost nation-state from which the diasporic subject is exiled—an absent nation-state sublimated (as Kwai-Cheung Lo has proposed) into the ideal, dematerialized body of Bruce Lee.[75] Given what I have written so far, Lo's argument can be extended, noting the ways that Lee's ideal body signifies according to the logic of a nationalist (or "mass") body. However, in particular in the wake of the comedies of the early 1970s with their new attachment to Hong Kong, the comedic kung fu body involves the dissolution of these ties and the identification with a different body, one altogether less attached to the (absent, Chinese) nation-state or its physical ideals. The kung fu comedy's "carnival" body is an expression, if you like, of the loosening of these attachments. Detached from the singular ideal of the identical national mass, Hong Kong cinema's comedic kung fu body celebrates instead the impurity, heterogeneity, even cultural (if not precisely racial or ethnic) hybridity that might typify the experience of identity in the colony—suspended as it was between China and the West, and situated in the midst of global economic, cultural, and migrant flows.

Carnival, Comedy Kung Fu, and the Popular Body

In the kung fu comedy, then, with its heterogeneous, even unruly corporeality, we are faced with what I would like to term a "popular" rather than a "mass" body. In this, comedy kung fu accords with the "all-people's character" that Bakhtin accorded the grotesque body of carnival. For Bakhtin, "the material bodily principle is contained not in the biological individual, not in the bourgeois ego, but in the people, a people who are continually growing and renewed," and the grotesque body refers us "not to the private, egotistic, 'economic man,' but to the collective ancestral body of all the people."[76] It is such an incorporated self-image—literally "ancestral" in its projection back into the past—that the comedy kung fu film perhaps provided for its Hong Kong audiences and for diasporic Chinese audiences more generally.

Some thirty years on, Bakhtin's description of such an unruly "all-people's" body is reprieved in the inhabitants of "Pig Sty Alley," the primary setting in Stephen Chow's 2005 nostalgic reworking of the martial arts comedy genre, *Kung Fu Hustle*—one of the most prominent places where we might trace the "legacy of the Drunken Master" in contemporary Hong Kong cinema. Pig Sty Alley—with its aptly carnivalesque name—is a poor slum tenement, obviously based on that depicted in *House of 72 Tenants,* with all the suggestion that this might carry of the slum as an allegorical image of Hong Kong. Amongst the inhabitants live—unnoticed until the events of the film unfold—three unlikely-looking and ageing kung fu masters: a ragged coolie, an effete tailor, and a balding cook. The landlady and landlord of the tenement turn out to be even more powerful martial artists: she a fat, middle-aged woman with curlers constantly in her hair and a cigarette hanging from her mouth; he a skinny, lecherous, perpetually henpecked, and rather unprepossessing man. The coolie turns out to be a master of flying kicks, the tailor of "hard" fist styles, and the cook of spear and pole fighting. The landlady has developed the special "internal" skill of the "lion's roar"—a shout so loud and powerful that it not only shatters glass but shreds all physical objects before it, while the landlord has a rubbery "tai chi" flexibility and softness that allows him to absorb any attack on his body and redirect its force back to his attacker.

These figures emerge from, and belong to, the larger, collective, grotesque body of the inhabitants of the alley. When we are first introduced to them at the start of the film, it is as they perform their morning ablutions at the communal water pump, in the midst of food, flatulence, sexual innuendo, bum-cleavage, oversized underwear, and all the Bakhtinian processes of the "lower bodily stratum." When, later, the film's hero Sing (Stephen Chow) comes into conflict with the inhabitants there, the grotesque possibilities of the image of the "all-people's" body embodied in the crowd offer Chow much opportunity for humor. Pretending to be from the notorious axe gang in order to extort money from them, Sing challenges anyone in the gathered crowd to fight him (fig. 1.4). Each person who steps forward (only to be rejected by Sing as an opponent) turns out—through CGI trickery—to have a distinctly peculiar body. Sing attempts to choose weak-looking people but each time is foiled—he first selects a woman from the crowd, but when she steps out, she is a tough peasant made strong through work. He picks out what looks like the shortest person, who stands up to reveal that they are in fact bizarrely tall, but had simply been sitting down. A character wearing glasses (who Sing assumes is therefore a "wimp") turns out to have the overdeveloped muscularity of a bodybuilder, and when Sing picks out a small child instead, the child steps forward displaying a similar physique. Each time, the individual bodies of the slum-tenement crowd, once they are drawn out of the anonymity of the "collective ancestral body," turn out to be marked by excess and disorder. Just as in the drunken master comedies of the 1970s, the popular body refuses good form.

Petrus Liu's arguments about the politics-beyond-nation of martial arts literature in his book *Stateless Subjects* may help us further understand the signification of such a grotesque, "popular," communal body and its difference to the national, "mass" body. Liu argues that the Chinese martial arts novel, as it emerged in the twentieth century, has consistently refused narratives of the desire for a strong nation-state, as expressed in the literary and intellectual modernism of the early twentieth-century New Culture Movement, which sought to modernize China and reject its feudal past in favor of Western models of rational efficiency. (Early twentieth-century martial organizations such as the Jingwu movement discussed above, of course, were a part of this modernizing

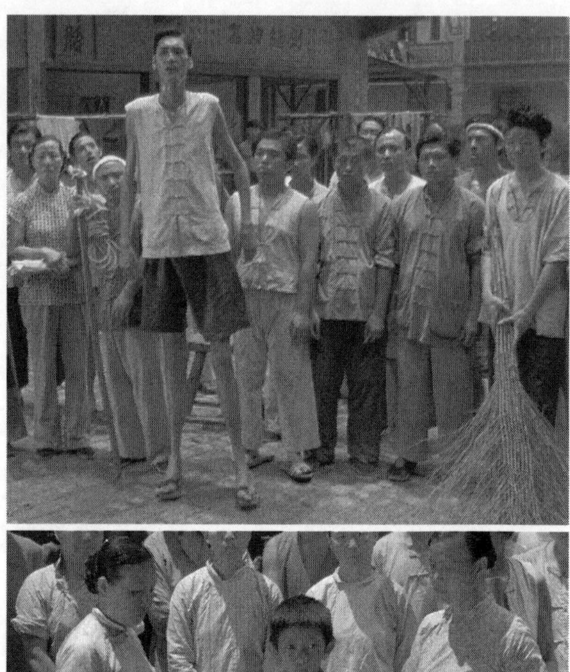

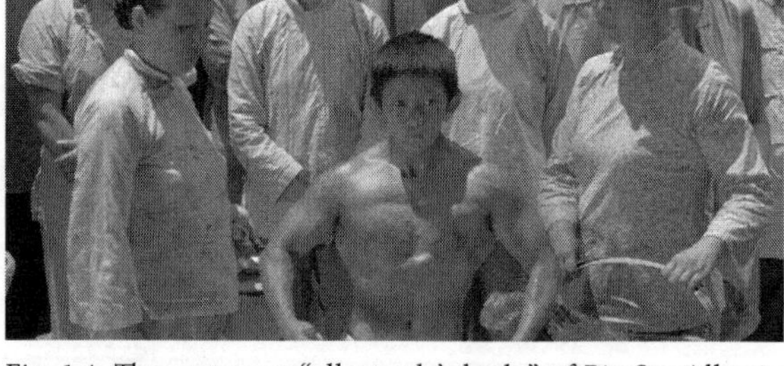

Fig. 1.4. The grotesque "all-people's body" of Pig Sty Alley in *Kung Fu Hustle*. Video stills. © Columbia Pictures Film Production Asia 2004.

nationalist discourse.) Instead, suggests Liu, the martial arts novel often contested this version of modernity, positing forms of community, belonging, social organization, and meaning beyond the organization of the nation-state—holding out a model of what it would be to become "stateless subjects."[77] With regards to the cinema of the 1970s, such a fantasy of life and identity beyond the state may have been strong in Hong Kong under colonial rule, and in particular in the shadow of the Cultural Revolution in the PRC and the White Terror of the GMD in Taiwan, neither of which, perhaps, would have offered the image of more benign governance or a more attractive pole of identification. The "impurity" of such a body may also have made it such a favorite in particular for marginalized audiences abroad—the African American contingent, for example, who were so important in the US reception of Hong Kong martial arts cinema.

However, in spite of a certain refusal of the state, there may nonetheless remain something "fascizing" in such a populist vision. The body in such films remains—perhaps all the more so in imagining it as organic rather than politically constituted—almost exclusively an ethnic one, genetically Han Chinese and, even more restrictively, fundamentally Cantonese. Where we see other ethnicities—whether Chinese minorities such as Tibetans or Manchurians, or whether these be Japanese, white, black, or South Asian foreigners, they appear in a demonized guise, for ritual carnival abuse. In all this, the "abstract nationalism" that Stephen Teo discovers in Bruce Lee's movies (a nationalism that subsists in the cinema of greater China and in the wider Chinese diaspora, but which does not attach itself to any of the nation-states that claim to represent a "Chinese nation") takes on a rather more alarming and reactionary face.

Beyond the Protestant Ethnic?

This chapter, then, has set the kung fu comedic aesthetic of the grotesque, carnivalesque body against that of the heroic martial arts films of the late 1960s and early 1970s. During the chapter, I have understood this latter aesthetic—one emerging from the idealizing, normative, and nationalist tendencies of the early twentieth-century martial arts cultures of China—through Rey Chow's notion of the "protestant ethnic." Chow's critical concept upsets the narratives that are often told about the development of kung fu comedy as a fall from a more "authentic" and properly militant assertion of national identity in the martial art cinema of the preceding decade. It allows me to develop a more nuanced sense of the kung fu comedy not simply as a reflection of, but also as a nuanced and partially resistant response to, Hong Kong's conditions of capitalist and (post-)colonial modernity.

Though the literal religious reference of Weber's phrase on which Chow plays for her terminology may seem oddly out of place in the Chinese context, the "Protestantism" here is apt not only in terms of the play Chow makes on the "protest" that is so often associated with ethnic identities. Inasmuch as Protestantism was a religion of individual conscience and subjectivity—a form that remains central to the capitalist self—this is profoundly at odds with the popular collectivity of the carnival.

Carnival, then, I have argued here, takes us beyond a politics of the militant, nationalist body. But it doesn't take us beyond politics as such. The nationalist body of kung fu was a certain response to an experience of Western imperialism and, in the Hong Kong context, to more directly colonial conditions. However, the grotesque body of kung fu comedy, I have argued here, can also be read as a colonial or postcolonial response to conditions which were rapidly changing as new forms of capitalism developed. Within the context of changing relations to the mainland and increasing ambivalence to "Chineseness," the body as we meet it in kung fu comedies seems to express an emerging hybridity, fluidity, and complexity of identity, as well as the "doubleness" of colonial life. Its disorder and lack of fixity resisted the order and conformism that such a colonial world imposed upon the body, but largely without nostalgia for an imagined "purity" that nationalism might provide. Picking up forms of carnival inversion, it enacts a celebration of a popular body beyond the nation-state and its identifications at a point when nationalism must have seemed increasingly problematic and when "people" and "nation" were increasingly difficult to conflate. This popular body offered a pole of identification and political subjectification in many ways separate from (and implicitly in opposition to) that produced by the governmental rhetoric of the nation-state. If heroic kung fu films such as *Fist of Fury* refer identity back to "roots" in an essentializing maneuver, kung fu comedies such as *Drunken Master* seem instead to define their audience (both at home in Hong Kong and abroad) in terms of the intercultural "routes" within which they are travelling or on which they are located as a staging post. Nonetheless, as I have described them here, antiauthoritarian and anarchic though the films might be, their politics are made up of a complex mixture of both progressive and regressive forces, as popular culture perhaps always is. If an aspect of the carnival body is its ever-unfinishedness, then this might also be true of its political valence, which is also to a large extent indeterminate—and which may in any case depend not only on what was done with it *then,* but also what we might wish to do with it *now.* It is in this regard precisely a question of "legacy"—as signaled by the title of this book.

It is these aspects of the open, the in-transformation, and the unfinished in the grotesque body that I will pick up in the next chapter. This will turn away from Bakhtin's conceptualization of such characteristics in terms of carnival and think about them instead with reference to Walter Benjamin's discussions of the body as it was found in early comic cinema—in the films of Buster Keaton or Charlie Chaplin, as well as in the cartoon bodies of Mickey Mouse in the first Disney films. The relation—often clearly self-conscious—between Jackie Chan's physical craft of performance and that of Buster Keaton, as we shall see, is a frequently noted one. Benjamin, however, offers us a path to understanding such a relationship, posing provocative questions about how we might evaluate the "utopias of the body" we encounter in such performances as responses to "modernity." I will pursue this modernity, with regards to Chan at least, as one that can be reinflected, just as Bakhtin's carnival can be, as globalizing and (post-)colonial. The following chapter, then, will continue the exploration, begun here, of what kind of a response to the conditions of Hong Kong life the kung fu comedy might be, and why it might have a relevance to us beyond that context.

CHAPTER 2

Utopia

> On the one hand, film furthers insight into the necessities governing our lives by its use of close-ups, by its accentuation of hidden details in familiar objects, and by its exploration of commonplace milieux through the ingenious guidance of the camera; on the other hand, it manages to assure us of a vast and unsuspected field of action.
>
> —*Walter Benjamin*

In the last chapter, I argued that to begin to think about the politics of kung fu comedy—which I am approaching in this book in the light of the politics of the body—we need to shift away from approaches that read this in terms of the nationalist bodies of the modern era. I proposed that the striking resonances between the bodies in Hong Kong comedies of the 1970s and the "grotesque body" of European medieval carnival might help us open up new ways of thinking about the politics of the body there. Nonetheless, I proposed, these parallels to carnival imagery do not in themselves valorize the martial arts comedy. Carnival was itself a complex and contested terrain, crisscrossed by both emancipatory urges and also forces of social conservatism. As much as carnival offered its peasant participants a mode of expression and experience that stood in contrast to—and opened up a critical angle on—the restrictive official culture of the time, carnival also functioned as a regulating mechanism, only serving to reinforce and naturalize the cultural norms and ideologies of the elite, even as it transgressed these. The recognition that kung fu comedies may function according to a similar logic suggests that a further analysis of the *particular* opposing forces that crisscross the visions of the body in these films is necessary. For this, we need to look further at *particular* aspects of the films, and we need to draw in further theoretical materials to think about them.

In this chapter, I wish to pursue possible resonances between the kung fu comedy of Jackie Chan in particular, the silent-era slapstick films that emerged from vaudeville, and the anarchic violence of early twentieth-century cartoons.

(Bey Logan has gone as far as to write that "Chan was born a real-life cartoon character.")[1] Though starting once again by analyzing Chan's initial drunken master films, this angle will allow me to trace one of the "legacies" of these in his ongoing work, in particular through an analysis of his film *Project A,* which marked a new stage of his career in the mid-1980s.

Such parallels between Chan and Hollywood slapstick have often been drawn in discussions of kung fu comedy, both in academic discourse and its more vernacular counterparts, though usually the comparison remains a surface one rather than a matter of in-depth analysis.[2] Marking parallels between forms of early Hollywood comedy and 1970s kung fu cinema begs, rather than answers, the question about the meaning of any similarities between the two.

The reference to these older cinematic genres is often, of course, an explicit one within the films, especially with regard to slapstick. Chan himself has cited Keaton as a reference point for his work in numerous interviews,[3] and a number of stunt sequences in his films pay direct homage to the "silent greats." In *Project A* (dir. Jackie Chan, 1983), for example, after being entwined in the gears of a clock in a manner that might remind a viewer of the famous scenes in *Modern Times* (dir. Charlie Chaplin, 1936) where Chaplin's factory worker is sucked into the bowels of a machine, Chan dangles from the hands of a clock tower (fig. 2.1) in what can only be an intentional replay of Harold Lloyd's iconic stunt from *Safety Last!* (dir. Fred Newmeyer and Sam Taylor, 1923) (fig. 2.2). To underline the explicit nature of these references to the silent screen, in his sequel *Project A II* (1987) Chan restaged Buster Keaton's famous trick where the façade of a house falls down around him; he is saved from a grisly death only because he is standing in the precise spot where space is left by an open window when the wall hits the ground. Similarly, it may tell us something about the cultural investments of Chan's long-term collaborator Hung Kam-bo that the nickname he took on and by which he is better known—"Sammo"—is drawn from the name of the hero of one of China's most famous cartoon strips, Sam Mo, or "Three Hairs," a scrawny street orphan whom Hung was thought to resemble.

Chan's persona, then, is assembled by replaying slapstick stunts, and Sammo fashions his in the image of a comic-strip character. Each, in this regard, self-consciously activates a particular cinematic and popular-cultural legacy in their work. But what are we to make of their "elective affinities" with these moments from the cultural past? Can they be understood as more widely significant than the particular (and arbitrary) tastes of individuals?[4] My argument here will be that there *is* indeed something worth analyzing in such a historical relationship. To understand these relationships as more than arbitrary, I will think about them in terms of the historical connections between Hong Kong in the 1970s

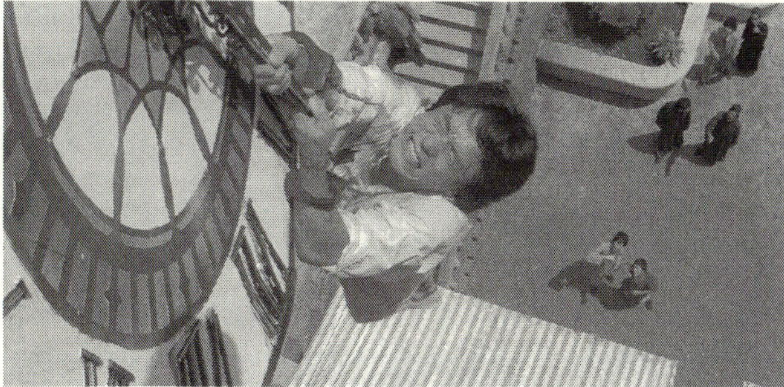

Fig. 2.1. Jackie Chan hangs from a clock tower in *Project A*. Video still. © 2010 Fortune Star Media.

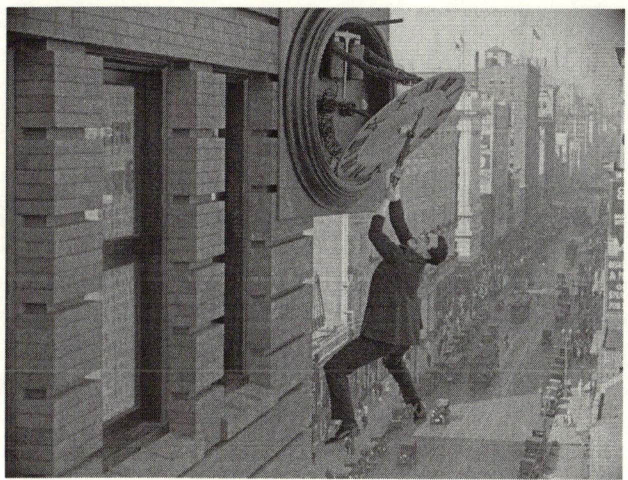

Fig. 2.2. Harold Lloyd hangs from a clock tower in *Safety Last*. Video still. © 1923 Harold Lloyd Trust / 2013 Criterion Collection.

and the early twentieth-century European and American context of slapstick and cartoon comedy. This throws us into the set of historical connections and continuities (as well as disconnections and discontinuities) that we began to establish in the previous chapter. At the heart of this historical relationship are questions about embodied experiences of modernity and modernization at these two different moments and geographical locations—and about the ways that modernity is inflected by the Hong Kong experience of (post-)coloniality and capitalist globalization. This last is something that Man-Fung Yip has discussed in his book *Martial Arts Cinema and Hong Kong Modernity,* and my account of the kung fu comedy in this chapter will build on his insights there.

With regard to the previous chapter, we might also understand Hollywood slapstick and cartoons of the 1920s and 1930s to offer a link to the popular carnival tradition itself, drawing on the same utopian "grotesque realist" iconography of an anarchic body and world in flux. Central in my analysis in this chapter, however, will be an examination of cultural critic and philosopher Walter Benjamin's engagement, throughout the 1930s, with the early Mickey Mouse cartoons. Benjamin's shifting positions on Mickey Mouse—as Disney's own output changed and as the political situation in Europe grew ever darker in the rising shadow of National Socialism—offer us a number of ways to think about the politics of the body in cinema in general, and they open up useful perspectives on the kung fu comedy, on its "cartoonesque" violence, and on the elastic, resilient bodies of its characters and stars, who are seemingly as impervious to permanent harm as Donald Duck or Wile E. Coyote. Bakhtin, as we have seen, explored the resonance of a popular culture of the body in relation to one modern totalitarian regime; Benjamin (who was born just three years before Bakhtin) complements this with an investigation of folk culture's antagonistic relation to another such dictatorship. Benjamin was a canny analyst of both the utopian potential of the ways that human experience was being transformed by new modes of technology—technologies of representation as much as any other—and also their nightmare potential for mass domination. Benjamin's meditations on Mickey Mouse, within such a context, will offer us an entry point, in Chapter 3, to thinking further about the roles of derealized comic violence in cinema. They also, however, open up an understanding of the very transformability of the body in the kung fu film. In the last chapter, we saw how this physical as well as mental flexibility has been understood as a prime capitalist virtue, and Benjamin—a key thinker of the ways that the human body is subject in the modern world to a new regime of shocks and dislocations—helps us think further about the ways that the kung fu comedy's corporeal iconography might either embrace or transcend such a virtue.

Benjamin's "On Mickey Mouse": Fascism, Capitalism, and the Alienated Body

Benjamin's first discussion of Mickey Mouse came in a short, unpublished fragment, written in 1931, "On Mickey Mouse."[5] Benjamin's interest had been aroused by the German release of the first Mickey Mouse film the previous year, which launched a veritable craze for the cartoon rodent. While Disney today is something of a watchword among the critical left for reactionary mass culture,[6] the German intelligentsia's reaction to the company's first animations was altogether more positive. The films were widely lauded for their technical avant-gardism and for their surreal, jazz-age anarchy. Mickey Mouse—who in the German context seemed to carry with him a cosmopolitan glamour—was even taken up as an anti-Nazi symbol, with left-wing publications during the rise of Nazism advising supporters to wear Mickey Mouse badges on their clothing, as an alternative to the swastika. The pro-Nazi press in its turn attacked Mickey Mouse as anti-Aryan and—in terms that resonated with the racialized language of abjection through which the Jewish were denounced—complained about a cinema that celebrated "vermin."[7]

It was, perhaps first off, this very impurity with regards to Aryan racial hygiene that Benjamin, the anti-Nazi Jewish intellectual, enjoyed in the cartoons, understood as an antidote to the idealized bodies of both Nazi ideology and a broader bourgeois humanism. For Benjamin, Mickey "disrupts the entire hierarchy of creatures that is supposed to culminate in mankind."[8] Or, as Esther Leslie puts it, he is "spirited and insubordinate . . . a pesky, ratty creature, creating mischief, indulging in vaudeville and low-life."[9] He's not a million miles in this from the "kung fu punks" played repeatedly by Jackie Chan in his breakthrough moment, or their descent into the "animal" discussed in the last chapter. This suggests that Mickey Mouse (like Jackie Chan) is a creature connected to Bakhtin's "grotesque body" and its subversion of forms of ultimately totalitarian body idealism. (We hardly need Leni Riefenstahl's films to remind us of the ways that Nazi Germany's eugenics program was powerfully invested in idealist physical culture movements profoundly concomitant with the nationalist body discussed in the last chapter.) Such a position is only reinforced by Benjamin's reading of Mickey Mouse as a modern version of the fairy-tale imagination.[10] Benjamin and Bakhtin, faced by modern forms of totalitarianism, both looked to a popular "folk" past as its antidote.

However, Benjamin's interest in Mickey Mouse penetrated beyond the racial politics of 1930s Germany, and Disney cartoons afforded him an analysis of the wider nature of experience, subjectivity, and embodiment in capitalist modernity. Benjamin, struck by the enormous popularity of Mickey Mouse, surmised that "the explanation for the huge popularity of these films . . . is simply the fact that the public recognizes its own life in them." For Benjamin, this was to say that the Mickey Mouse cartoons registered something of the peculiar alienation of the body and the self that he elsewhere diagnosed as characteristic of the capitalist, industrial, and urban world of the twentieth century. Subtitling his note on Mickey Mouse an analysis of "property relations" in the cartoon, Benjamin foregrounded the way that the body had become not an integral and inalienable part of the self but an object for others. Benjamin writes that in Mickey Mouse films, "we see for the first time it is possible to have one's own arm, even one's own body stolen." He proposes that Mickey's movements, rather than being propelled like the athletic and intentional body of a "marathon runner," are more like that of an "office file." Our bodies, and by extension our lives, Benjamin seems to be suggesting, are often passively and helplessly subject to the same impersonal forces of bureaucracy and economics as paperwork as it flies from desk to desk.[11]

Benjamin would go on, most prominently in his work on Baudelaire, to extend this insight, developing analyses of the human body and self as increasingly subject to (and objectified by) the traumatic shocks and deadeningly inhuman rhythms of modern life, from trench warfare through to the stop-go lights of urban traffic systems and the mechanical discipline of the Taylorized factory floor.[12] Such an experience is, of course, parodied in the work of silent comedians. This is done most famously in *Modern Times,* where Chaplin's worker is subjected to the discipline of the factory and the rhythms of the production line. Harold Lloyd's tussles with the motor car in *Get Out and Get Under* (1920) and Keaton's famously "mechanical" physical performance style might also register the way that the body is transformed into an object by these new forms of industrial technology, and might start to embark on a mimesis of it, turning the body into a mechanism and a thing.[13]

Surpassing the Wonders of Technology

However, for Benjamin, Mickey Mouse seems to do more than simply reiterate the human body's pacification at the hands of the machine. The blurring of the boundaries between the animate and the inanimate set up by slapstick and early Disney films cuts both ways, involving a reanimation or re-enchantment of objects, machines, and nature itself, as well as an objectification and deadening of the life world. The mimesis of machinery by the human body seems to overshoot the mark of reification, taking on the new and fantastical powers unleashed by capitalist industry itself. Chaplin's body in *Modern Times,* after all, refuses to be pacified by the factory. The mechanical cadence of the pathological twitch he has taken on after a prolonged period tightening nuts on a tyrannically paced production line takes on a surreal libidinal dimension, and the end of the film's factory scene has him pursuing a woman with nut-shaped buttons on her dress out into the streets, his wrenches still in his hands, still convulsing to the machine's now obscenely sexualized rhythm. Keaton's machinic performance style itself can also be seen as opening up new vistas in imagining the abilities of the human body, and hence a new freedom of movement. As well as recording the alienation of the modern condition, Mickey Mouse and slapstick thus also bring to light a set of utopian fantasies lodged in the heart of the very same technology that otherwise seemed a tool of oppression.

Benjamin, then, returned to Mickey Mouse in his essay of 1933, "Experience and Poverty," arguing that

> the existence of Mickey Mouse is . . . a dream for contemporary man. His life is full of miracles—miracles that not only surpass the wonders of technology, but make fun of them. For the most extraordinary thing about them is that they all appear, quite without any machines, to have been improvised out of the body of Mickey Mouse, out of his supporters and persecutors, and out of the most ordinary pieces of furniture, as well as from trees, clouds, and the sea. Nature and technology, primitiveness and comfort, have completely merged.[14]

Property Relations in Jackie Chan Films: The Training Montage

Can such an analysis be extended to the kung fu comedy? During the 1970s, Hong Kong was certainly experiencing a period of rapid modernization that in many ways rivaled the upheavals of the European metropolises in Benjamin's lifetime. The colony was at the forefront of the convulsions of globalization and the shift in the world economy from a "Fordist" mode of factory-line production (often still located in the old heartlands of the developed world) to the present-day variation of capitalism, which has been dubbed the regime of "flexible accumulation." In this system, international capitalists move industry to wherever labor is cheapest, with the minimum investment in machinery that might hamper their future mobility, and they make highly differentiated products in small batches, in ways that track shifting demand much more nimbly than the older, more standardized "mass" forms of production.[15] Though large-scale and high-tech mechanization is thus less important under flexible accumulation than in the more immediate aftermath of the industrial revolution, work is increasingly precarious—and corporeally intensive—for those in the global sweatshop hubs, such as Hong Kong was becoming in the 1970s and 1980s, when "Made in Hong Kong" became a familiar mark across the world on low-cost plastic, textile, and electronic goods. With labor cheap, and working conditions relatively unprotected, one might indeed expect some of the kinds of experience of the dehumanizing and alienating nature of work, and the violence that it wreaks on the human body, to come to the fore again in Hong Kong culture of this period.[16] Indeed, such is the argument of Man-Fung Yip in his work on martial arts cinema during this period, which he diagnoses as "marked by a more emphatic corporeal focus" than its predecessors. In this, he argues:

> The robust bodies of the action heroes, with . . . their use as an instrument for overcoming adversity and achieving success, conjured up in many

> ways the capitalist ethos of hard work, competition and conquest, and ascetic perseverance widely considered as the driving force for Hong Kong's phenomenal economic growth in the 1960s and 1970s. In particular, the spectacle of physical mastery and empowerment spoke to the main target audiences of the films, namely young, blue-collar workers for whom the body, as vehicle of physical labor, was often the only "tool" which they could count on to improve their economic and social standing. [17]

In the early Jackie Chan comedies we certainly see something of this. Admittedly, the direct thematic exploration of "labor" is often avoided—with its Marxian overtones, it may well have been an incendiary theme in the 1970s, when politics became famously taboo in Hong Kong culture. Here, though, I will follow Yip in arguing that the figuration of "kung fu" and its training presents us with a displaced image of the laboring body—of both its alienation (as we have seen Benjamin put it with regard to Mickey Mouse, "it is possible to have one's own arm, even one's own body stolen"), and also of the ways that such a body might be reappropriated.[18]

The theme is perhaps introduced most clearly in the genre-defining opening film of the drunken master cycle, *Snake in the Eagle's Shadow* (dir. Yuen Woo-ping, 1978). Its hero, the orphaned Chien Fu (Jackie Chan), works as a janitor in a martial arts school, where he can only fantasize about training. Chien Fu is not only given demeaning and physically punishing work to do while the school's clients—spoiled children of the town's wealthy merchant class—get to practice martial arts, but he is further objectified by being made the school's "human punch bag" (as one character in the film puts it). For the instructors, their kung fu is a commodity for sale on the open market, and when they wish to make themselves or a student look expert in order to sell their school, they wheel Chien Fu out as an "opponent" who is forbidden to fight back in earnest and made to take a beating. Chien Fu is someone whose body—to echo Benjamin—really is no longer his own. Also adapting Benjamin's claims that Mickey Mouse films were popular because "the public recognizes its own life in them," one might read this as offering an analogue for the experience of labor in Hong Kong's many sweatshops—and perhaps offering broader resonances for a transnational audience increasingly subject to the same economic imperatives.[19]

But if work in such films is often alienating and physically brutal, it has its opposing image in "kung fu" itself. The term "kung fu" (or, in Mandarin, *gongfu*), which, as well as denoting a cinematic genre, has come to name Chinese combat systems themselves in the Western vocabulary, more properly does not actually designate martial arts specifically, and has a significant etymology with regards to questions of labor. The word more generally refers to skill: you can have *gongfu* in flower arranging or making tea, for example, as well as in fighting, where these things are raised to the status of an art. Furthermore, it refers especially to skill that is developed over long periods of repeated work. The first character of the term, 功 (*gong*), which takes on a range of meanings including merit, accomplishment, and power, is homophonous with and includes the radical 工 (*gong*), which on its own means "work," "labor," "worker," or "craft," among other things. The *gong* of *gongfu,* however, as we meet it in the martial arts comedy, certainly seems to entail a rather different mode of work or labor to that experienced under capitalist conditions.

As noted in the previous chapter, a key trope in the genre is the "training montage," and it is in this that we most clearly meet the distinction between kung fu and capitalist labor. Ironically, such training seems at first sight to be just like the brutal alienation of exploitative work. It is physically punishing and seems to involve giving one's life over as property to a master.[20] The student's body is no longer their own; rather, it is made into an object of manipulation by the technology of training, and by the outlandish mechanical apparatuses that often serve as its adjunct, which carry with them an uncanny, if distant, echo of the modern factory. The formula was already established in *Snake in the Eagle's Shadow,* but developed in Chan's and Yuen's follow-up, *Drunken Master* (dir. Yuen Woo-ping, 1978). Here, the film's hero, Wong Fei-hung, is given over (against his will, and as a punishment) by his father to the teacher Beggar So. Wong hears the rumor from a classmate that So is sadistic and delights in injuring and even maiming his students under the pretext of training, and attempts to flee. When by chance he encounters So, he is kidnapped by him and forced to train, initiating the famous scenes where Chan's body is put through one ghastly punishment after another. It is from the seeming cruelty of these scenes that Leon Hunt (among others) would seem to have the impression, noted in the last chapter, that So is amoral and sadistic.

However, the training is not simply alienating. The body (and by extension the self) is not only the *means* for the work of kung fu, it is also the *object* upon which kung fu works, its raw material *and* its product. The benefit accrued in this work passes to the student—unlike in capitalism, where the fruits of labor are appropriated from those who toil by those who own the means of production. The result of kung fu is a transformation of the practitioner's body, which becomes newly powerful. The point is perhaps made most famously not in a Hong Kong film, but in an American appropriation of the martial arts genre, The *Karate Kid* (dir. John Avildsen, 1984). In this, the young hero, Daniel (Ralph Macchio), becomes the student of karate expert Mr. Miyagi (Pat Morita). It seems at first that

Daniel is simply put to work varnishing Miyagi's fence and cleaning his car for free. It's only later that "Daniel-San" realizes that the movements of the work he has been doing—"wax on, wax off," "paint fence, up, down"—have been conditioning and programming his body for a series of powerful karate blocks and strikes. If Mr. Miyagi seems at first to have misappropriated Daniel's labor, it turns out that he has instead been gifting him an invaluable lesson. Similarly, while Chan's Wong Fei-hung in *Drunken Master* breaks nutshells with his fingers for the lazy Beggar So, who guzzles down the food contained in them, he is also developing the power to grasp and crush an opponent's body with his bare hands.

Another example is *Return to the 36th Chamber* (dir. Lau Kar-leung, 1980), in which Gordon Liu's Chu Jen-chieh attempts to enroll at the Shaolin monastery in order to fight injustice, only to be refused the kung fu training he hopes for. He is instead put to work repairing the walls of the monastery. However, watching the monks train and integrating the style of their movement into his work, he comes to develop a new martial arts style, based on the skills and strengths fostered in his construction of the bamboo scaffolding necessary for this, and to use this to defeat his tormentors. This is, in fact, a film that is more broadly organized around themes of work and its appropriation. The film's conflict is initiated in the struggle over ownership of a dyeing factory, which is being taken over by ("foreign") Manchu occupiers during the Qing dynasty. The struggle over the factory and the profit that it produces is thus a matter of class, setting workers against their bosses, but also of "colonial" occupation and ethnic tension, which may have been resonant in the Hong Kong situation. Here, the monastery is set up as an alternative space to that of the dyeing factory, in which a different, non-exploitative logic of labor is at work, and it is through such labor, even, that the means of production are wrestled back. Of course, this ethno-nationalist, anticolonial narrative in the film locates it within the tradition that, as I proposed in Chapter 1, was replaced somewhat by the kung fu comedy. It is worth noting in this respect that the film's director Lau Kar-leung, though himself a pioneer of the kung fu comedy, was an influential figure in developing the cinematic and choreographic style of the heroic martial arts film during the late 1960s and early 1970s, and the film itself continues a cycle of Shaolin Temple films that served as a mainstay of this, so both director and film serve as something of a bridge between the two genres.

Of course, one way of reading such depictions of kung fu as work in the comedy film might insist on the way in which this symbolic "solution" to alienated labor reiterates capitalist ideology. Yip, for example, argues that for all the extent that kung fu films reimagine what is essentially the experience of factory work as an ascetic practice leading to emancipation—and therefore present it as "an emblem of 'liberated labor,'" —this remains, in the final account, no more than a "fantasy" that "constitutes in the end a regulatory and disciplining mechanism that is anything but liberating."[21]

We might add that the only alternative to exploitation, it seems from the kung fu comedy, is to become a micro-capitalist owner of one's own body.[22] What we have is in this regard no more radical than (and perhaps serves as an extension of) the antiheroes of the Hui Brothers comedies, discussed in Chapter 1, who attempt to flee the world of wage-labor by becoming small-scale entrepreneurs.

However, from a Benjaminian perspective, in the transformation of the body through training we have an example of a certain mimesis (a copying) of a technological and economic logic, embedded now in the body itself, that reappropriates its productive powers for the purpose of the transformation of self and reality. As in Benjamin's account of Mickey Mouse, "miraculous" powers that "surpass" and "make fun of" those of the industrial and capitalist world are "improvised out of the body." I hesitate to call this a "human" body, in that, just as with Mickey Mouse, the body here subverts the "hierarchy" of beings, plunging into the inanimate and mechanical (in its alliance with and imitation of machinery), into the animal (in becoming snake, cat, monkey, or the like), and also into the super- or post-human in its assumption of new powers (in becoming dragon[23]—or even drunken god).

As imagined in the training sequences of films such as *Drunken Master* and *Snake in the Eagle's Shadow,* then, it is paradoxically through an excessive mimesis of the objectifying powers of (post-)industrial capital that the body becomes more than an object, and is rehumanized, as we are reconnected with deep, animal aspects of our life. It is only through the alienation of the body that it can become an object of the work, manipulation and discipline that allows for its transformation and its ultimate return, in altered guise, to the subject.

In the Miracle Fighters series of films, made by Yuen Woo-ping and his brothers in the 1980s in the wake of their work on the drunken master films, images of technology—both archaic and modern—become increasingly scrambled in films notable for their sheer hallucinogenic absurdity.[24] The "kung fu" that the protagonists and their enemies practice is no longer straightforwardly a martial art as we might understand it, but, as it is integrated into supernatural plots, becomes ambiguously a matter of fighting skill, trickery, the conjurer's sleight of hand, and actual magic. In a Méliès-like (or early Disney–like) reiteration of the *fantastique,* paintings of waterfalls can gush out real water, origami butterflies take off, pet fish talk (and even die for their masters), giant poison toads are controlled by playing music, human bodies can be folded down flat so their toes point out from under their chins, pancake dough can be made by simply throwing flour through a stream of water pouring from a bottomless pail, and roast chickens fly through the air and burst into flames, all in a manner that seems to extend and dovetail into the unreal physical virtuosity and dexterity of the films' performers, as miracles both magical and martial are "improvised" from their bodies. That such miraculous magical-martial artistry might explicitly serve to "not only surpass the wonders of technology, but make fun of them" is underlined in the many devices that serve as premodern analogues of industrial technology—such as, for example, the magically powered car driven by a drunken monk in both *Taoism Drunkard* and *Shaolin Drunkard.*

In Benjamin's early drafts of his most famous essay, "The Work of Art in the Age of Mechanical Reproduction," the figure of Mickey Mouse was introduced once again in order to emphasize the utopian powers of such an image of transformation, which entailed a rejection of the "prison-world" of everyday experience, which strikes us, with all the force of the given, as incontestably true. For Benjamin, Disney cartoons played a role in developing an understanding of the redemptive powers he understood to lie at the heart of cinema itself. Mickey Mouse was excised from later drafts of the essay, and this insight about the transformative powers of cinema was preserved only in terms of an "optical unconscious" revealed by the technical powers of the camera to show us the world from unimaginable angles. These reveal previously invisible aspects of reality that "shatter" the ordinary appearance of the world that we carry around with us and that limits our understanding of it. In the essay's first version, however, Benjamin grounded this explosive logic of the "optical unconscious" in its parallels with the surreal, re-enchanting, fantastical transformations of body and world—and hence the "unsuspected field of action" Benjamin discusses in this chapter's epigraph—that are to be found in the first Mickey Mouse cartoons and American slapstick, and that are, I have been arguing here, preserved in kung fu comedies.[25]

Benjamin, then, expresses a complicated, dialectical ambivalence to technology—to both the productive technologies of the new industrial world and the reproductive or representational ones of the emerging mass media. I will thus now turn to further discussion of Benjamin's understanding of technology, in order to further understand the nature of the mimesis of technology in the kung fu comedy.

First Technology, Second Technology, Kung Fu

In his second version of the essay, Benjamin, in fact, divides technology into two types: "first technology" and "second technology." The kinds of modern, industrial mechanization with which the term technology is usually associated constitute what Benjamin calls "second technology." This is defined in relation to older forms of technology—"first technology"—associated with magic, myth, and ritual, and rooted primarily in the intensive use of the human body itself. For Benjamin, such things as magic or ritual served as technologies inasmuch as they stood, at earlier stages of human development, as attempts to control and conquer nature, which still held humanity within the violent grip of necessity. If premodern forms of technology served as a means by which humanity emancipated itself from such want, in Benjamin's always-dialectical thought, such technology also has negative dimensions: the connections to myth and ritual pin it to conservative, authoritarian and mystificatory forces, forces that Benjamin worried were being resurrected by fascism in its manipulation of the mass image as a means of social control.[26]

Second technology, in its operational rationality, for Benjamin seems to open up ways beyond these now regressive technological and cultural forms. However, this, too, is ambivalent. As many modern commentators stress, such forms of technology are often experienced in terms of the domination, alienation, and exploitation that I have discussed above as a part of capitalist life. Nonetheless, for Benjamin—writing as a messianic revolutionary—these do not encompass the "essence" of (second) technology. Rather, this lies in its utopian, revolutionary potential—the potential to free humanity by developing new productive powers, ending want and opening life out into the realm of dream and fantasy. For Benjamin, then, the essence of such technology is "play," in particular the playful renegotiation of the relationship between humanity, nature, and technology itself.[27] If Yip, as discussed above, condemns kung fu cinema's depiction of kung fu as emancipated labor as (mere) fantasy, in the Benjaminian sense we might now accord it, "fantasy" is not just falsehood—it is a productive and transformative power.

As Benjamin emphasizes at the end of the essay, technology only takes on a nightmare form where an exploitative elite, unwilling to let technology play itself out in this way, appropriates its powers as means to dominate the rest of humanity. It is this organization of the industrial base of society by capitalism and fascism that sets technology against the human body.[28]

In Miriam Hansen's incisive analysis of the theme of technology in Benjamin's work on cinema, she argues—piecing together passages from a range of his fragments—that Benjamin sees the reintegration of aspects of "first" and "second" technology as key in humanizing the latter. Hansen points to Benjamin's fascination in a number of places with intensively corporeal practices that might be closely associated with the "ritual" origins of first technology. While martial arts are not discussed—although certainly known in the West, they still had a rather low profile within the European cultural consciousness during the inter-war era—Benjamin does, in a couple of places, discuss the parallel, "Eastern" practice of yoga in ways that might suggest the role that kung fu might have taken within his thought. In a passage from *One Way Street* entitled "Antiques," Benjamin values the way that yogic breath control and Buddhist chanting might serve as ancient technologies of physical self-control that are key to the production of forms of imagination and power, and the self-creation of the human will.[29] Hansen thus argues that

> regulating the interplay between humans and (second) technology can only succeed . . . if it reconnects with the discarded powers of the first, with mimetic practices that involve the body, as the "preeminent instrument" of sensory perception and (moral, political) differentiation. . . . Negotiating the historical confrontation between the human sensorium and technology as an alien, and alienating, regime requires learning from forms of bodily innervation that are no less technical but to a greater extent self-regulating.[30]

This is, perhaps, a key part of Benjamin's fascination with both the physical discipline of the slapstick comedian and the way that cartoons are rooted in forms of reimagined corporeality. In both, we are faced with reinventions of the body, impossible without the mediation of the new mass-reproductive technology of cinema itself. We are faced with both intensely corporeal and highly mechanized practices, and cinema's emancipatory potential appears precisely in its power to combine these two aspects within its images.

Hansen's argument here also provides a way of understanding representations of physical self-transformation in the kung fu comedy. These transformations are grounded in intensely corporeal practices that are certainly coded within their cinematic representations as rooted in tradition and in ancient forms of mystical knowledge, even if there is some debate by contemporary martial arts historians about just how "ancient" or "mystical" they really are.[31] These representations are also, of course, themselves rooted in second technology. Within the world of the film, as I have argued, the techniques of training are imagined in ways that echo the industrial organization of capitalist modernity. Such representations are also entwined within the high-tech cinematic apparatus itself and its ability to represent, replicate, and refigure the human body, enhancing its powers through all the trickery of film and its narrative power.

This analysis allows us to return and say a little more about the definition of "kung fu" itself and its relation to ideas of "labor," as discussed above. If, as

I argued, kung fu does not simply equate with capitalist labor, this is because the work involved belongs not to the era of "second technology" but to the older world of "first" technology. The work of kung fu is not that of the proletarian "worker"; rather it is artisanal in nature. In this regard, Yip (as cited above) perhaps overequates martial training and modern labor; the former, perhaps, *also* carries something heterologous that his argument does not fully capture. The etymology of the term—and its broader meaning beyond the designation of the martial arts—points to this fact, with "craft" being one of its significations. The radical for work (工) contained within the character *gong* (功) is in fact a pictogram depicting a carpenter's measure. It is the artisan, the value of whose labor resides in their long-acquired, embodied expertise, who has *gongfu* in their trade. "Kung fu" thus evokes a whole preindustrial realm, and its romantic appeal (both within and beyond cinematic representation) lies precisely in its power to evoke a wider realm of practice that escapes the alienating logic of modern production. Perhaps the appropriate Benjaminian translation of *gongfu* would thus not be "labor" (which is too crude and misses all this) but rather "experience." For Benjamin, experience—the slow, layered integration of what happens to us into our very being and identity, in transmissible form—was being threatened in modernity, emptying life of depth, wisdom, and meaning, and leaving us helpless in the face of the onrush of baffling and seemingly patternless new impressions. If experience equates to mastery (drunken or otherwise), then in the modern world, we are left without the resources for command over our lives or our realities. Experience and its transmissibility might be a key to the thematic of training within the kung fu comedy film, and of the relationship between master and disciple, which is also so often central in its narrative.

Project A: Kung Fu and the (Post-)Colonial Landscape

So far in this chapter I have explored a number of ideas in the work of Walter Benjamin that offer, I have argued, useful ways of interpreting the kung fu comedy and the ways that it is situated as a response to the experiences of capitalist modernity. In particular, the kung fu comedy becomes legible as an insubordinate reaction to experiences of the alienation of the body within the world of work, and as offering a redemptive image in which the new powers of the industrial world are incorporated (or in Benjamin's terminology, "innervated") into the body itself, through a process of mimesis, to rehumanize them. These powers, within the cinematic imagination at its most emancipatory, open up a critical vision that refuses to accept the world as it is (and as the current regime would like it to stay), envisioning the possibility of transformation not only of the body and the self, but also of the whole world of things within which we live. Such a cinematic dream-world (opposed to the "prison-house" of the everyday) begins to resemble the utopia of carnival in which all things are involved in constant transformation.

This certainly helps think about the ways that the kung fu comedy might offer an image within which a global audience subjected to the ongoing processes of alienation within the neoliberal regimes of transnational capitalism "recognizes its own life." However, the analysis has not yet taken account of some of the *differences* between the particular context of Hong Kong that surround the production and first reception of the kung fu comedy and the moment in which Benjamin was writing. To do this—and to understand the kung fu comedy not just as repetition, but as taking up and transforming a legacy within a new context—we need to shift the analysis to take into consideration questions of colonial history and experience. What happens, then, when we start to understand the forms of violence, alienation, objectification, and unfreedom to which these films respond not just as entailing a new regime of technology, but rather forms and experiences of *colonial* modernity? To start to unravel this question—while also testing out the usefulness of a Benjaminian approach through more extended application—I will turn in this final section of the chapter to the analysis of a particular film, Jackie Chan's *Project A* (1983).

Project A is an unusual film within the kung fu comedy genre in its specific historical location and the explicitness with which it offers us an image of the colonial world. While many comedy films are located somewhat imprecisely in time and space, in a slightly loose vision of late Qing or early Republican southern China, *Project A* is clearly set at the height of British Empire—as is made clear in the very first image of the film, depicting the front of an Anglo-colonial-style building and marked with the subtitle "In Early Hong Kong." Though unusual in the explicitness of its colonial setting and its colonial imagery, I take *Project A* as useful in revealing the colonial experience latent within the wider genre of which it is a part.

The film—made during the early stages of a period that has been characterized as dominated by the looming handover of Hong Kong back to Chinese rule and by consequently intense cultural reflection on the history of the British rule of the territory[32]—revolves around the conflict between the local police and coastguards, and the attempts of the latter to capture a band of pirates who have brought trade to and from the island to a near halt. Though in many ways somewhat tender and nostalgic in its detailed reconstruction of the past, the film is nonetheless satirical in the images of the corruption, incompetence, and muddle of colonial life, as exemplified by both its European and Chinese representatives. Overall, however, for the purposes of my analysis here, which will seek to apply Benjaminian insights into representations of the body, the film's plot is rather less important than an attention to physical performance.

Chan's signature style of comedy action, as it had been developing up to this point, had increasingly become organized not simply around arranging fights and choreographing martial arts moves, but around the creative use of objects and environments with which he is now most commonly associated. It has been argued that something very similar was at the heart of Charlie Chaplin's comedy, which often built its humor out of the transformation of objects from their mundane uses to new and surprising ends, based not on convention, but on the morphology of the object itself.[33] Chan and Chaplin here can both be read in Benjaminian terms as presenting us with a new mastery of the modern environment and with a rehumanization of the alienated world of things, which lose their "essential" and tyrannically fixed nature.

This all happens, in hyperbolic form, in the action scenes of *Project A,* as is exemplified in the many reconfigurations of the relationship between the human body and the simple chair within the film (just a few of these are shown in fig. 2.3). In the restricted, "normal" use to which we should put them, chairs can be understood as tools for the discipline and socialization of the body, and the constant commands of adults to children should alert us to this fact. ("Sit up straight!" "Don't tip the chair backwards!" "Don't put your feet on the table!" "Stop shuffling and sit still!" etc.) Chairs in this sense rule, determine, and order the human body through use. However, rather than something to be sat on in the "proper" manner, a chair in a Jackie Chan film is also for leapfrogging over, rolling across, or even for a momentary headstand. With a strike coming toward one, the body may well spin around to lie on the chair, ducking underneath the strike. And tipping the chair back in what would normally be a disastrous fall, the acrobatic kung fu comedic body might turn the upturned seat of the chair into a form of shelter behind which the body might momentarily nestle before rolling away or flipping around to move into a new position for attack or retreat. Wielded in the hands of the stars of *Project A,* Jackie Chan, Sammo Hung, and Yuen Biao, the chair is no longer a chair, but a shield, a tool for disarming or trapping an opponent, or simply a heavy bludgeon. Tucked rapidly under the body, it might become, again, a launchpad, or a perch on which to posture and pose before the next exchange with an opponent.

Similarly, in *Project A* coat stands become polearms; vases become Indian clubs; bamboo poles are no longer for hanging washing on, but become jousting lances for knights mounted on bicycles; bedpans become missiles, fired with a flick of the foot using a bicycle wheel as a launching device; tables become battering rams or vaulting benches; windows become portals to exit and enter a space.

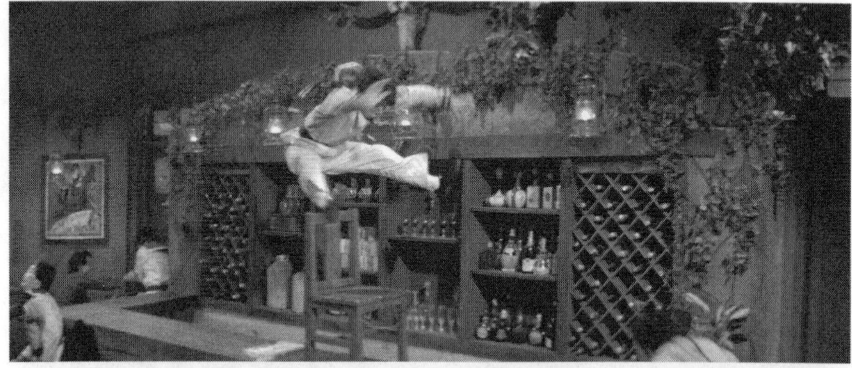

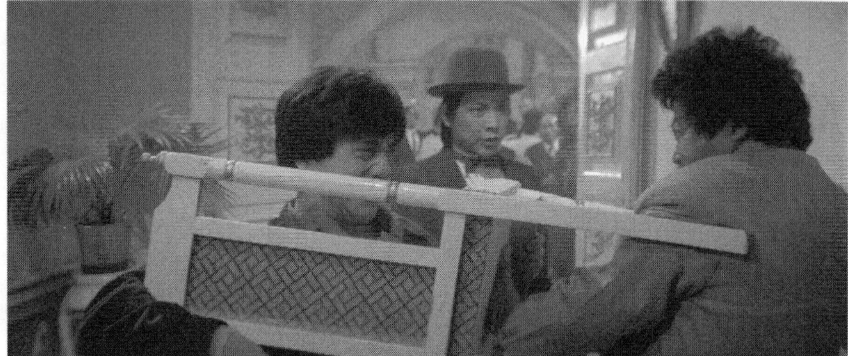

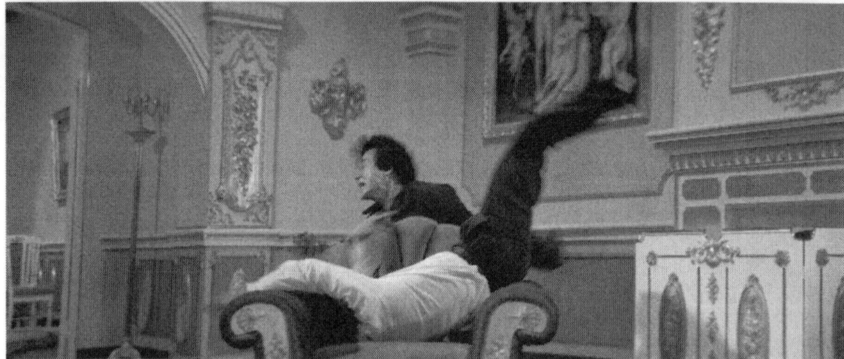

Fig. 2.3. When is a chair not a chair? When it's in a Jackie Chan film . . . Video stills from *Project A*. © 2010 Fortune Star Media.

Banisters are for vaulting over or sliding down; flagpoles are for climbing up, out of harm's way; awnings break your fall; chandeliers are useful to swing from . . . If Benjamin describes how the camera offered the potential to shatter the "prison-world" of the everyday landscape and our habitual traversal of it by showing us that world from previously unimaginable angles, so revealing an "optical unconscious," Chan's physical performances reveal another, corporeal unconscious, buried in things themselves and our habitual physical relationships with them.

To carry out this transmutation of things, Chan takes on the "cunning" and "high spirits" that Benjamin praised as the essence of the fairy tale.[34] As with Mickey Mouse, "miracles" are conjured from Chan's body, those of his "supporters or persecutors," and "out of the most ordinary pieces of furniture."[35] However, it is no longer the world of industrial machinery that these miracles "make fun of," but rather a colonial order and its material and spatial instantiation.

In his influential critique of colonialism, *The Wretched of the Earth,* Frantz Fanon argued that domination in the colony is structured through spatialized forms of exclusion and control, and that it is through such spatial domination that colonial violence is instituted and made a part of the everyday experience of the colonized subject. The world such a subject inhabits is, in Fanon's words, a "narrow world, strewn with prohibitions."[36]

Project A certainly doesn't offer the kind of open anticolonial and ethnonationalist revolt against such an environment that Bruce Lee's *Fist of Fury* does, with Lee kicking to pieces a sign on a park gate that reads "No Chinese and No Dogs" and beating unconscious the foreigners who attempt to keep him out and humiliate him through his exclusion. Chan's character in *Project A,* "Dragon" Ma, is in contrast a loyal member of the official colonial law enforcement services, dedicated to upholding the status quo. However, Chan as Dragon Ma nonetheless introduces an element of anarchy into colonial spaces through his physical traversal of them and his refunctioning of their logic.

Hong Kong was, in comparison to the French-held Algeria that Fanon knew and on the basis of which he developed his critique of colonialism, far less repressive. However, what at the very least had a very literal dimension in the context of the overcrowded enclave was the sense of the "narrowness" of colonial life.[37] This seems to have left a stamp on Chan's performance style, and in *Project A* this is perhaps most spectacularly envisioned—and most obviously brought to the fore as a choreographic concern—in the bicycle chase through old Hong Kong's narrow alleyways, where the protagonists have to zigzag their ways through the cheek-by-jowl lives of its inhabitants, navigating impossibly tight right-angle turns as fantastical leaps, or climbing up walls to escape speeding pursuers (fig. 2.4). At speed, ordinary aspects of the landscape such as opening doors or shutters, ladders, street stalls, or debris on the ground become both mortal hazards and tactical opportunities. The relation between the human body and the bicycle itself becomes radically refashioned to make them tools for a superhuman traversal of the colonial metropolis.

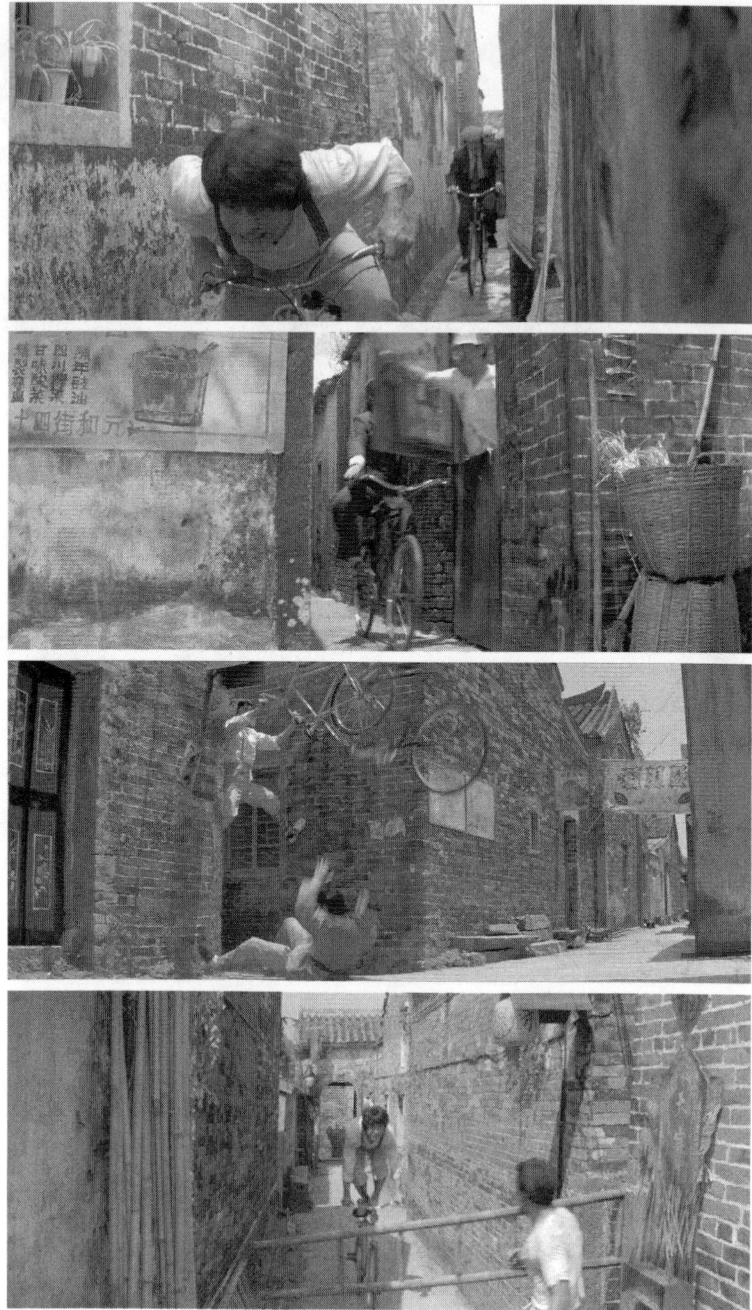

Fig. 2.4. *Project A*'s bicycle chase through the narrow streets of old Hong Kong. Video still. © 2010 Fortune Star Media.

The logic that pits the body against the colonial organization of space, however, is even set up in the very opening sequences of the film, for example, as we see Ma, in his colonial coastguard uniform, rushing to a meeting at the police and coast guard headquarters. After leaping from his still-moving bicycle, which crashes madly into a bicycle rack, disintegrating as it does so, Ma rushes up the evocatively colonial staircase of the building and along its wooden balconies. He vaults and spins over a handrail to get past oncoming employees within the narrow space available, without breaking his stride, defying the "proper" function of the architecture. His wild running contrasts to the neatly regimented marching columns of his colleagues and, as he reins himself in in front of a superior officer, it becomes clear that his mode of propulsion is a transgression of correct protocol.

The architecture of the colonial police headquarters is also renegotiated by Ma later in the film, when he decides to spy on his superior officers, hoping to hear good news about the reinstatement of shelved plans to attack the pirates. Ma transforms a chimney into a tunnel that takes him into the heart of the administration, bypassing the normal security that keeps social inferiors away from the private discussions of their superiors. Ma, however gets more than he bargains for when the (English) governor steps aside from his (Chinese) commanders into a side room to do a deal with a wealthy businessman who is in fact in league with the pirates. The governor's inner-sanctum-within-an-inner-sanctum sets up a further spatial divide in rank and privilege between him and his high-level subordinates. Ma, however, has come into this very room, and it is his illicit eavesdropping, discovering his superior's guilty secret—and his superior's discovery that he has done so—that allows him direct access to the ears of the very highest level of colonial authority. Being in the center of the administration, Ma gets the privilege of putting the moral case to the governor for fighting the pirates rather than doing a deal with them. Chan's/Ma's physical renegotiation of the environment thus undermines the normal hierarchies of the film's world, which are realized in the architecture of the police headquarters and its regime of physical exclusion.

Another location in the film where the colonial ordering of space is clearly at stake is an exclusive club, in which one of the film's most spectacular set-piece fights takes place. The police (including Ma) have arrived to arrest a suspect harbored by the club's well-connected owner. The staff at the club's door make it clear that this is a space from which the police are normally both economically and linguistically excluded—the head waiter, for example, insists on talking to them in English rather than Cantonese. Then, when the fight breaks out, we have a tour-de-force of the transformation and reuse of its fittings and furnishings, from the Rococo-style staircase through the antiques that litter its walls, to the furniture itself, as all these things are, in their turn, transformed into weapons. Central to the visual spectacle of the scene is an extended display of the acrobatic falls for which Chan's stunt team is so well known, crashing the human body (thrown, spinning, often from great heights, and with great kinetic force) into the various props or scenery provided. In most cases, although the body certainly gets an awful punishment, it is ultimately the club itself that comes off worst. The initially opulent environment is reduced, by the end of the scene, to little more than fragments of wood, ceramic, and plaster (fig. 2.5). A kind of a "kung fu revenge" has been enacted upon this space of class and colonial privilege through its collision with the rubbery bodies of the stunt team and their cartoon-character-like resilience. In fact, the film overall seems to have a point to make through our extra-diegetic response to performance, in the ways that (even where taking a thrashing) the performers' bodies take on new, fantastical relationships to their environment, performing unusual forms of movement through it at new velocities, and in the ways that the threats of injury by which that environment disciplines the body are made trivial.

This setting of the body against the colonial landscape *within* the cinematic narrative, then, can also be read on the level of performance *outside* narrative. On this level, they present a fantasy not only of real-world repossession of the spaces and objects of the everyday, but also of "Third World" film production itself, in opposition to the hi-tech and capital-intensive mechanisms of Hollywood. Here, the cinematic miracle of the depiction of the marvelous itself is conjured not from sophisticated special effects, but rather (to slightly paraphrase Benjamin one last time) improvised straight from the bodies of the stars and their team of

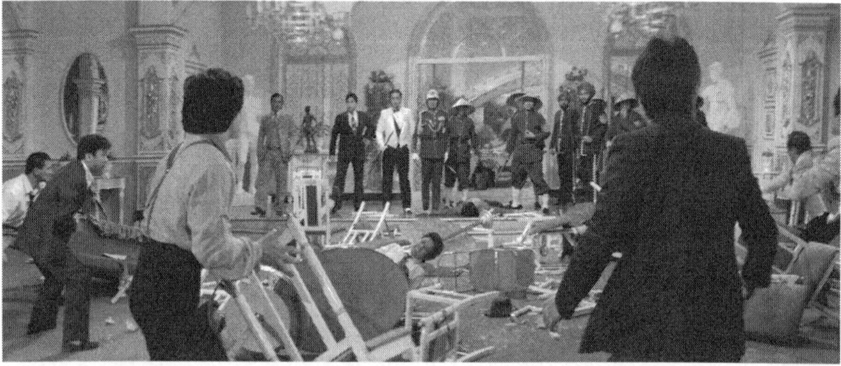

Fig. 2.5. Toward the end of the fight sequence in a high-class club in *Project A,* the previously opulent environment has been largely reduced to matchwood through collision with the rubbery bodies of Chan's stunt team. Video still. © 2010 Fortune Star Media.

stuntmen in a way that mocks, through its rivalry, the multi-million-dollar American movie business—and, by extension, the technological and industrial might of the "First World." This opposition between the two forms of film production was underlined when Jackie Chan, in interview, discussed meeting Stephen Spielberg. Chan reports how he admiringly asked about the computer-generated effects for *Jurassic Park* (1993), and Spielberg said it was easy, requiring simply the push of a button, and then expressed admiration for Chan's own stunts. Chan apparently, self-effacingly, said that this was even easier: "Rolling! Action! Jump! Cut! Ouch! Hospital. Easy, right?"[38] Chan's anecdote is humorous and lighthearted (if tinged with an image of a physical precarity of the body that, as his autobiography makes further clear, is ultimately connected to the economic circumstances into which Chan was born), but nonetheless provides a vivid image of the resources of the colonized subject, in the face of the conditions of their life and the huge forces that are stacked up against them. These resources, of course, are constituted by the body and its wily use: as the title of one film puts it, *He Has Nothing but Kung Fu* (dir. Lau Kar-wing, 1977). The image that Chan gives of the difference between his filmmaking methods and Spielberg's are at the core of his "myth," his performance style, and the meaning of his star persona, which had enormous Asia-wide appeal long before it spread to Europe and America.

This chapter, then, has sought to tease out, through a series of parallels with early Hollywood, and through Benjamin's thought-provoking analyses of these, some of the ways in which the representation of the body in kung fu comedies involves both the registration of the exploitation and domination at the core of modern life but also a utopian dream-image of an emancipated life beyond this. I have argued that in Hong Kong during the 1970s and 1980s such conditions were no longer simply a matter of industrial modernity, but also of its colonial or neocolonial forms and those of the newer condition of globalized neoliberalism. The reading here has tended to draw primarily from one side of Benjamin's highly dialectic thought, focusing on those aspects of his analyses of popular cinema that highlight its liberatory potential. In the next chapter, some of Benjamin's countervailing warnings about popular culture will form a starting point for a broader discussion of what are often seen as some of the more problematic aspects of the kung fu comedy: its lighthearted embrace of violence.

CHAPTER 3

Violence

> A primary difficulty reviewers, critics and some adults have in dealing with the Kung Fu films is that their performance is based upon violence, destruction and death.
>
> —*Stuart Kaminsky*

In the last chapter, I examined the ways Walter Benjamin's first responses to the early Mickey Mouse cartoons open up a reading of the kung fu comedy as harboring forms of resistance to the alienating regimes both of industrial-capitalist and postcolonial modernity. Though far from the direct ethno-nationalist challenge to colonial or even class oppression that might be read in films such as Bruce Lee's *Fist of Fury*, I suggested that the kung fu comedy, as exemplified in the work of Jackie Chan, harbors fantasies that challenge the givenness of the everyday world of domination and dream of forms of physical liberation from it. Such fantasies imaginatively reconcile the objectifying logic that underpins capitalist economics and colonial social control with the artisanal concern with the body in a hoped-for process of rehumanization.

In this chapter, I will turn away from such readings to examine some of the more troubling dimensions of kung fu comedies; in particular, their acceptance—and comic exploitation—of violence. After all, as Stuart Kaminsky has argued of the kung fu genre more generally, violence is surely "at the core of the meaning and appreciation of these films."[1] If the ecstatic identification with the body in motion is key to the pleasure of the martial arts film, this is also a body in *violent* motion—the source, as Kaminsky notes in the quotation at the head of this chapter, of quite some disquiet with the genre within liberal discourse on film. So how might we start to understand the politics of images of the violent body—and of the body subjected to violence—in kung fu comedies?

These questions around violence in the kung fu comedy open onto the darker side of the relationship such films have to the popular slapstick or animated genres of early twentieth-century Hollywood discussed in the last chapter—whether such relations be understood as a matter of influence or structural similarity.

Indeed, the problem of the evaluation of the comedic violence of such films also played an important part in the work of Walter Benjamin. Benjamin offers not one but a series of perspectives on cinematic violence, each developed in response to the changing historical circumstances in which he was writing. These positions—and those developed by Max Horkheimer and Theodor Adorno, who Benjamin engaged in a dialogue on his work—present in their variety a set of different approaches to evaluate the valences of violence in the kung fu comedy, on which I will draw—and then hope to move beyond—in this chapter. Capitalizing on this plurality of perspectives, I will be arguing here that violence in these films is inherently an ambiguous, overdetermined phenomenon. Accepting such overdetermination is, of course, consonant with the larger position of this book, which treats popular culture as a compromise formation between the vested interests of the elite who finance and control its production and the desires of the audiences that must buy it as a commodity in order to ensure its financial viability. However, the motif of violence, as we shall pursue it here, exacerbates such structural polysemy. Violence is, after all, always a matter of the irrational. It is linked to an aggressivity at the core of our being that can neither be conjured away nor simply accepted, and resists neat theorization in terms of the logic of the reason of a conscious mind whose very existence, according to Freudian theory, relies on the repression of such urges into the unconscious. This chapter will therefore have to hold in tension with each other a number of different approaches to thinking about the inherently contradictory and perhaps ultimately insoluble question of cinematic violence, each offering a certain, partial understanding.

My approach here, as in previous chapters, does not seek to treat "violence" (or "comic violence") simply as abstract and ahistorical categories, but will rather attempt to root its analysis in both the continuities and discontinuities of aesthetic form and historical context, to attempt to grasp the particularity of the violence we encounter in kung fu comedies from late 1970s and 1980s Hong Kong. Violence itself, after all, is a multifaceted phenomenon, with a range of very different historical manifestations both on screen and off, each with very different meanings or ramifications.

My analysis will begin by working through the clashing positions of Benjamin and Adorno, which each offer a more sophisticated way than the knee-jerk liberal responses of the mainstream media to understand the links between cinematic and social violence, and the sadistic and masochistic fantasies that this might address in its audience. Adorno and Benjamin certainly, at least, open up angles more suitable to a "radical" rethinking of violent representations. These lead me to comment on the tensions that might be useful in understanding images of violence in the era of globalized neocolonial capitalism. To this end, as means of understanding the comedic kung fu body as subject to as well as a source of violent forces, I contrast the recent arguments by Mark Neocleous about a neoliberal agenda that promotes "resilience" with Howard Caygill's arguments that highlight the importance of maintaining a "capacity to resist." These help position the kung fu comedy within a contemporary politics of affirmation or revolt. However, it is using Leo Bersani's analysis of cultural images of violence from sources as disparate as ancient Assyrian sculpture and European art-house cinema in his account of the "Freudian body" that I can make sense of the position that kung fu comedies take in relation to the sadistic and masochistic fantasies identified in the Frankfurt School thinkers' accounts of slapstick, and the kind of "politics" this might entail within the particular context of the making of these films. This is a politics, of course, very different from that of the "heroic" martial arts movies of the late 1960s and early 1970s, with their more direct attachment to the historical violence of nationalist and anticolonial revolt. Nonetheless, they help us locate the kung fu comedy with regards to a context that includes the unfolding history of the Cultural Revolution, colonialism, the violence of Chinese history, and the ongoing nature of capitalist exploitation. Among the films whose violent imagery this discussion allows me to evaluate are *Knockabout* (dir. Sammo Hung, 1979), *The Young Master* (dir. Jackie Chan, 1980), and *Thundering Mantis* (dir. Teddy Yip, 1980).

Walter Benjamin, Kung Fu, Violence, and "Positive" Barbarism

Cinematic violence has primarily been understood by critics—especially critics in the more popular media—as a matter of (lower-class) youth and delinquency. As James Kendrick has argued, anxieties about real-world criminality being encouraged by seeing its onscreen counterpart have often triggered oversimplified knee-jerk moralizing responses from critics.[2] David Desser's research has shown that this was certainly the dominant register through which Hong Kong martial arts cinema was initially received in the West, with *Variety,* for example, referring, in epidemiological language, to its first mass release in the United States during the "kung fu craze" of 1973 as a "rash" of imported movie releases whose box-office success could be explained in terms of the appeal of a "sheer violence" that paralleled the pornographic draw of "sheer sex."[3]

As we have seen, Walter Benjamin's first response to the violent content of early popular cinema was rather more hopeful. In the fragment "On Mickey Mouse," Benjamin describes cinema more as a reflector than a director of the violence of modern life. The violence of exploitation (which reduces the human being to an office file or a cog within the factory machinery) or of the rise of fascism (which mobilizes both technology and mythology in a project of mass destruction) both pre-exist the cinematic image, which gains its truth-value from what it reveals about this world. According to Benjamin, the public "recognizes its life" in the violence that Mickey Mouse has to survive. In the potential for this recognition, popular cinema raises the brutalized condition of our existence to visibility.[4]

His early writings on "the funnies" also, however, went beyond this in their optimism. Mickey Mouse opens up a hope for transformation in our existence not only beyond but also *through* such a violent present—for a transcendence of modernity through modernity itself, even in its unfeeling brutality. Mickey Mouse, he argued, offers hope in that he poses the possibility that "a creature can survive when it has thrown off all resemblance to a human being."[5] Even the "barbaric" laughter of the cinema audience at everything Mickey suffers, and at all the suffering he dishes out, offers a potential for rehumanization. Benjamin attempted to reconceptualize a new form of "positive" barbarism emerging (in both Mickey himself and in the audiences that laughed at his debasement), in the face of bourgeois ideals of "humanity" that had become the pretext for war, exploitation, and imperialism. For Benjamin the lie of a barbarous "humanism" could only be countered in a humanized barbarism. In popular comic cinema, Benjamin saw the image of new barbarians, who had had everything "human" stripped from them by capitalism, setting out with nothing but the improvisatory cunning and "spirit" of fairy-tale heroes to adapt themselves to their world and reinvent it.[6]

Though cinema may be brutal, then, Benjamin suggests, it is only through this that an already brutalized audience can come to feel again at all. As he wrote elsewhere, it is through cinema and advertising that "sentimentality is restored to health and liberated" and "people whom nothing moves or touches any longer are taught to cry again."[7] Kung fu cinema is, of course, deeply sentimental, just as it is violent, and in many ways, violence serves precisely as a tool for its larger project of sentimentality. Alex Clayton has similarly argued, in the context of his analysis of the Hollywood slapstick tradition, for the power of violent comedy more broadly in inculcating a capacity for feeling that is at once corporeal and also emotional: "the brutal force of a slapstick pratfall has the capacity to reawaken us to the fundamental physicality of the world. . . . Ironically, the very brutality of slapstick has the potential to engender a heightened sensitivity to the world."[8]

This, then, might suggest one evaluation—partially useful at least—of the kung fu comedy. In its mimesis of the laissez-faire conditions of the Hong Kong society of the 1970s, the kung fu comedy envisions just such antiheroes as Benjamin enjoyed in the cinema of the 1920s and 1930s, and their embrace of violence is a part of their movement beyond bourgeois humanism. Such kung fu tricksters have often been understood by critics—in contrast to the heroes of the epic martial arts movie who clearly fight for a cause—as fundamentally without morality. In one of the earlier American scholarly responses to the kung fu genre, for example, Stuart Kaminsky sees the kung fu film as centered on revenge without recourse to justice.[9] In attempting to reconstruct the interests of "ghetto" audiences, Kaminsky proposes that any "moral posture" must be dropped, and kung fu itself is just "dirty, graceful fighting."[10] The pleasure of the genre is simply in the "respect" that attainment of physical prowess accords the hero, with whom the viewer identifies.[11]

Though Kaminsky's rather paranoid vision of the kung fu audience as a ghetto mob is rarer in contemporary scholarship, the reading of kung fu comedies as amoral continues within the critical literature to this day. Leon Hunt, for example, suggests that Beggar So in the drunken master films has "inner strength but nothing resembling virtue," displays "few redeeming features," and is "cunning, violent and mean."[12] For Hunt, both the young, undisciplined heroes and their lazy, vagrant masters in the kung fu comedy are simply out for what they can get, like everyone else in capitalist society. But such readings miss the positive value of such characters. Beggar So, for example, in *Drunken Master,* is in fact vicious and mean only in rumor rather than reality. As the film develops, he and Wong Fei-hung develop a close and even caring relationship, and this is the general pattern of vagabond teachers in the cycle of films *Drunken Master* inspired. One might understand this as a reinvention of human relationships, and of the master–pupil bond in a world where traditional forms of patriarchy are in decay, as evidenced in Wong's starchy father's inability to discipline him and Wong's own inability to respond to such discipline to become a "filial son." Wong Fei-hung and Beggar So are in this regard precisely those who are thrown back on "barbaric" resources to recreate humanity, in the face of a bankrupt "civilization."

There is also a world of difference in the films' universes between the minor tricksterism of many of the genre's heroes and its truly unpleasant villains. Some of Sammo Hung's films of the late 1970s might seem to offer the clearest examples of what seems an amoral universe. Man-Fung Yip, for example, takes *Knockabout* (dir. Sammo Hung, 1979) as a clear example of a film where the protagonists' relation to their "master" is entirely cynical and "business-like."[13] The film's two heroes, the brothers Yipao (Yuen Biao) and Taipao (Leung Kar-yan), are in fact introduced to us pulling a con on a greedy pawnbroker, who is only drawn into the trick by his own attempt to cheat them. Yipao and Taipao then lose the money they have made through this scheme when Fat Beggar (Sammo Hung) takes advantage of their distraction by their mutual attempts to defraud each other over the lion's share of the gains, to pull his own trick on them. We are thrown into a world where everyone is out to put one over on everyone else, and Yipao and Taipao's behavior seems endorsed as a necessary (if somewhat hopeless) strategy for people with no other means of survival.

The scenario, of course, echoes that of the films of the Hui Brothers, with their chancers and small businessmen struggling to survive in the dog-eat-dog world of modern-day Hong Kong, which I suggested in an earlier chapter provided much of the blueprint for the kung fu comedy. The extent to which *Knockabout* might also provide a portrait of such conditions remains basically transparent. However, the seeming amorality of such survivalist trickery is belied by Yipao and Taipao's meeting with "Old Fox" (Lau Kar-wing), a criminal in hiding who (as Yip notes) takes them in as students only to help him do away with his enemies. When this has been achieved, Old Fox murders Taipao, with only Yipao managing to escape. Old Fox belongs to an entirely different order of greed, criminality, and viciousness from the relatively benign (and ultimately "human") antics of the two brothers.

In more traditional Chinese cosmology—and its theatrical manifestations—the comedy of clowning and the violence of the "martial" (*wu*) alike are both profoundly associated with the "yin" forces of chaos. As discussed by Ashley Thorpe, the exorcistic or ritual function of comedy in operatic traditions works through a homeopathic principle where the inversions of comedy serve to inoculate the community against the larger and more dangerous disorder of evil.[14] With regard to the distinction between the amoral antiheroes and immoral villains of the kung fu comedy, Thorpe's distinction between the fool and the villain in Chinese drama is useful. This suggests that while the villain is usually brought to justice and often sentenced to death at the end of the play, the fool is defined as "he who is none the worse for his slapping."[15] Such an analysis also suggests the conservative functions that such drama may have. The chaos of foolery or violence alike (or their combination in the figure of the martial clown) is important and powerful only because it is the means by which evil can be overcome and order restored. As with Benjamin, in Chinese theater it is through a passage into the "barbaric" world of chaos, violence, comedy, and conflict—and not bourgeois morality—that evil might be countered and humanity redeemed.

For critics such as Hunt and Kaminsky, the final showdown, in which, to defeat Old Fox, Yipao teams up with Fat Beggar (who turns out all the time to have been an undercover policeman), all that may be at stake is personal revenge, but, within the film's moral order this is clearly a matter of justice, too. And if the film, as Yip notes, includes the absolutely inhuman master–student relationship with Old Fox, this is nonetheless contrasted with that between Yipao and Fat

Beggar, which, just as with Wong Fei-hung and Beggar So in *Drunken Master*, slowly develops in a much more benign and warm direction. Rather than simply an amoral universe, what we seem to have is the distinction between the apparent, false morality of convention and a "deeper" morality based in human feeling, which exists beyond given rules.

The same structure is retained in Stephen Chow's more recent *Kung Fu Hustle* (2004), where once more the hero, Sing, starts out as an impoverished chancer looking to eke out a living through petty crime. Like Yipao and Taipao, he is ultimately not very successful in doing so. The ultimately good-hearted Sing is contrasted to the altogether more irredeemable bad guys of the film, the axe gang, who are ruthlessly running the organized crime of Shanghai. Sing, instead, is very much Thorpe's fool, who is only bettered by the beating that he takes throughout the film.

Adorno, Outtakes, and the Problem with Cinematic Violence

Such arguments already take us further into the complexity of violence in the kung fu comedy than paranoia about copycat crimes. However, while his early writings seem to embrace violent comedy in the cinema, Benjamin's analysis of popular cinema seems to have taken an increasingly cautionary note as it developed under the shadow of the rising tide of Nazism.

In the first version of "The Work of Art in the Age of Mechanical Reproduction," written in 1935, Benjamin still hoped for a therapeutic effect from the violence of popular cinema, in relation to such historical events. He proposed that the audience's laughter at such films constitutes a pre-emptive release of the "sadistic fantasies and masochistic delusions" that were contributing forces to the catastrophe already threatening to overtake Europe. In contrast to those detractors who see cinematic representations of violence as contributing to its real-world effects, Benjamin hoped—at the very least in the dire circumstances in which he was writing—that channeling destructive urges into the realm of representation might ameliorate their expression in life. As he puts it, "American slapstick comedies and Disney films trigger a therapeutic demolition of the unconscious" and a "psychic immunization . . . against mass psychosis." These things no longer lurk as unacknowledged forces deep in our psyche, determining our behavior through symptoms of obedience to and identification with the totalitarian state.[16]

However, between this version of the essay and his redraft of February 1936, Benjamin had started a dialogue with Theodor Adorno and Max Horkheimer of the Frankfurt Institute, with whom he sought to republish it.[17] Adorno understood the nature of the cinema audience's "barbaric" laughter—and its relation to sadistic impulses—in a much less rosy light than Benjamin.[18] Whether because of Adorno and Horkheimer's objections or because of the worsening situation in Germany, Benjamin appended a new footnote to his essay, balancing his affirmations of mass-appeal comic cinema by criticizing its "cozy acceptance of bestiality and violence as inevitable concomitants of existence." For Benjamin now, the characters in slapstick and cartoon films began to resemble "the dancing hooligans to be found in depictions of medieval pogroms."[19] Benjamin stressed how Nazism was displaying the power to appropriate even potentially radical aspects of cinema. Rather than preventing fascist identification, popular film was now imagined as contributing to it.

Perhaps with these caveats in mind, we would have to remember that to a certain degree, rather than necessarily bringing us "beyond" bourgeois moralities, even films such as *Knockabout,* in their very sentimentality, ultimately serve to reinforce these. Yibao is motivated by the "wholesome" and traditional value of family loyalty and the duties that stem from this, and the final showdown is sanctioned by the moral authority of Fat Beggar's role as a policeman, capturing the story of revenge within the remit of the law. In the end, the lines between good and evil are, it seems, ultimately unproblematic.

Of course, one might well question the applicability of Benjamin's arguments, both about the possible cathartic power of laughing at cinematic images of "barbarism" and about their potential role within the mania of fascism, to the Hong Kong situation. Is there any equivalent here to the rise of Hitler that might make such clearly located observations meaningfully transferable? We will have to do quite a bit of further work in this chapter before we can return to this point later in the argument, in order to draw conclusions about the significance of the kung fu comedy's mode of representing violence as a response to the historical context in which it developed.

However, Benjamin's interlocutors Adorno and Horkheimer, writing in the context of mid-century America and the rise of "mass culture" there, would go on to observe something of the same routine masochism and sadism Benjamin saw in Nazi culture as a more general aspect of capitalist life and its media imagery. In *Dialectic of Enlightenment,* their verdict on Disney was that "Donald Duck in the cartoons and the unfortunate in real life get their thrashing so that the audience can learn to take their own beating."[20]

Like more popular discourses on the effects of cinematic violence, Adorno and Horkheimer's judgment assumes that this takes place through audience mimicry of the images they see. However, it also offers a more nuanced version of this, which reads these effects not in terms of the spectacular criminal behavior of the lower classes, but through a normalization of the everyday brutality of social and economic exploitation, domination, and alienation. Cartoons turn out not only to offer us training in bestiality toward others but also reconcile us to the violence to which we are subject ourselves, inuring us to conditions we should not accept. The problem with Donald Duck cartoons is not so much their sadism, but the masochistic mode of identification they elicit. However, as Esther Leslie has noted, Adorno would go on in his work on the "authoritarian personality" to draw a psychological correlation between the petty bully's conformist acceptance of society's brutality toward himself and his consolatory readiness to mete out the same punishment to others on behalf of that society.[21]

This analysis may well reveal a lot about the functioning of the kung fu comedy. Jackie Chan's *The Young Master* (1980) would seem to be a good example of this. First off, as with *Knockabout* (discussed in the last chapter), the characters throughout the film are cynical and manipulative in their dealings with others, each setting out to outsmart their rivals. Rather than reading their "amorality" as "positive barbarism," following Adorno and Horkheimer we could see it as inculcating the normal and proper behavior within late twentieth-century Hong Kong's laissez-faire capitalism—and so as being far from subversive. Violence in the film may largely be understood to be a part of the instrumentalized manner in which characters treat each other. As the parallel with *Knockabout* suggests, such a moral universe is hardly unique to *The Young Master* within the kung fu comedy genre, but what perhaps sticks out is the nature of the final fight scene and the victory of its hero, Dragon (Jackie Chan), within this.

As I have argued, in most comic martial arts films of the period, victory over the villain entails a form of self-transformation (whether moral, physical or mental) through kung fu training. It is such a theme of transformation that marks the films out, in Benjaminian terms, as having a particularly strong utopian content. Little such sense of transformation, however, seems to be involved in *Young Master*. In contrast to Chan's earlier films (such as *Snake in the Eagle's Shadow* or *Drunken Master*), there is no "training" section in the film, so to defeat the villain, Dragon doesn't have to learn a new style of combat, hit on a new insight into the forms of nature, or take on a new kind of "becoming." Rather, in the final fight, in which Dragon squares up against the terrifying Master Kam (Hwang In-sik), it is primarily his ability to take a beating—and stand up again—that allows him to win. Nihilistically enough, the reversal of fortunes only comes when Dragon is given "pipe juice" to drink instead of water, and his body flips into a nicotine-fueled, crazed state, in which he simply ignores the blows rained on him by Kam, to the extent that he can land enough counterstrikes to overcome his opponent, who is too expert to be used to getting hit himself.

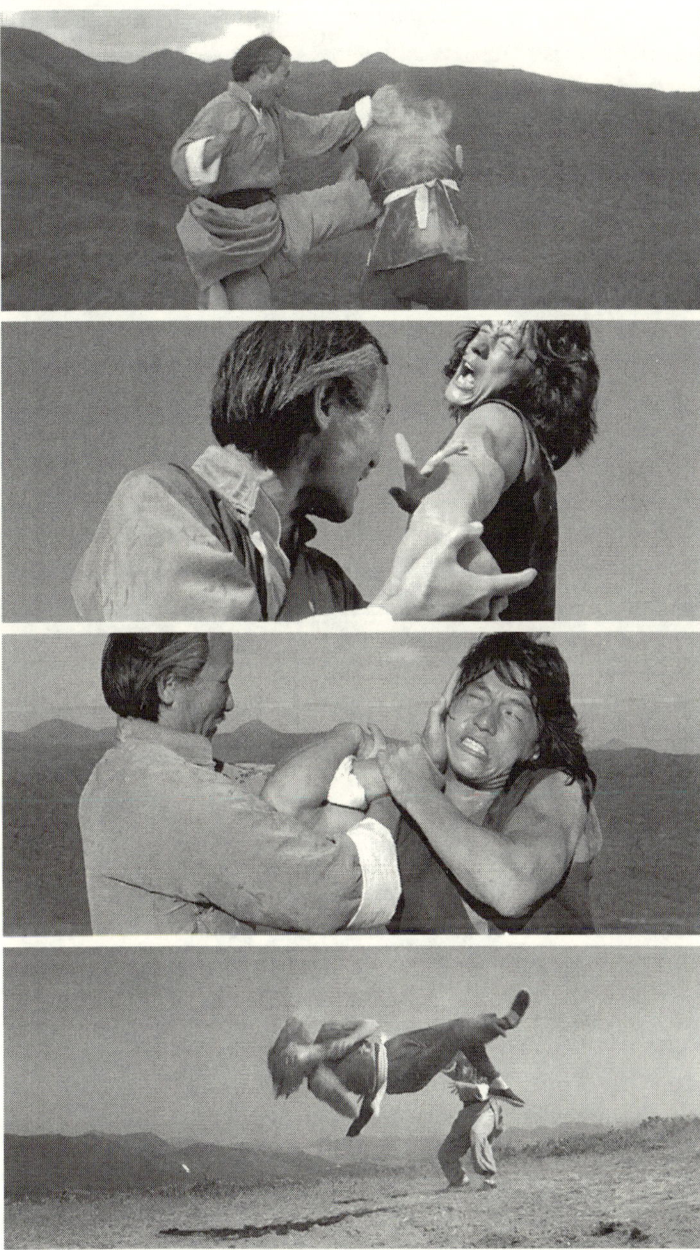

Fig. 3.1. Jackie Chan takes a severe beating in the final fight of *Young Master,* as he's subjected to a punishing series of strikes, locks, and throws. Video stills. © 1993/2004 Star TV Filmed Entertainment / 2015 SelectaVisión.

The first three-quarters of the fight is filmed very much as a showcase for Hwang's impressive martial arts skill, with Chan himself playing the part of the crash-test dummy through whom we see its results (fig. 3.1). Chan is first subjected to a series of Hwang's trademark lightning Taekwondo-like kicks. Then, to show that this isn't all that he can do, Hwang switches to a series of arm locks, with close-ups of Chan's agonized face and contorted body, as he is bounced from one position to another. Next, Hwang goes on to display a series of throws that send Chan repeatedly crashing into the ground.

If in *Snake in the Eagle's Shadow* the character Chien Fu is pitiable because he is made to play the role of a "human punch bag," Chan himself seems to have chosen this as a real-life task for himself in the construction of this fight scene. The punishment that Dragon receives within the film's world blends into the extra-diegetic spectacle of Chan's own performance, not so much as an athlete with a refined skill, but rather in terms of the physical "authenticity" of his ability to soak up the blows and take the falls.[22]

In the very final scene, after he has defeated his opponent, we see the "victorious" Dragon, led in a procession, but bandaged from head to foot (fig. 3.2). Then, breaking the "fourth wall" in a final shot (and in doing so blurring again the distinction between character and star), Dragon/Chan, still in his bandages and reclining in a chair, waves farewell to the audience, while the credits roll, and, in a series of inset split screens, scenes from the film are replayed, anticipating the "outtake" reels that would become another trademark feature of Chan's later works.

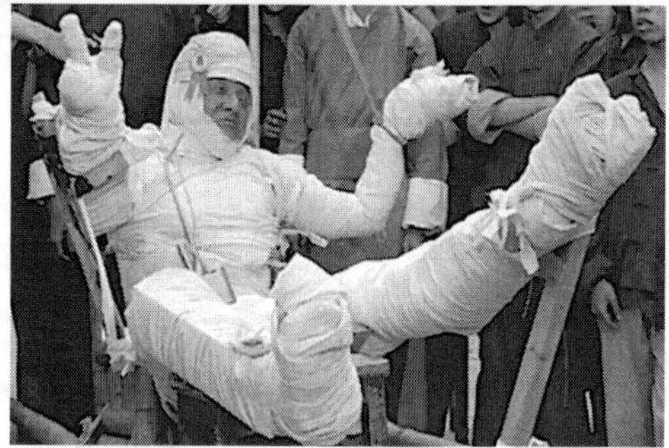

Fig. 3.2. Dragon (Jackie Chan) returns home in triumphal procession, bound from head to foot in bandages at the end of *Young Master*. Video still. © 1993/2004 Star TV Filmed Entertainment / 2015 SelectaVisión.

The slide here between diegesis and performance exemplifies the ways in which the moral of such a film (that the utmost virtue and the path to success is to accept Donald Duck's "thrashing") becomes a matter of the meaning of Chan's star persona itself, and the performance style he developed. Chan's plots would increasingly emphasize not skill or strength but perseverance, determination, and what in the Chinese martial arts is called "eating bitter." Chan became known as the star who does all his own stunts, and for the various bones that he broke in the production of his films. Famously within Chan's own narrative of his career, the grueling training scenes he pioneered were based on his own tough education as a child at the Beijing opera school of Yu Jim-yuen, which is detailed in all its brutality in his autobiography.[23]

Chan's outtake reels further leverage these blurred boundaries between Chan and the characters he plays on screen. In these, the scenes we have just been watching as fiction are replayed, but now we are presented with the spectacle of real bodies soaking up real blows. The caricatured, semaphored signs of pain in the film's comedic reaction shots, designed as they are to reassure the audience that this is not "for real," are replaced with the sight of the genuine effects of impact where the stunts have gone wrong, as Chan and his stunt team writhe in authentic agonies. If characters such as Dragon in *The Young Master* offer us an image like that of Donald Duck, Chan himself and his team of stuntmen play the role of the "unfortunate in real life" whose suffering also presents us with the lesson of our own existence.

Cinema is often understood as involved in the production of an illusion that erases its own production—and the foregrounding of the means of representation are often taken in a Brechtian tradition as a means of critically empowering a viewer in the face of the ideological effects of such illusion. Such a perspective might be associated with a wider Marxian critique, which emphasizes the way in which the commodity form replaces the reality of work and exploitation with the glossy surface of its products, seeming as they do to spring into the world pristine and untouched by human hands. However, the effect of Chan's revelation of the labor involved in the production of his films appears to have a far-from-demystifying function. The "fetishism" of the untouched cultural commodity is replaced with a fetishization of Chan's auratic, suffering, enduring body itself.

Leon Hunt has usefully anatomized the different registers in which "authenticity" is pursued in martial arts cinema.[24] Drawing on his schema it is clear that the authenticity fetishized in Chan's outtake reels is far from either the "authenticity" of martial skill fans discover in Bruce Lee ("he can really fight") or the authenticity of the historical roots of the martial arts styles depicted by Lau Kar-leung ("what he does is real, traditional Hung Gar"). With Chan it is, instead, the authenticity of physical knocks that is at stake ("he really jumped from that building, and he really broke his leg/arm/back doing it"). An Adornian reading would understand this suffering as exemplifying—even celebrating—the nature of work within capitalism and the destruction that it wreaks on the body. Emerging from the tough, macho, competitive conditions of stunt work itself, and expressing its ethos or ideology, Chan's outtake reels suggest that to earn or to produce value one must suffer violence on the self; it is the ground of the laborer's claim to be worthy of pay. Chan's extreme suffering—his entrepreneurial taking of risks with the capital of his body itself—is also what elevates him to a special level of recompense, beyond that gained by the normal worker, slowly offering up the working powers of their body and their life force in measured, calculable dribs and drabs. In Chan's performances and the minor industry of documentaries and DVD extras surrounding them,[25] the violence to which the working body is subjected is not only normalized but also celebrated and made a marker of a version of "manliness."

Resilience and the Capacity to Resist

However, such a vision can be understood in different ways. The Adornian critique just offered is consistent with Mark Neocleous's recent analysis of the promotion of "resilience" as a desirable characteristic for contemporary subjects to attempt to foster. Often, in a transformed echo of the physical culture movements of the early twentieth century, resilience is pursued through physical practices such as "boot camp" fitness programs, mindfulness classes, or even the study of martial arts. For Neocleous, "resilience" is a character trait privileged within a neoliberal rhetoric that expects its subjects to endure and accept the harsh reality of the "austerity" measures, precarious labor, poverty, and unfreedom that characterize contemporary capitalist life. Such traumas are naturalized as merely the way of things, rather than a result of the chronic insecurity and instability of a particular economic system, and they are made a problem to be faced not at the level of the political, but the individual, and in fact serve a further conservative function, as the fostering of resilience in individual subjects becomes a concern of the state within the context of the maintenance of its own institutional resilience.[26]

This said, questions of "resilience" might be understood more positively as linked to Benjamin's reading of Mickey Mouse as emblematic of the potential of *survival* through and beyond capitalist life. Resilience—survival—after all, is a prerequisite of any possibility of resistance or revolt. The military strategist Carl von Clausewitz—whom Howard Caygill has foregrounded as a theorist not only of Napoleon's triumph in Europe, but also of the forms of guerrilla warfare that developed to fight him, and so of the emergence of a "people's war of resistance"—defined the aim of war as being to "render the enemy incapable of further resistance." Caygill's argument is that for Clausewitz, war is fought not against the enemy, but more precisely against their "*capacity* to resist."[27] Resilience can be understood as a necessary—though far from adequate—part of such a capacity to resist. One reading of postmodernity is as the continuation ("by other means") of the war by the powerful against the weak into the terrain of culture; mass culture, inasmuch as it is (partially) managed by a powerful elite, can be understood as serving to quash capacities for revolt. Caygill suggests that while the powerful seek to strike the final blow, the strategy of the weak (whether Maoist guerrilla or Ghandist *satyagraha*) is "temporal distension," avoiding, displacing, and extending conflict, putting off such a final blow further and further into the future.[28]

The kung fu comedy, of course, emerged in precisely such a moment of extreme weakness, where the political movements of the 1960s were no longer available to support "radical" culture. (Perhaps it is the similarity of our condition in the present that lends kung fu comedies their continuing resonance.) In the light of this context and through Caygill's notion of resistance, we might see the kung fu comedy as involving a retreat of the campaign to preserve the capacity to resist from the impossible terrain of political conflict into the realm of culture and into the body itself. The fantasy of kung fu training contained in these films can be understood as the preservation of the capacity for violence within the embodied self, rather than allowing this to become a perfect monopoly of the state.

The extent to which such a reading is viable may vary from film to film, and it may depend on the extent that such films articulate a set of values that are autonomous from those of the state itself. Films that imagine—as I have earlier suggested much of the drunken master cycle has done—a "popular body" beyond the state, and that keep alive a set of carnival strategies of the comic inversion of power, may have some degree of this value. To my mind, however, *Young Master* would be relatively weak in this regard.

Adorno and Benjamin's arguments, then, present us with dialectically opposite ways of grasping the phenomenon of violence within the kung fu comedy. The poles of their disagreement may be understood to lay out an antinomy structural to modern culture. Such an antinomy would be, by definition, irresolvable within the confines of the present, but instead presents us with a contradiction that structures our existence.[29] As such, we may read the answers that the two thinkers offer us not in terms of a choice, but as overlaid aspects of the same overdetermined, contradictory, and multivalent phenomenon.

Benjamin and Adorno alike, however, rely on their wider diagnoses of a social totality of the particular moments within which they were writing, into which they attempt to fit their analysis of violent cinematic images, in order to come to their particular judgments about the functions, effects or meanings of films they analyze, and there are methodological problems with this projection from the general to the particular. Adorno and Benjamin's arguments—certainly, at least, as I have rendered them here—also both remain rather abstract in their engagement with "violent" imagery. They have so far not taken us far enough into thinking about the particular contents or formal nature of the particular representations that we are dealing with. Not all cinematic violence is the same, and it may—as film scholar James Kendrick notes—be doing quite different things in different places.[30] Given what I have been suggesting here is an instability and multiple coding in such violent imagery, it may also take on quite different meanings for different subjects in different moments.

In the second half of this chapter, then, I wish to turn first to a further examination of the particular forms of the violent body in the kung fu comedy and then, on the basis of this, to turn to a psychoanalytic reading of violence that will take us further in pinning down the particular dominant valences of the kung fu comedy.

The Stylization of Violence in the Kung Fu Comedy

I have, earlier in this book and elsewhere, argued that the blood-drenched "new era" swordplays of late 1960s and the early, epic kung fu films that followed in their wake sought—often self-consciously—to offer an analogue to the political and social turmoil that marked their era.[31] Registering colonial unrest, such films, critics have noted, held a wide appeal for the marginalized across the world, and they could be read in terms of a rebellious, countercultural, and anti-establishment politics.[32]

This "politicization" of the heroic Hong Kong martial arts film was accompanied by an increasing emphasis on graphic violence; on what the publicity discourse around the films itself referred to as a new "realism" in relation to fighting (contrasted to the more "theatrical" techniques, borrowed from opera, which dominated up to this point); and on cinematic effects, from stage blood to constructive editing, that gave an added materiality and visceral corporeality to action sequences and sunk the films increasingly into the bodies of its stars and audiences alike.[33]

In many ways, the kung fu comedy departed from this model. As we have already seen with *Young Master*, a certain mimetic "realism" of the body remained core to the pleasures of the film, and inasmuch as the kung fu comedy foregrounded phenomenally acrobatic performances there is a degree to which the body (and its performances of violent movement) became even more central to the genre.

However, what perhaps begins to separate violence in the kung fu comedy from its predecessors is an exacerbation of the *stylization* of violence. Stylization is, perhaps, endemic to the martial arts genre—and even to the martial arts themselves, which arguably always involve a theatricalization, aestheticization, and formalization of combat.[34] However, the kung fu comedy seemed to reverse the trend to increased "realism" and return to the deliberately theatrical elements of opera that the films of the early 1970s had eschewed.

Sometimes, fighting becomes much more like dancing—with Jackie Chan, for example, almost as frequently compared to Fred Astaire or Gene Kelly as he is to Buster Keaton.[35] Aaron Anderson has stressed this relation to dance in Chan's films, citing Chan himself in interview, who stresses the importance of rhythm and "music" in his fight scenes, and the importance of a process of aestheticization:

> Everything is pretty. It's like dancing. Even fighting somebody, it's all pretty. At the end you have a pose like a ballet. That's what I want. I want to show audiences fighting is an art. It's not like, "I want to kill you." It's an art.[36]

Chan, of course, is hardly alone in making fighting into ballet—in *Crippled Avengers* (dir. Chang Cheh, 1978), for example, several scenes of combat are taken to such a degree of abstraction that they are transformed into an ensemble dance, or even a *pas de deux* for two male bodies. The training sequence with hoops, performed between the blind Chen Shun (Phillip Kwok) and the mad Wang Yi (Chiang Sheng), is a case in point. It is creative and exuberant in its physical movement, blending the acrobatic with the humorous, and Kwok and Chiang move in split-second harmony with each other, often mirroring or echoing each other's movements, or allowing momentum to pass from one body through the other and back again in a way that seems to blur the boundaries between the two. Martial technique takes a backseat, and the effect of the perfect synchronization between the two performers—who were in reality lifelong friends from their days in opera school in Taipei—is almost tender, as they perform a scene that sketches out the erotics of the homosocial bonding of martial "brotherhood" that constituted such an insistent theme for the film's director, Chang Cheh.

At the other end of the spectrum, the stylization of violence in the kung fu comedy brings it closer to clowning than dance. Often fight sequences (in particular, for example, in the style developed by Sammo Hung in the late 1970s)[37] create their characteristic rhythm through the alternation of spectacular martial arts techniques—often with a highly acrobatic inflection—with either verbal repartee or physical slapstick from outside of a martial arts canon of movement. Punches and kicks are interspersed with jabs or pokes, slaps across the cheek, farts in the face, pulling an ear or nose, pulling a hat down over the eyes, smearing food on an opponent, or pushing their face in the dirt. Reaction shots on characters play up the effects of violence in a caricatural manner (crossed eyes and pulled faces) that again derealize its effects. Sound effects—drums, gongs, and whistles—further key us into this unreal circus mode and its rhythms, and some devices—the oversized lump that appears on the head or the exaggerated makeup showing a black eye, for example—seem to be drawn from the language of cartoons, turning the body into an abstract signifier rather than a mimetic copy of the world.

Both the comic and the balletic dimension of the new choreography of the kung fu comedy, then, share an aestheticization and abstraction that serves to make violence less "real." In Chan's interview, the intention appears paradoxically to be to remove violence itself from fighting. In what he says, the extent to which we are faced with an art (with something "pretty") is a matter of the negation of the sense that the sentiment of martial arts might be "I want to kill you."

However, this stylization is not the end of the matter—and certainly not if we simply imagine the kung fu comedy as presenting us with a "watering down" of violence that might better be approached in a "realist" manner, staged in all its gravity. Mirroring the narrative structure, which takes us from small-time tricksterism to the final showdown with a film's evil archvillain, the performance style in the kung fu comedy typically shifts from the comic-balletic mode to more conventional styles of martial arts choreography, with fighting techniques no longer mixed to the same degree with "gags" or grandstanding acrobatics, even if they often remain, even in the final fight, much more fantastical in their envisioning of combat than in a "straight" martial arts film. Certainly, this is the shift in register we see in *The Young Master*. In the early part of the film we see spectacular displays of trickery and of manipulation of props by Chan—in one scene juggling several swords at once as he combats a group of corrupt and inept police sergeants and in another defeating an opponent through a virtuoso performance with a folding fan—and by Yuen Biao in his dazzlingly inventive play with a bench as a weapon. These, however, give way as the film draws to a close to the spectacle of the damage that Chan's body can soak up in the barrage of kicks, locks, and throws that Hwang inflicts on him.

Perhaps the most extreme and clear example of this logic of narrative and performance structure, however, is in *Thundering Mantis* (dir. Teddy Yip, 1980). *Thundering Mantis* follows the basic format of the drunken master cycle. In it,

Leung Kar-yan plays Ah Chi, a boisterous and anarchic fishmonger's apprentice who befriends a street urchin, The Kid (Wong Yat-lung), whom he catches one day attempting to steal fish. Ah Chi and The Kid come into conflict with a local gang who terrorize the town, sparking off a series of comedic scenes featuring Leung's performance of "shrimp" kung fu and Wong's impressive acrobatic skills. As they are then confronted with the increasingly powerful villains who back the gang, Ah Chi learns Mantis style from The Kid's grandfather (Chin Yuet-sang), a drunken and disheveled street performer, in order to defeat them. Finally, the head villain, Shiao Tse-tung (Eddy Ko), arrives on the scene, kills the grandfather, captures Ah Chi, and tortures The Kid to death in front of him. These last scenes begin to shift the mood of the film and the register of its depictions of violence away from the comic. Overcome by horror and grief, Ah Chi falls into an insane rage to take his revenge on Shiao and his subordinates, and the resulting sequence is one of the kung fu comedy genre's most striking—even shocking—displays of violence, with all the lightheartedness of the earlier part of the film falling suddenly away. The choreographic style shifts, and the villains no longer offer comedic reactions; instead, we see their bodies being battered, mangled, and broken in Ah Chi's fury.

Ah Chi's mimesis of the mantis in this final sequence—though seeming to fit into the genre's pattern of strange becomings—plunges into a depth of inhuman animality that most other martial arts films stop short of. In these, the hero's becoming animal is usually a way to truly become human and to retain what is important in the face of a barbaric civilization. However, in *Thundering Mantis,* we see what it really is to lose one's humanity as Ah Chi reverts to a predatory insect level of existence.

Violence is no longer consequenceless as before—it is clearly painful, crippling, and lethal. We even see Ah Chi tear off one opponent's leg, for example, as the fight progresses. As Ah Chi comes face to face with Shiao, and as he himself begins to take a battering, the loss of humanity is further exacerbated. He no longer responds in a familiar, mammalian manner. He refuses to react at all to a number of pounding and clearly damaging blows, instead clenching his muscles into an insensate exoskeleton, which no longer offers soft, fleshy purchase for the talons of his opponent's "eagle claw" technique. The injuries he receives are registered instead in other pathological, submammalian symptoms—foaming at the mouth, for example—and in an increasing automatism. The fighting movements start to lose their resemblance to the repertoire of punches, kicks, elbows, knees, locks, or throws that we might recognize and descends instead into manic twitching. At one moment, cornered, Ah Chi lies on his back convulsing in a way that nonetheless stops his opponent coming near. Ultimately, he doesn't "wrestle" or "box" Shiao—who clearly becomes more and more disoriented and terrified—but instead bites and tears at him. In the final shots, we see him drag his unconscious enemy out of the camera's view, so that only the shadow he casts on a wall is visible, revealing him dismembering and eating his foe. In this act of cannibalism—the final freeze-frame ending of the movie—the transformation into mantis and the loss of humanity is, it seems, symbolically complete, just as the register of comedy has now given way fully to that of horror.

However, the relationship between comedy and horror here is not simply a matter of the one giving way to the other. The shock effect of the fight scene at the end of *Thundering Mantis*—precisely in the hyperbole of its horror—would perhaps be impossible outside of the comedy genre, and is profoundly marked by the comic performance style that dominates the hour of the film running up to this. Leung's performance retains the manic energy and exaggerated vivacity of these earlier scenes. He still moves with a "bounciness" and an irregular staccato rhythm that seem more suited to a clown than a warrior. His face pulls a series of absurd grimaces—caricatural laugher or tears, insane glee—that though now emptied of humor might otherwise fit well within the comic mode, and these elements only render the scene more uncanny. The exaggerated unreality of the earlier comic scenes offers an alibi for the extremity of a performance of more "earnest" violence that would have been difficult within a film that up to this point had been played "straight." Perhaps, furthermore, the comedy—as a kind of foreplay for sadism—softens us to accept its violent content.

Violence and the Freudian Body

The kung fu comedy, then, does not involve only comic depictions of violence, and if we are to understand violence within such films, we need to make sense of this tension between its comic and non-comic modes. To work further toward an answer to this—and to that of the politics of violence in the kung fu comedy—I will turn, in the final pages of this chapter, to the work of literary theorist Leo Bersani and to his analysis, in particular, of representations of violence in the rather different contexts of ancient Assyrian art and Pier-Paolo Pasolini's *Salò,* a filmic retelling of Sade's (in)famous *120 Days of Sodom.*[38]

Making a close deconstructive reading of Freud's *Beyond the Pleasure Principle,* Bersani proposes a truth that he believes Freud had uncovered, but was himself too conservative to admit. For Bersani, what Freud terms the "death drive" evidences a fundamental masochism and self-destructivity at the heart of human desire and subjectivity itself. The ego is, after all, formed in a process of the repression of that which is excluded from it, the *id,* and such a divided self, profoundly invested in its war against itself, experiences its own "shattering" as a fundamental basis of "pleasure." As a result, Bersani proposes, "we are, ontologically, implicated in violence almost from the beginning." The "choice between violence and nonviolence" is a mirage.[39]

The choice, instead, is a matter of different libidinal "economies" into which these drives to aggression might enter. These economies involve different kinds of temporality, and in turn these are instantiated artistically in different narrative or aesthetic forms. Bersani argues that sadism—as exemplified in its master text, *120 Days*—involves a fixation of such destructive energies onto an object and moves to a climactic state of release. This release, of course, unleashes destruction on the object of fixation. If such energies are understood as taking on social and historical manifestations, Bersani's analysis offers strong moments of accord with both Benjamin's hope of the "premature" spending of sadistic energies in cartoon violence and his anxiety that such images can serve to reinforce a sadistic "text" that was coming to dominate German cultural life with the rise of Hitler—the primary (though far from exclusive) object of sadistic fixation within Nazism being the Jew. (Such an equation between Sade and fascism is certainly made within Pasolini's *Salò,* which transposes *120 Days* into the dying moment of Mussolini's rule in Italy.)

The aesthetic form that Bersani associates with such a Sadean temporality is narrative, with its movement toward closure. We may, of course, see something of this logic structuring the kung fu film—comedic or otherwise—with its initially slow escalation of violence, building up to the climactic battle in which the film's villain is killed. This may be one way of reading the narrative arc, and the shifting registers of violence, in *Young Master* or *Thundering Mantis* with their initial lightheartedness and shockingly brutal endings. This progression echoes the structure of Pasolini's *Salò* itself, which starts with relatively mild forms of dominant-submissive imagery, before escalating to its horrendous ending in which we see graphic depictions of the libertines torturing their victims to death—scenes that caused the movie to be banned in many countries.

However, Bersani also argues that other aesthetic forms allow artworks to remain within the inescapable orbit of violent content but nonetheless resist this dangerous Sadean logic. Bersani's primary examples—aside from Pasolini's ironic mimesis of Sade in *Salò*—are the ancient Assyrian friezes held in the British Museum, depicting the Assyrian state's military victories and the ritual lion hunts in which its rulers displayed their authority as protectors of the nation. For Bersani, these friezes are singular in their relish for violence and the relentless, minute attention to physical suffering or brutality that they demonstrate—a relish that has elicited "distaste" in many scholars and bolstered the image of the ancient Assyrians as an "intensely nationalistic, imperialistic, and violent people."[40] However, Bersani suggests, what is interesting about the depictions of violence in these friezes is their abstraction, which repeatedly transforms narrative content into formal or aesthetic pleasure. Due to such formalism, the interplay of shape or line often ends up distracting from the depicted image, and the eye is led through and past the sadistic narrative incidents that are their ostensible focal points.[41]

For Bersani, this involves a restless, unfixed gaze that counters the logic of sadism. While the latter moves us to destructive fixation and closure, the former, though it remains captivated by a violent death-instinct that we cannot in any case renounce, resists such a closure, keeping us looking. For Bersani, this aestheticism offers us a "moral perspective" on sadism similar to that of Pasolini's *Salò.* As Bersani puts it with regard to Pasolini, the "saving frivolity with which we simply go on looking" allows "a promiscuous mobility thanks to which our mimetic appropriations of the world are continually being continued *elsewhere* and therefore do not require the satisfyingly climactic destruction of any part of the world."[42]

This may open a more generous reading of films such as *Young Master* and *Thundering Mantis.* Such films may, like the Assyrian lion hunts, be understood as held in a tension between narrative and formalizing (comedic/aesthetic) modes, and the maintenance of such a tension may be the "moral perspective" (as Bersani puts it) of their relationship to their violent source material. In this regard, it is worth noting the often-observed disdain for narrative form that is typical of the genre—and that frustrates so many viewers. In Aristotelian terms, "episodes" and set pieces (whether these be fight sequences or comic routines) often threaten to overwhelm the overall arc of the plot. The films are often structured around repetitions rather than the orderly movement of the drama toward an ending.[43] And then, of course, there are the (in-)famously abrupt freeze-frame endings so common in the genre, usually as soon as the villain is killed. These on the one hand seem to highlight the consummation of violence as the purpose of the film; however, they often undermine the very satisfaction of the sense of an ending itself, unlinking such a climax from the creation of a satisfactory aesthetic whole, and often leaving any number of narrative threads unresolved.

An interesting counter-example of narrative structure to *Young Master* or *Thundering Mantis* (or even *Knockabout*) is Karl Maka's *Dirty Tiger, Crazy Frog!* In this, the fight with the chief villain, toward which the drama seems to be escalating, happens three-quarters of the way through, and ends up short and anticlimactic; instead, the final set piece is a competition between the two heroes, Frog and Tiger (played by Sammo Hung and Lau Kar-wing, respectively), which is altogether more nonlethal and comic in tone. The film thus overshoots its climax and returns to the more lighthearted mode in which it starts out, and even, narratively, ensures that it sets us down in a place similar to where it started, as if the film could begin all over again on a new caper. Narrative closure and climax here are clearly resisted, and viewing desire—in its very "saving frivolity"—remains in circulation.

Rehistoricizing the Violence of the Kung Fu Comedy

But how might we think about such a treatment of violence (or, in Bersani's terms, even a "moral perspective" of representation in regard to it) historically and politically, rather than just psychologically or psychoanalytically? Recalling the arguments of Adorno and Benjamin discussed earlier in this chapter might take us back to this question of the relation of a film to its historical context. The context of Hong Kong cinema of the 1970s and 1980s, however, is of course rather different to that of the rise of European fascism that Benjamin watched growing up around him, or even the McCarthy-era American society that provided a context for Adorno's anxieties about the "authoritarian personality." We may well, therefore, ask if there is any kind of equivalent historical phenomenon to which the kung fu comedy film should be related.

One answer may be to relate these to the ongoing trauma of the Cultural Revolution, which was still in progress in mainland China, and which overshadowed Hong Kong politics during the period. The horror of the Cultural Revolution made its mark most decisively on Hong Kong in the Leftist Riots of 1967, and in their wake politics itself became increasingly taboo. As well as eliciting a regime of tight censorship of political threats from the colonial authorities, the Cultural Revolution and the repressions of the Maoist state could be understood to have created a blockage for radical or even progressive politics in Hong Kong, which would rapidly be associated with the excesses of Mao and the Red Guards. If there are dangerously destructive energies that (in Benjamin's terms) are being prematurely released, or to which (in Bersani's terms) the stylizations of the kung fu comedy might allow its spectators a mobile rather than fixated relationship, then the Cultural Revolution might at least offer an initial image through which to name them.

However, quite what I mean when associating these historical and psychic energies with the Cultural Revolution may be rather complicated. A detailed assessment of the Cultural Revolution—without which pronouncements on it would be necessarily platitudinous—is beyond the scope of this book, but it seems impossible to think about the "historical" nature of images of violence in Hong

Kong films without reference to it, one way or another. One Benjaminian perspective on it, however, would read it as exemplifying the logic that "The Work of Art in the Age of Mechanical Reproduction" recognizes in fascism. According to Benjamin here, the elite, wishing to keep their power intact, offer the people not freedom or progress but "self-expression" as a people. From such a perspective, it is in this "aestheticization" of politics that the root cause of war and destruction should be sought—whether what emerges is the image of the Nazi *Volk* or the Marxian proletariat, whether the cult of the auratic leader be that of Hitler or Mao, and whether the elite in question be the industrial bourgeoisie of 1930s Europe or the new class of bureaucratic functionaries who emerged in the mid-century Communist Bloc. Both Nazis and Red Guards constructed enemies within, on whom violence was focused in order to create the fiction of a "people," whose violent historical struggle becomes itself a total work of art in a moment of artistic self-alienation that—certainly in Benjamin's account of fascism—allows its fixation on and reflexive contemplation of its own epic self-destruction as sublime aesthetic spectacle.[44] A mobile psychology like the one Bersani describes, and which I have suggested may be at play in the kung fu comedy, may be a meaningful response to such violent fixation.

However, this destructivity can also be understood as, in its turn, having roots in the unfreedom, poverty, and exploitation suffered by those who are to become this "people." In Bersani we discovered violence as something inherent to the human condition. In the anticolonial writings of Frantz Fanon, however, we find that there is a historical dimension to the form in which it is implanted within us. The violence at the heart of the colonial subject, within his account, is created by the conditions of colonial life, which are themselves nothing if not brutalizing. According to Fanon (again mirroring Bersani's argument about a broader psychological mechanism), for the colonial subject there is no simple choice between violence and nonviolence. This led Fanon to his controversial belief in the importance of "native" violence in the removal of the oppressor; and critics of Fanon might, indeed, see the Cultural Revolution as an example of the disastrous outcome of such a revolt from below, though certainly his supporters may well understand it as far too much manipulated by a political elite to be legible in such terms. Whatever we make of Fanon's embrace of violence, however, it is worth noting that Fanon himself—in an argument that parallels some of the readings I have offered here—saw stylized, culturalized, aestheticized, and ritualized forms of violence nurtured in the African context—in, for example, ecstatic mystical dances—as serving to channel away necessary energies of revolt to merely cultural ends, dispersing and neutralizing them.[45]

Underlying the fascist harnessing of aggressivity, then, is a more authentically "popular" anger and resentment. And under these, in turn, lies the violence of oppression itself. In Fanon's work, this is primarily the direct violence of colonial domination. However, in this book overall, I have been arguing for a broader continuity between Fanon's understanding of colonial violence and the wider violence of economic, cultural, and sociopolitical subordination that characterizes capitalist modernity. I have been arguing that it is such a set of continuities that account for the continuing appeal of kung fu cinema—and all its echoes in transnational cultures.

Within the Hong Kong context, certainly (and ultimately in ours, too, I would wager), the neutralization or dispersal of the energies of political violence would have appeared—and in fact been—by no means as simply negative a thing as Fanon suggests. Bersani's argument—inflected through Benjamin—suggests that what the kung fu comedy may offer, in stylizing violent action to make it beautiful, funny, and physically astonishing, is the mobility of an unfixed relationship to this complex of historical violence at once suffered by the subject and wished on others, at once harboring radical energies of anti-imperial revolt in relation to the state and the fascizing tendencies of popular mobilization.

CHAPTER 4

Hysteria

> Drunken boxing, a real form of kung fu, mimics the swaying of the drunkard, but the film actually requires the character to get inebriated in order to fight. Chan's scenes of doing just that are absolutely hysterical.
>
> —*Clyde Gentry*

> What does it mean to be hysterical? . . . Isn't it a malaise, a great distress, caused by the desire for an impossible *something?* In that case, all of us who have imagination are afflicted with it, with that strange sickness.
>
> —*George Sand*

The starting point for this book's analysis of kung fu comedic cinema has been the recognition of the role played in it by a "grotesque body," akin to that of European carnival. The following two chapters will return to aspects of such a grotesque body, though my aim will be to think about it in rather different terms, and terms that will open up different aspects of the ambiguous and ambivalent politics of the kung fu comedy initially introduced through the notion of carnival. The central concept I will be using to do this is *hysteria.* In this chapter, I will be exploring the question of the hysterical body—and of whether it might help make sense of the kung fu comedy—in primarily theoretical terms. In doing so, I respond to attempts that have been made by Bhaskar Sarkar and Mark Gallagher to use the notion of hysteria to discuss Hong Kong action cinema, and to Kwai-Cheung Lo's investigation of gender in martial arts films. In the following chapter, I will be setting out a series of "hysterical" analyses of films in which, I will be arguing, issues of colonialism, modernity, class, masculinity, and Hong Kong identity are at stake, articulated around a thematic of inheritance (in other words to the question, once more, of "legacy") and the relation to the father.

If the misery of a mental illness and the celebration of carnival seem at first poles apart, the possibility of bringing them together is at the very least made more plausible by the work of Allon White, who was not only one of the most important figures in the Anglophone debates on Bakhtin, but also a lifelong sufferer of hysterical attacks, brought on by witnessing the death by drowning of his sister in childhood.[1] Looking at Sigmund Freud's casebooks, White was "fascinated by the carnival debris that spills out of the mouths of those terrified Viennese women in Freud's *Studies of Hysteria*."[2] Tracing profound echoes between the grotesque iconography of carnival and that of the hysterics' fantasies, White "was struck forcibly . . . by how many images and symbols, which were once the source of vigorous pleasures . . . have become transformed into morbid symptoms of private terror."[3] Even as popular carnival imagery became repressed by the strictures of bourgeois culture, it re-emerged, in transformed guise, as nightmare, physical symptom, and neurosis.

In making this connection between hysteria and carnival, White's work lifts the former out of a realm of pathology and into that of cultural analysis. Drawing on such an approach, using the notion of hysteria to think about cinema does not necessarily entail a pathologizing function.[4] It does not suggest that in some literal sense the viewers or creators of the Hong Kong comedy suffer disproportionately from particular illnesses, but rather finds in hysteria a model for the representational, narrative, and aesthetic forms of the genre, which may be indicative of their meaning and function. Following such a culturalizing logic, the surrealists Louis Aragon and André Breton went as far as to value hysteria as "a supreme mode of expression."[5] More recent feminist reappropriations—discussed in detail below—return a political dimension to this cultural thinking of hysteria, seeking to make it legible not simply as an illness, but rather as a series of complex and subtle forms of resistance, as well as acquiescence, to patriarchal power.

Such cultural rather than medical approaches to hysteria are further supported by the Lacanian traditions that have treated it less as an illness than as a modality of discourse. As Gérard Wajeman put it, "the speaking subject is hysteric as such."[6] But if this might suggest hysteria to be something of a universal in the human condition—something that, in George Sand's terms, "all of us who have imagination are afflicted with"—my argument here will be that kung fu comedies, in particular, are especially ripe for analysis in its terms, and that it is a notion that makes particular sense of the special kind of imagination that such films display. To make this argument, however, will require me, first, to further conceptualize the notion of hysteria.

Hysteria and Common Sense

There are a number of ways in which, in the most everyday sense, we might claim that kung fu comedies are hysterical. Most simply and commonly we might make a claim for them as "hysterically funny." Clyde Gentry, for example, in the passage quoted at the head of this chapter, makes such a judgment in his fan-oriented biography of Jackie Chan, calling Chan's performance in *Drunken Master* "absolutely hysterical."[7] On the surface, this merely offers a vaguely hyperbolic form of approbation, registering that Chan's performance is not only mildly amusing but laugh-out-loud funny. Beyond its simple affirmation of Chan's comedy, however, this use already signals a set of qualities that, even in its everyday and nonspecialist usage, the term carries with it. Hysteria, commonly understood, refers to behavior that is compulsive, extreme or excessive, unrestrained or even uncontrollable, feverish, erratic, and overemotional. The laughter Gentry claims to experience when viewing *Drunken Master*—racking the body into involuntary spasms—is of this order. By extension, however, we might find many of these hysteric qualities in Chan's physical performance itself, with all its melodrama, manic energy, and anarchic grotesquery.[8] The precise grammar of Gentry's claim is in fact not that his own laughter was hysterical, but that Chan's performance (what he is "doing" in his "scenes") is, and there is a conflation here of performer and spectator, as if Chan's corporeal enactment produces a contagion on the body of the viewer, locating the hysterical affect somewhere between the two, rather than in one particular body or on one particular side of the screen. The kung fu comedy more generally, with its sudden shifts in tone from the flippant to the gruesome, its exaggerated pantomime acting, its heightened violence, and its absurdism, might well be described with this rather loose, lay conception of hysteria, and it would certainly seem to be in such a "hysterical" register—rooted in the irrationality of the body itself—that such a cinema attempts to address its audiences. Whether it is successful or not, of course, is another matter, but the very notion of the "kung fu craze" that is supposed to have swept America (and the world) in the 1970s—suggesting as it does a form of "mass hysteria"—might signal an anxiety about this form of address and the potential psychosomatic contagion of kung fu's theatrical and corporeal excess. In this regard, is even the "motion emotion" David Bordwell discovers in martial arts cinema—his "delusion" that he can "vault, grave and unflappable, over the cars parked outside the theater"—itself a kind of hysterical symptom?[9]

This "hysterical" mode of martial arts performance (quite different from the stoicism of the typical hero of the "serious" martial arts film) is most obviously brought into the narrative itself and thematized in another of Jackie Chan's early films, *Fearless Hyena* (dir. Kenneth Tsang and Jackie Chan, 1979). In this, the hero, Sing Lung, learns a style of "emotional kung fu" in which power is generated and the enemy is disoriented by excessive and unstably alternating displays of sorrow, anger, laughter, and happiness. In a more proper sense of the term, then, it is in this film rather than *Drunken Master* that Chan's performance might be said to become "absolutely hysterical"—though certainly his performance in the latter is well on the way there.

Hysterical Histories

My premise here, however, is that the notion of hysteria can be used in a more "technical" sense and that this will help us further understand the qualities just described, and their significance. There are of course problems with attempting to do so. During its flowering in the late nineteenth century, hysteria became one of the most frequent diagnoses for mental illness; however, as a medical term it has been largely obsolete (even discredited) since the early twentieth century.[10]

Over a long history stretching back to the ancient world, the term came to be associated with an impossibly wide range of causes. For Hippocrates, it described the effects of a dissatisfied "wandering womb" on other organs of the body.[11] In the middle ages, it was a term associated with demonic possession—primarily of women and in terms of the sinfulness of their sexuality.[12] The concept was remedicalized in the seventeenth and eighteenth centuries, increasingly being understood as a "nervous" disorder.[13] During the nineteenth century, one of hysteria's most famous investigators, Jean-Martin Charcot, spent much of his career attempting to root it in physiology and in poor genetic stock, though increasingly it became defined as a disease that, though manifesting in a variety of bodily symptoms, had no physical etiology and was ultimately mental in cause.[14] As such a mental illness, hysteria would prove to be the initial field on which Freud developed the core concepts and approaches of psychoanalysis.[15] Freud located the roots of hysteria first in traumatic experience, its symptoms repeating in mutated form an event too awful for the subject to have admitted into consciousness. Increasingly, however, Freud located hysteria in the existential trauma of the human development of sexuality itself, with the hysterical symptom not only marking a site of trauma, but also simultaneously expressing and masking a repressed desire.[16]

If such questions of causation produced little consensus regarding the nature of hysteria, threatening the coherence of the concept as a meaningful diagnosis, then its protean symptoms were hardly more stable ground. Hysteria was, almost by definition, difficult to locate in a clear and repeated set of phenomena. Its effects were manifold and in different patients may have included fainting, tears, paralysis, vomiting, hallucinations, blindness, deafness, loss of speech, tics, epileptoid fits, inexplicable pains, uncontrollable laughter, or even odd effects such as suddenly being able to speak a language that the patient did not know they knew. It seemed often to mimic other diseases, and the main sign that the symptoms indicated hysteria rather than anything else was that there seemed to be no underlying physical cause for the illness, so diagnosis was, in many respects, by default.

The history of hysteria, then, offers a concept so profoundly inconsistent and variant that it has been largely abandoned.[17] Worse than this, however, hysteria has consistently been a term involved in the subjugation of women and carries with it a highly problematic gendering that has run from ancient understandings of hysteria as caused by the womb, through the medieval period's (quite literal) demonization of women's sexuality, to eighteenth- and nineteenth-century conceptions of hysteria as a symptom of weakness and femininity.[18] The treatment of female hysterics has involved, repeatedly, an attempt to subject women to the knowledge and authority of men—most spectacularly, perhaps, in the clinic of Salpêtrière, where within Charcot's attempts to visually document and categorize them in a display of his own, masculine mastery over their feminine madness and weakness, women's voices and their own accounts of their symptoms were largely silenced and ignored, reduced to the status of meaningless "babble."[19] If Freud gave such patients a "voice" in the talking cure, this was nonetheless, as his feminist critics have since noted, only within the context of analytic sessions that often amounted to a battle of wills in which he attempted to impose his interpretations on their discourse and to return them to their "proper" place within the bourgeois, patriarchal home—a place which their very symptoms suggest could never be an entirely happy one for them.[20]

Hysterical Resistance

However, it is precisely these problems with hysteria that make it useful for my analysis of martial arts comedies. As understood through feminist reworkings of Freud, the "problem" of hysteria is not so much to be found within the body or the psyche of the (female) patient, as within the conditions of bourgeois patriarchy itself. The disease rose to prominence, after all, precisely as these conditions developed and primarily among young women, those most silenced and powerless within the stifling world of the middle-class home and the nuclear family. Its symptoms emerged as responses to the forms of power and authority that structured not only those family relations—primarily relations to the patriarch—but also those relations of "transference" within which they were presented to the patriarchal representative, the doctor, as he subjected his patient to diagnosis and treatment. All this is to say that hysteria is a matter not simply of the subjective, but of the intersubjective—and even of culture.

Such symptoms, then, can be understood to mark the extent to which such women were the victims of Victorian patriarchy; but they can also be understood as constituting a complex form in which they negotiated their relationship to masculine authority and power. This is certainly not as simple as a form of overt "rebellion"—the hysteric is far from a feminist in her challenge to her subjection[21]—but it certainly signals the place where "politics" re-emerges. The hysteric's symptoms have in fact been understood as being in many ways profoundly complicit with male authority. Charcot's patients in his Salpêtrière clinic obediently acted out the elaborate, standardized symptomatology that he wrote about, displaying a compliant desire to please the "master" and to submit to his authority.[22] Charcot's symptomatology was only undermined as science by the fact that his patients' particular set of symptoms was entirely specific to his clinic—they were notoriously found nowhere else. His patients' compliant address to a paternal authority, however, seems to have been far less unique. Hysterical symptoms varied over history, in line not only with changing medical theory but also with changing ideas of femininity. In typical symptoms (fainting, paralysis, fits of tears) the female hysteric often—in exaggerated, pantomime form—reiterated what was expected of her as a woman: weakness, delicacy, irrationality, emotionality, and the like.

Nonetheless, the compliance and conformity of the Victorian hysteric was complicated by a relationship to power that was far more ambivalent than evident at first sight, and hysterical case histories often seem to be marked by subtle forms of defiance that made the hysteric a heroine figure for a number of feminists during the 1970s.[23] It is perhaps no accident that Freud's conception of "resistance" emerges first in his casebooks on hysteria, shifting gradually from a military metaphor describing the defensive attitude of his patients to take on its increasingly technical, psychoanalytical sense.[24] Even in her compliance, in fact, the hysteric resists, telling the doctor what he expects to hear, rather than speaking the truth that would afford him the mastery of knowledge—thus performing a paradoxical form of evasion, a little like the kung fu practitioner who bends to the force of an opponent, seeming to give them the advantage they seek, but precisely in yielding makes sure that the attack does not meet its mark. If this simile seems slightly forced, its value might perhaps be enhanced by considering hysteria as a strategy (like kung fu) by which the weak may avoid being overpowered by the strong. In this, hysteria can be understood as one strategy by which the overpowered can maintain, if not a state of outright warfare, then at least the "capacity to resist" that I have discussed in a previous chapter.

Even more fundamentally, the hysteric's symptoms disrupted and threatened the order of the bourgeois home. French feminist Hélène Cixous saw the hysteric as making "permanent war" and hysteria as "a disturbing force which means that the little circus [of patriarchy] no longer functions."[25] As Carroll Smith-Rosenberg notes, while young women were expected to wait docilely and silently upon the needs of their elders and of men, the bedridden hysteric commanded care and attention from others in ways that were otherwise not socially open to her.[26] As Julia Borossa has summarized it, then, hysteria was not simply a matter of acquiescence, nor of rebellion, but involved "a problematic, paradoxical relationship to conformity, played out primarily in the arena of the body: gendered, out of control, and refusing easy categorization."[27] Might this not be an apt description, too, of the kung fu comedy?

At the outset of this book, I noted the frequently posed argument that the kung fu comedy marks a retreat from the "political" content that was found in the Hong Kong martial arts films of the late 1960s and early 1970s. Taking such a position, commentators have often understood kung fu comedy as expressing an increasing conformity to the values of the capitalist culture of the rising "tiger" economy, acquiescing to the dictates of colonial rule and the taboo on political dissent. However, if, as I have suggested, "carnival" content suggests that politics continued in other forms, then "hysteria" might be a way of further thinking through the form that this continued "resistance" took. Certainly as described by the critics who find kung fu comedies apolitical (or even apologist), the social conformism of Hong Kong in the late 1970s seems to offer us something much more like the seemingly docile, silenced young women of the Victorian era than anything akin to Rey Chow's "protestant ethnic." If there is "resistance" here of some sort, then, it is likely to be on something of the same grounds as that of the hysteric rather than the radical activist. The position of the colonial subject with regards to a strong and efficient colonial paternalism, and the position of the Third World proletarian in particular, contains parallels to the position of woman within patriarchy. Both are denied a voice—denied in many respects a legitimate position with regards to the "language" of the master—and made "others" (if in racial or class rather than gendered terms), objects of knowledge rather than its subjects.

Hélène Cixous, discussing Freud's perhaps most combative hysteric patient, Dora, has written a striking sentence that helps us think further about the Hong Kong situation in terms of hysteria. She proposes: "I am what Dora would have been if the history of women had begun."[28] Such a "history of women" would have to be one in which women were fully the subject. It would be a history made by women "as" women, and as self-conscious agents. It would also be a history critically grasped and known by those women, one in which women could see and understand themselves reflected. What marks, then, the beginning of the "history of women" and distinguishes Cixous herself from Dora is the advent of feminism as a political movement, through which such subjectivity might be articulated.

There are ways in which we may well understand non-elite Hongkongers of the 1970s, inasmuch as they were colonial subjects, to stand, in some respects, in a similar position "outside" their own history. In the most basic terms, Hong Kong was certainly not a democracy, and its "history" was the history of the colonial government, and of the small coterie of native businessmen who had their ear. Hong Kong certainly saw a developing "public sphere" in the 1970s, but this was at the expense of a powerful taboo against politics and against anything that rocked the boat.[29] In the wake of the anticolonial and leftist riots of 1966 and 1967, the administration had enforced a swingeing crackdown on oppositional groups, and even beyond this, in the shadow of the horrors of the Cultural Revolution on the mainland, self-censorship outstripped the regime's official mechanisms in enforcing a culture of conformity to the status quo, creating the "politics of disappearance" documented by Ackbar Abbas, in which political energies were rechanneled into conspicuous consumption and the pursuit of economic gain.[30] Within such a situation, political subjectification was profoundly blocked; politics itself could be understood as having become too traumatic to bear conscious engagement, with historical agency becoming a now-unthinkable desire—an "impossible *something*" of the sort mentioned in the quote from George Sand with which I started this chapter.[31]

If, in Freud's classical model, the hysterical symptom is a displaced image of a trauma and a desire, the political situation of post-1967 Hong Kong may well serve as the primary referent to which we can understand Hong Kong culture responding in the ensuing decades. It is, of course, a trauma overdetermined by others: by the dislocation and diaspora that had brought the bulk of the population to the enclave; by the wider civil war that had racked China throughout the preceding century and that had in turn driven the diasporic scattering that had brought people to Hong Kong; by the meetings with Western modernity and the imperialist depredations that had seen China itself fall from the richest nation in the world to semicolonial status, the "sick man of East Asia," triggering difficult renegotiations of racial and national identity; and of course by the disruption of traditional modes of life by the capitalist economy.

Writing not of kung fu comedies in the 1970s, but of the resurgence of swordplay (*wuxia*) films during the 1990s, Bhaskar Sarkar has in fact set out to use the notion of hysteria to understand Hong Kong action cinema as a response not only to the rising anxieties of the 1997 handover of Hong Kong to the control of mainland China, but also to just such experiences of physical displacement, cultural dislocation, and the perpetual instability and insecurity of living conditions in Hong Kong's deregulated economy.[32] Although his account of hysteria tends to its more everyday sense, rather than a technical one, and although it often seems to border instead on an account of postmodern schizophrenia,[33] Sarkar draws from Baudrillard to understand hysteria primarily in terms of the "exacerbated staging of the subject" and of a "theatrical and operatic conversion."[34] For Sarkar, this hysterical theatricalization was evident in the 1990s swordplay film in its "dizzying pace," its dramatic, often tilted camera angles, its "soaring" music, the gravity-defying bodies produced by wirework, the increasingly outrageous special effects, and the rapid crossing of genres and genders alike.[35] However, Sarkar not only understands the films he discusses in their formal particularity and that of their context in 1990s Hong Kong, but he also treats this as an "intensification" that speaks of a broader phenomenon of which they were a part.[36] For Sarkar, hysterical qualities are implicitly to be found in the longer history of Hong Kong martial arts cinema and in fact reflect a wider, emerging "transnational Asian" experience.[37] Beyond this, the conditions Sarkar describes (displacement, precarity, and the like) have increasingly been a part of a global landscape and are already named in his essay as forming a wider "postmodern" condition—perhaps explaining the rise of international interest in Hong Kong movies during the 1990s and the ways in which its film style has become increasingly absorbed into a "transnational" cinema language.[38]

Given this wider potential application of the term, it is striking that in many respects the kung fu comedy is an even better candidate for a "hysterical" cinema than the swordplay. What defines hysteria most fundamentally is its corporeal dimension—what Freud termed the "bodily conversion" of the symptom, where, with the silencing of the voice, it is left to the body to speak and to take on the burden of communicating the subject's trauma.[39] If, as Sarkar and Baudrillard emphasize, hysteria involves theater, the medium of its drama is the corporeal. Similarly, while the characteristics of the swordplay that Sarkar associates with hysteria are primarily matters of cinematography, in the kung fu comedy—as I have argued throughout this book—it is primarily the performing body that bears the expressive burden. The "exacerbated staging of the subject" and "theatrical and operatic conversion" of Baudrillard and Sarkar in fact describe well the exaggerated, formalized, and dance-like qualities of the martial arts performances of the kung fu comedy, as discussed in the last chapter.

Indeed, although hysteria is more often associated in the popular imagination with "feminine" weakness, fainting, or tears, what is striking in examining Charcot's attempts to create a photographic iconography of his patients' enacted symptoms is the intense athleticism evident in many of his plates (of both men and women hysterics) and the resultant echoes between these images and those of the comedic martial arts body (see figs. 4.1–4.8).

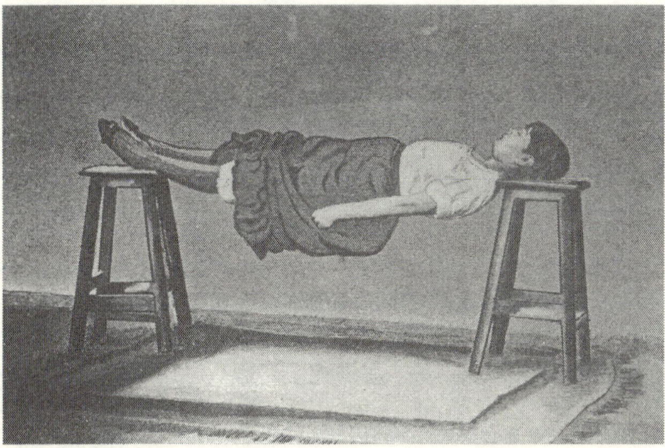

Fig. 4.1. "Spasms in all the muscles of the body of Paule G…" Photogravure from Albert Pitres, *Leçons cliniques sur l'hysterie et l'hypnotism* (Paris, 1891), vol. 1, p. 501. Digitized by the Wellcome Library, London, made available on Creative Commons Attribution-only 4.0 License.

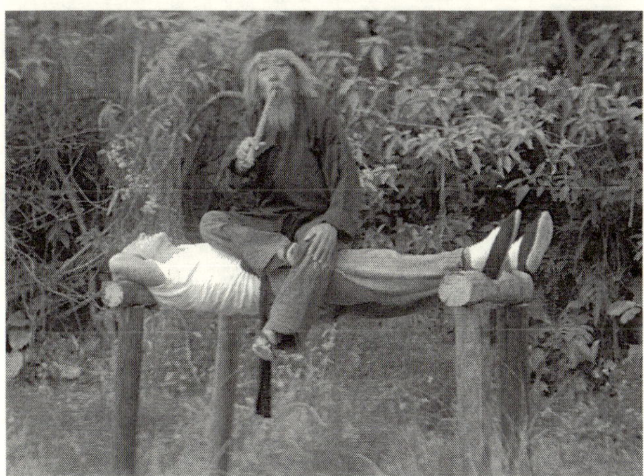

Fig. 4.2. "Spasms in all the muscles of the body of Jackie C…" Video still from *Snake in the Eagle's Shadow.* © 1979 Seasonal Film Corporation / 2018 Koch Films.

Paraphrasing Charcot's treatises on hysteria, Elisabeth Bronfen thus describes "a period of *grands mouvements,* of contortions and bodily dislocations" in which "the hysteric would exhibit an extraordinary expenditure of muscle

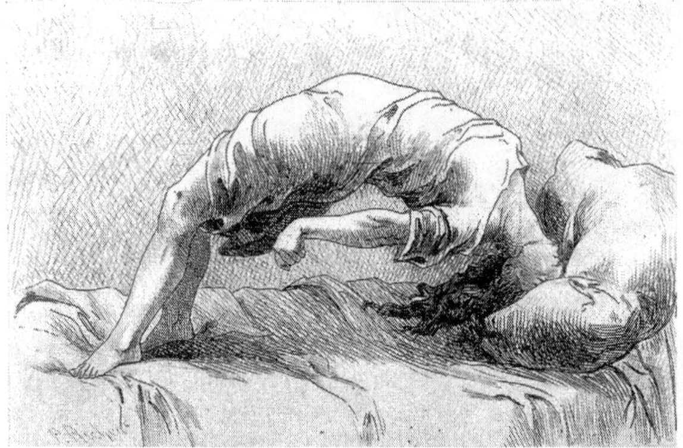

Fig. 4.3. The "arch of hysteria," one of the most famously typical movements of Charcot's patients' hysterical fits. From the "period of clownism," as illustrated in Paul Marie Louis Pierre Richer's *Etudes cliniques sur l'hystero-epilepsie ou grande hysterie* (Paris, 1881), Plate III. Digitized by the Wellcome Library, London, made available on Creative Commons Attribution-only 4.0 License.

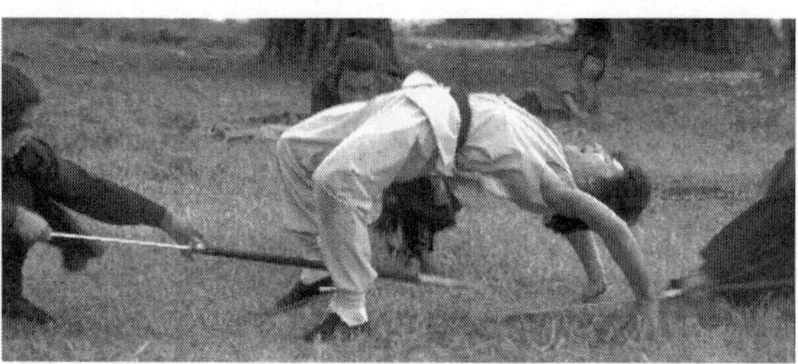

Fig. 4.4. Jackie Chan makes an "arch of hysteria." Video still from *Fearless Hyena*. © 2010 Fortune Star Media.

power." Bronfen comments that in this phase of *grands mouvements,* "Charcot thought to have detected eccentric body turnings and grotesque body postures, marked by an unusual flexibility, mobility, and sheer physical force."[40]

If this might also be an apt description of a comic kung fu performance, the parallels become even closer with Charcot's understanding of the actions of his hysterics as "a theatrical miming of passionate emotions such as anxiety or fear, in an embittered battle with an imaginary enemy" and in the parallels Charcot drew between "the hysteric and the animal, as though the entire body had transformed into a dislocated foreign body," echoing the strange becomings initiated by kung fu training in Hong Kong films.[41] In these, just like Charcot's patients, the body of the martial arts comedian departs from its proper and "normal"

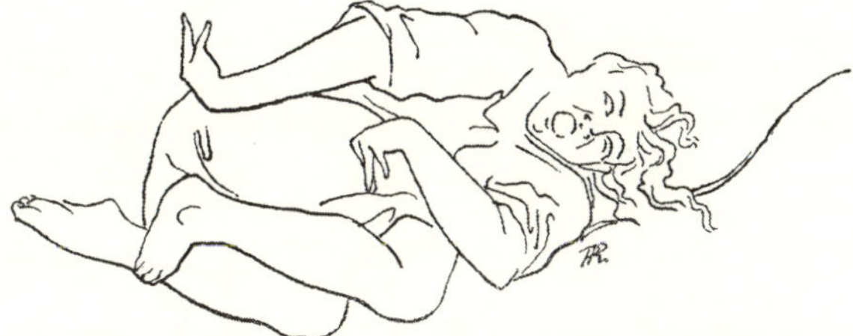

Fig. 4.5. "Phase tonique. Grands mouvements toniques." Illustration from Paul Marie Louis Pierre Richer, *Études cliniques sur l'hystéro-épilepsie ou grande hystérie* (Paris, 1881). Digitized by the Wellcome Library, London, made available on Creative Commons Attribution-only 4.0 License.

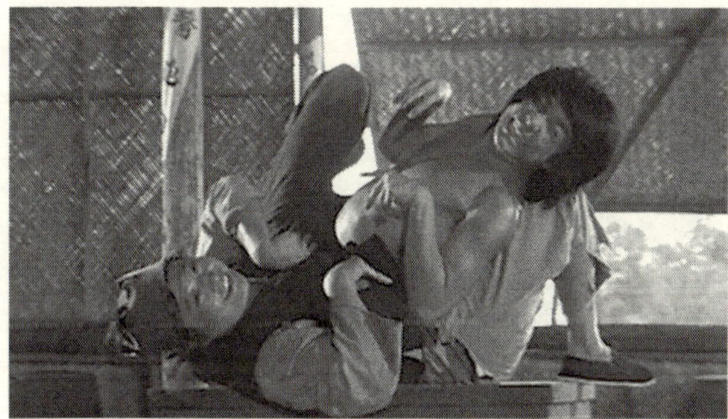

Fig. 4.6. Yuen Biao and Sammo Hung performing some "absolutely hysterical" monkey-style kung fu in *Knockabout.* Video still. © 2004 Star TV Filmed Entertainment.

upright posture to engage in strange crouching, bending, rolling, and flipping actions, to a fit-like, staccato rhythm.[42] The eccentricity and acrobatic excess of such movement stands in powerful contrast to the rational, economic, and efficient movements of a boxer or, in terms of cinema, even in relation to the more pared-down and "realist" fight aesthetic, for example, of Bruce Lee's final showdown with Chuck Norris in the Roman Colosseum in *Way of the Dragon* (1972)—though even this is open to analysis as somewhat hysterical. Charcot's use of a metaphor from the comic theater to name such a cluster of symptoms, terming them "clownism," has strong resonances with the kung fu comedy performance style and its roots in the operatic martial clown (*wuchou*) roles.

Through the parallel I have articulated above to Victorian hysterics and their position with regards to a locus of power from which they are excluded, such manic,

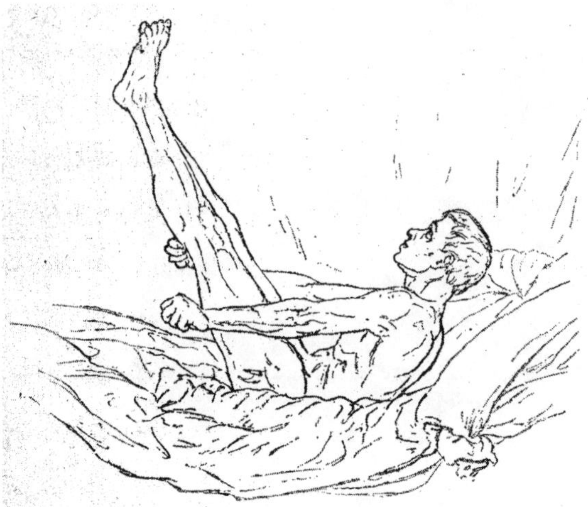

Fig. 4.7. "Positions of the hysterical attack. Arc de cercle. Emprosthotonos," from Jean-Martin Charcot, *Leçons du mardi* (Paris, 1887), vol. 2, p. 427. Digitized by the Wellcome Library, London, made available on Creative Commons Attribution-only 4.0 License.

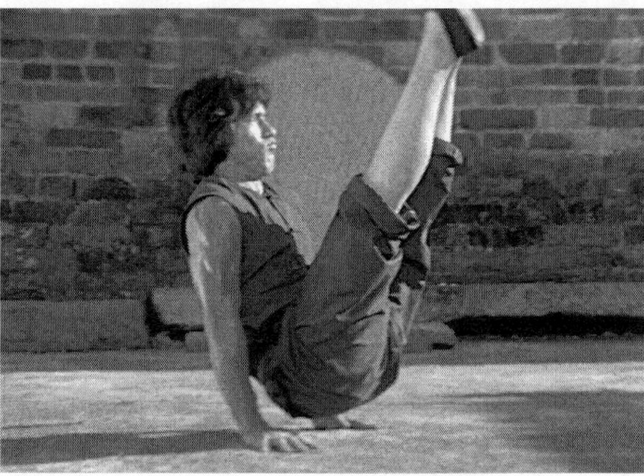

Fig. 4.8. Jackie Chan's "Arc de cercle. Emprosthotonos" in *Snake in the Eagle's Shadow.* Video still. © 1979 Seasonal Pictures / 2018 Koch Films.

"theatrical and operatic" physical performances of the kung fu comedy, in their very parallel to the "clownism" of Charcot's patients, become legible as displaced symptoms of a blocked political subjectivity, lodged in the body. With political self-determination denied, the desire for freedom re-emerges in the fantasy of the individual (and perhaps, my argument in this book so far would suggest, even collective) body, transformed by kung fu.

Hysteria, Complicity, and Subversion in *Project A*

Such a notion of hysteria as I have discussed here might offer a way of further understanding the distinction I made between Jackie Chan's role as the loyal police officer, Dragon Ma, in the *Project A* films, and Bruce Lee's anti-imperialist rebel in *Fist of Fury*, as analyzed in Chapter 2. In terms of a reading of Chan's wider career and the trajectory of kung fu comedies, this is all the more significant in that Chan, of course, would become increasingly synonymous with this role of the dutiful cop—a faithful civil servant and upholder of (colonial) law and order—throughout the 1980s and 1990s. He plays the role not only in the sequel, *Project A II* (dir. Jackie Chan, 1987), but notably also, for example, in a more modern setting, in the Police Story films, and in his appearance in the first three of the Lucky Stars series, as well as in the films in which he made his crossover to stardom in America, *Rumble in the Bronx* (dir. Stanley Tong, 1996) and the Rush Hour series.[43]

If in *Project A,* I have argued, Ma and his rather ramshackle cohort of coastguards accept and uphold the colonial order, it is only simultaneously to subvert it. Ma upturns a proper order that is both spatial and social-hierarchical through his inversionary body practices. His subaltern, *bricoleur* creativity in the refunctioning of bodies and objects, though obediently at the service of the colonial state, is articulated around a logic that is corrosive to colonialism itself and its technocratic systems of power or discipline, as they are enacted on the colonial body.

This is exemplified in the film's parodic reinvention of the kung fu comedy's training montage—already, of course, by 1983 a well-established and even overfamiliar trope of the genre. When Ma's unit of coastguards is disbanded and merged into the police force (their former rivals and, in a series of slapstick fights toward the start of the film, their antagonists), they are assigned to return to basic training, to acquire the discipline that they lack. The kung fu training of the drunken master films is now, however, transposed into the realm of colonial administration and its corporeal regulation.

This training is no longer aimed at developing "kung fu," but rather military discipline and subservience to authority. However, it takes on an increasingly carnivalesque nature as it goes on, as the new superiors also seek forms of vindictive revenge for their past conflicts. When two recruits on parade, for example, are discovered mouthing a lewd comment about a passing woman, they are punished by having to repeat the comment *ad nauseam,* only serving to multiply, rather than negate, its obscenity. Another recruit who fails to salute a superior officer

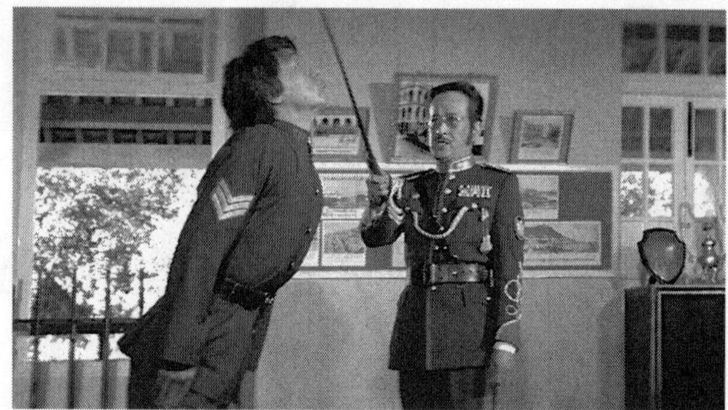

Fig. 4.9. Jackie Chan stands (hysterically) to attention in *Project A*. Video still. © 2010 Fortune Star Media.

correctly is made to salute repeatedly, but this makes the gesture of deference into an absurd and mocking simulacrum of itself. The three transgressors carry on their punishments into their sleep, muttering and twitching in their dreams, as the repeated actions become unconscious compulsions, ambivalent hysterical symptoms, addressed to the interpellating, authoritative gaze of colonial discipline, that have invaded the psyche of the colonial agent.

Ma's brigade is then stood on alert in the middle of the night by an officer who claims to be concerned that they have drunk too much soup, with Ma having to call an absurdly militaristic "charge" to the latrines that might have delighted Bakhtin in its reduction of the regimented and ideal order of the army to the level of the lower body stratum: physical drill is reduced literally to "toilet training." The next day, the recruits are ordered to strip naked to shower, and then interrupted, still only half soaped, and called out of the showers to stand for inspection with only phallically shaped water ladles to protect their modesty. The whole training section serves to relibidinize colonial discipline and to inject a sort of anarchy into it, through a failure of the "proper" mimesis of the colonial masters. This hysterical "failure" to conform and to perform—which, even within the obedient attempt to do so, seems to emerge from the colonized body—is celebrated throughout the film, as a productive, creative, and ultimately transgressive and liberating act. Even when Chan salutes his superior (fig. 4.9), his hysterical performance of subservience slips into subversion.

The return of the libidinal and of forms of perverse or disruptive pleasure, invested even in the conformity to colonial law itself, may also be read in terms of the fact that a symptom (hysterical or otherwise) is not only a message addressed to authority, but also an attempt to adapt. As understood within Lacanian psychoanalysis it is, in the words of Slavoj Žižek, "not only a ciphered message, but also a way for the subject to organize his/her enjoyment."[44] In Lacan's late work, the symptom, far from simply being a source of pain or disruption, can also be a means by which the subject avoids psychosis and annihilation in the face of trauma, allowing the sufferer to choose "something rather than nothing," binding desire and *jouissance* to that "something" (is it Sand's "impossible *something*" again?), and ensuring "a minimum of consistency to being-in-the-world."[45] The body in the kung fu comedy, subject as it is to colonial or capitalist discipline in military drill, in the constrictions of urban space or the rigors of deregulated work, becomes a source of symptoms and, through these, of new forms of (perverse, disruptive) pleasure.

In his analysis of the relation between carnival and hysteria, Allon White argues that many of Freud's early attempts at curing his hysterical patients amounted to the abreactive "reinflexion" of the grotesque aspects of their phobias into comic form, turning anxiety into "cathartic laughter."[46] This might well be a matter of the patient coming to enjoy their symptom. For White, carnival once allowed the ritual catharsis of the material repressed and othered by its society's symbolic systems, through just such means of abreactive humor. The bourgeois subject, after the repression of carnival, was left without the cultural resources to do this and thrown back on its own meager resources. Nonetheless, within White's text, even the neurotic's creation of hysterical symptoms, with all their "pantomime," amounts to a kind of attempt—partial and impoverished as it is—"to mediate their terrors by enacting private, made-up carnivals" as "therapeutic rituals."[47] The athletic dimension of the hysteric body in its moments of "clownism" in particular often stood in stark contrast to the restricted, "stiff and well-behaved" comportment of the body required of the Victorian bourgeoisie.[48] The kung fu comedy, then, though developing within a global hegemonic modernity that has generally repressed such folkloric traditions and their resources for catharsis, nonetheless retains a number of these and creates a collective articulation that can draw on resources unavailable to the nineteenth-century European bourgeois neurotic. These resources allow for a transformation of the symptom into laughter and physical joy, allowing a form of psychic adaptation and survival, and even cathartic healing; and even if, as in Chan's comedies, they bow to the paternalist authority of the status quo, they reintroduce carnival elements of excess and disruption into that order in their very pantomime enactment of acquiescence.

Jackie Chan in the USA

Given what I have argued here about the hysterical nature of Chan's repeated role of the loyal cop who nonetheless, in the performance of his duties and through the very "otherness" of his body, injects a chaotic element into the symbolic order, it seems highly significant that it is with such roles that Chan made his breakthrough to the American (and European) market with *Rumble in the Bronx* and the Rush Hour series.[49] Within such a context, the figure of the "dutiful Asian" takes on a further significance, fitting a series of pervasive racial stereotypes, often in contrast to both the wild and primitive African and to the white Westerner who is figured as "natural" master of both. In this regard, *Rush Hour*'s pairing of Jackie Chan as the conscientious and conservative Inspector Lee with Chris Tucker's portrayal of a reckless, fast-talking, womanizing, and rule-breaking African American detective seems highly predictable.

Chan, then, performs this obedient role obediently. In these films, he also situates himself within Hollywood action-movie conventions, playing out images of masculine strength and heroism. However, as Mark Gallagher has argued—in an article that once again links Chan to notions of hysteria—he inhabits these conventions in unconventional ways, disturbing the codes of masculinity that prevail within American action cinema.[50] Gallagher notes how Chan's performance, through its emphasis on rapid and agile movement, contrasts to the typical Western action star of the era. Gallagher reads the "statuesque," rigid immobility of the Western star as a fetishizing response to physical vulnerability, presenting in its face an image of sealed immutability and thus imperviousness to harm. In contrast, argues Gallagher, Chan's perpetual movement seems to mark him repeatedly as vulnerable—and hence "feminine." While American heroes stand and fight, Chan just as often creates action sequences by taking flight instead. Indeed, as Chan's career developed, his films became increasingly "chase" films, with the "kung fu" element receding proportionally. While American heroes command the action by being the still point around which it turns, often filling the frame of a shot to emphasize their dominance over their world, Chan (more, again, like Buster Keaton or Mickey Mouse than Arnold Schwarzenegger or Bruce Willis) is the acted-on and always out-of-control object of the forces around him, often framed as a small figure within a chaotic and dangerous environment. While American heroes overcome their enemies through sheer force, Chan is usually smaller and less powerful than his opponents, a master of flexibility rather than strength. In terms of acting, Chan's exaggerated facial expressions echo the frenetic mobility of his body and mark him as "emotional," in strong contrast to the deadpan stoicism of the typical American action star. Chan turns the action formula into comedy, and this, Gallagher concludes, ultimately involves a lampoon of the codes of action and the conventions of "masculinity" at its heart, in which they are destabilized and only adopted with a certain irony.[51]

To understand Chan's position with regards to the dominant structure of Hollywood action movies, Gallagher draws on Paul Smith's analysis of Clint

Eastwood's orangutan sidekick, Clyde, in *Every Which Way but Loose* (dir. James Fargo, 1978) to suggest that Chan provides a hysterical "burlesque" of masculinity.[52] According to Smith, action cinema primarily involves a "trial" of the hero's masculinity through a masochism that it must ultimately renounce, in order to return to the "ideal" body. However, for Smith this process is far from "seamless" and remains narratively "out of control" due to a "hysterical residue" introduced with the very corporeality that the films must first introduce in order to then conjure away. For Smith, the "burlesque" or hysterical body haunts the heroic body: rather than returning to the ideal, as the heroic body properly does, the burlesque body lingers within the sphere of masochism and corporeality that the heroic narrative is normally designed to exorcise. It enacts heroism with a "childish" levity that, through its parody, rejects and undermines the "adult" seriousness of violence and manliness. In its connection to masochism, this hysterical-burlesque body is also connected profoundly to powerlessness, and it is perhaps significant for my own analysis of Chan's postcolonial hysteria that Smith's analysis locates this powerlessness, in the case of Eastwood's character in *Every Which Way but Loose,* as a matter of his working-class background and environment. Clyde is interpreted as a split-off alter ego, expressing the hysterical symptom that is properly that of a troubled proletarian masculinity robbed of potency.[53] I have been arguing throughout that Chan's comedy is a response to just such powerlessness and symbolic marginalization, though, of course, within a context that is additionally colonial.

Gallagher's use of Smith might remind us that, as Kwai-Cheung Lo argues in his analysis of warrior women in Asian cinema, who he suggests perform a kind of "female masculinity," there is not only one masculinity but a plurality of masculinities.[54] One of the key appeals of Chan to much of his male, Western audience may precisely be in his doing masculinity *differently* to its hegemonic forms and in the valorization within his films of "other" ways of inhabiting the male position—what Lo calls "masculinity with a twist."[55] Lo suggests that the appeal to their fans of women martial arts stars—and the filmic texts in which they appear, where the "most secure and stable" forms of masculinity often seem associated with villains rather than heroes—suggests that "perhaps this steady and unchanging masculinity is the least attractive and interesting kind."[56] What such women action stars share with Chan is that their performance of masculinity emerges from a position of a certain otherness and exclusion, so is a matter of something achieved rather than simply given. This may well speak to the experience of a male audience for whom masculinity is also, inevitably, a task to be fulfilled (and, for most of us, with some difficulty) rather than a simple fact of birth.[57] Such characters are more "approachable" and ready for identification than the supposedly ideal exemplars of hegemonic masculinity, who may be experienced as "threatening."[58]

As Lo argues, such forms of nonstandard identification in many ways help support the very ideals that they depart from.[59] However, they also celebrate the "power to become other,"[60] and even as they serve to "fill the holes" in a system of gender, they also serve to expose and exacerbate its very inconsistencies.[61] To the extent that, as with Chan, they throw us into the "burlesque," they also foreground not the ideal but the very struggle with that ideal, and what comes to the fore are the elements of masquerade and theatrical play and the pleasures of the body itself in its very fleshy resistance to any ideal, with all the anarchy and subversion that emerges from the ultimate impossibility of its full capture within any symbolic order. In the bubbling up of its symptoms, we are placed on the ground of hysterical resistance.

From Hysteria to Masculinity

Where Gallagher's account differs from what I have offered thus far is in its treatment of gender. In this chapter, I have primarily been treating the "feminine" associations of hysteria, located within the context of patriarchal Victorian bourgeois culture, as offering a *metaphor* or a structural parallel for the colonial subject in its relation to power and authority. The Victorian woman and the proletarian Hongkonger of the 1970s alike occupy a silenced and marginal discursive position. Within such a situation, it is hard for the nineteenth-century woman or the colonial subject to envision themselves as fully historical subjects and agents. As a result, I have suggested, there are parallels between the representations that emerge from such Victorian women, on an individual level, and the wider cultural sphere of production in Hong Kong.

Gallagher, on the other hand, makes a much more direct link between Chan's "hysteria" and his "feminization" within Western discourse. Within his essay, Chan is feminized to the extent that his performance is hysterical, and he can be read as hysterical inasmuch as his performance appears in relation to dominant norms of action heroism as "feminine." The danger here is that the link between gender and hysteria may be uninterrogated, and that gendered norms and associations are simply reiterated in such an argument.

But should we understand the linking of gender (taken, at least as a sociohistorical construct rather than a biological fact) and hysteria in more-than-metaphorical terms? Certainly, within our culture, different binary oppositions function not independently of one another, but often overcode one another, with race and ethnicity often negotiated in gendered terms, and vice versa. Within Orientalist discourse, the East has thus been "feminized" and China in particular figured as the "Sick Man of East Asia," thus envisioning the Chinese people as deficiently masculine. The attempt to reclaim this position and the self-image of power and agency that "masculinity" entails in patriarchal ("phallogocentric") cultures was, of course, a core ingredient of the physical culture movements of the early twentieth century, discussed in an earlier chapter of this book, which sought to redefine Chinese national identity and reassert a place on the stage of global politics. Such physical cultures were also, of course, central in the development of the ethno-nationalist image of the powerful kung fu star, as embodied for many, for example, in Bruce Lee. In all this, if gender serves as a metaphor for other forms of identity, it does so in more than the work of theorists; rather, it is a metaphor that is deeply engrained in our culture and that is productive within our systems of representation. In the following chapter, then, I will build on the discussion of hysteria I have presented here in order to think further about precisely these issues of the interrelation of gender and nation, exploring the articulation, in the kung fu comedy, of Hong Kong and Chinese masculinities.

CHAPTER 5

Masculinity

> "Hysterical women suffered from an excess of 'feminine' behaviors, hysterical men an excess of 'masculine' behaviors." . . . In both cases their abundant or grotesque psychosomatic display revolved around their bodies' performance of the radical nothing that experiences of loss entail.
>
> —*Elisabeth Bronfen, quoting Mark Micale*

In the last chapter, I proposed the notion of hysteria as a way of understanding the complex ways in which Hong Kong kung fu comedies, eschewing strategies of political activism or radicalism, are involved in a complex relation to power, which is at one and the same time acquiescent but also perhaps subversive. In this, the concept of hysteria helps us further articulate the nature of the mode of politics of the kung fu comedy's grotesque body. In this chapter, I turn to the notion of hysteria in order to offer narrative analyses of themes of masculinity and of the relationship to paternal authority in a series of kung fu comedy films. Can the kung fu comedy be understood as constituting—as with the nineteenth-century male patients discussed by Bronfen, above—a hysterical response to the social discourses of masculinity and patriarchy? The relationship to the father that I will foreground—and to a phallogocentric order that names the hysterical subject, holding the key to their traumatic identity—is, of course, central to the hysterical complex, as articulated in psychoanalysis. Given the historical and sociopolitical inflection that I introduced to the notion of hysteria in the last chapter, however, I will argue that it is not only gendered identity at stake here, but also forms of "Hong Kong" identity, connected as these are to the complex and traumatic histories of modernity, the nation-state, colonization, and capitalism. Legacy or inheritance serves as the metaphor of such identities within the film texts that I shall pursue through the chapter, as they articulate these both in terms of "masculinity" as a (phallic) inheritance from the father and the historical legacies through which we come to ethnic or national identity. Within a patrilineal culture, after all, the relation to the father becomes the model and the medium through which other forms of inheritance occur.

Echoing this theme of inheritance, I will be drawing out the film-historical legacies of the drunken master cycle in genres that adapted its formulas to mix comedy and kung fu with elements of Gothic horror, in particular in the Miracle Fighters and Mr. Vampire film series of the 1980s. Within these films, I will trace a series of evil, castrating father figures and the structuring relations that the films' protagonists have with these. Before coming to these, however, I shall begin by laying out how theorists have proposed that questions of legacy, origin, and identity are entangled within the working of hysteria.

Origins, Desire, Identity, and the Body: The Hysteric's Questions

In her application of the concept of hysteria to the Gothic novel, Elizabeth Bronfen has proposed that the discourse of the hysteric and of hysterical symptoms revolves around three primary questions: (i) "What is the origin and solution of my legacy?" (ii) "What is the fate of my mutable body?" and (iii) "What is the origin and aim of my unsatisfied desire?"[1] These questions, then, may well help structure an understanding of the nature of Hong Kong cinema as a hysterical response to a historicopolitical trauma.

The second of these questions (i.e., "What is the fate of my mutable body?") perhaps most readily appears as relevant to the kung fu comedy, which throws us clearly into the concerns of the body, and of its "mutability," its fragility, and its susceptibility to death. As Man-Fung Yip notes, the kung fu body is always "poised between mastery and vulnerability."[2] Due to the genre's thematization of violence, the body of the hero is constantly threatened, and the specters of injury and death are kept at bay only through fantasies of martial mastery, which lend the possessor de facto invulnerability. As I have already noted in earlier chapters, such an existential anxiety takes on, within the Hong Kong context, the content of the body's subjection to the violence and precarity of the conditions of life and labor under late capitalist and postcolonial modernity. In the light of the psychoanalytical focus of the last chapter, we might add to this the threat of castration within patriarchy. We have also seen that the mutability of the body within the maelstrom of an ever-changing world is thematized, in the register of wish fulfillment, in the thematic of kung fu training, which grants not only invulnerability, but powers of corporeal self-transformation.

Bronfen's third question, about the riddle of unsatisfied desire (Sand's "impossible *something*"), has here been pursued within the Hong Kong context in terms of political subjectification and freedom, which, blocked by historical contingencies, I have discovered reinvested in the body and converted into images of corporeal exhilaration. In this chapter I will further pursue a reading of the films within such a sociopolitical register to develop this insight. As well as examining the other half of this question—i.e., the *origin* as well as the aim of such a desire—I will also explore the ways that it opens into Bronfen's first question: "what is the origin and solution of my legacy?" This question shares with the last the concern with origins, but this time is posed in terms not of desire but of "legacy." Posing these two questions of origin within the realms of politics and history foregrounds the problem of identity and the ways that rooting this in the past has become complicated in the Hong Kong context, suspended as it is between China and the West, between tradition and modernity, and even, perhaps, between hybridity and purity.

In these questions, then, unresolved problems of origin and legacy—of the past—fold into those of identity in the present, and through this into the futurity of desire and the problem of formulating the sense of self and agency on which basis desire itself might properly be fashioned. Concerned with this temporality of subjectivity, identity, and desire, Bronfen has foregrounded the extent to which the hysteric is haunted by the trauma of a "snarled knot of memory traces" that manifest themselves as an alien and "wandering" presence within the self and the body.[3] These memories are loose, in part, because they may well not be the memories of the self at all, but are a part of the legacy handed down to the emerging subject from those who went before them. In Bronfen's terms, these are foreign memories, "encrypted" within the hysteric's psyche and their body. These foreign memories haunt and possess the hysteric, passing not into consciousness, but directly from the unconscious of the parent straight to that of the child.[4] In this chapter, then, questions of Hong Kong identity and Hong Kong politics are overdetermined by the presence of the specters of its traumatic past, and that of a wider China.

Bronfen's proposition that the hysteric is concerned with such problems of identity is an elaboration on Lacan's more compact formulation in which the question the (female) hysteric addresses to authority, prompted by a perceived lack within the self, is, "What is woman?"[5] Transposed into the Hong Kong context, this question may well become, "What is a Hongkonger?"—or in the words of the title of Jackie Chan's movie, even more simply, "Who am I?"[6] Chan's movie was released in the year following Hong Kong's 1997 handover from British to Chinese rule, an event that lent such questions an amplified urgency and difficulty. For Sarkar, certainly, it is the deepening perplexity of issues around identity, history, and politics that the long run-up to the handover triggered that caused the intensification of what he identifies as "hysterical" traits in the swordplay films of the era. *Who Am I?* symptomatically has Jackie Chan playing an undercover agent who wakes in South Africa to find he has lost his memory. The native tribespeople who rescue him—and who cannot speak his language—take his incessant question about his identity as his statement of his name: "Whoami." It seems impossible not to read this motif, where an irresolvable question of identity (and hence both of history and belonging) becomes a proper name in and of itself, as an allegory of Hong Kong's self-image in the wake of 1997. This pursuit of the question of identity and self-knowledge becomes the driving problem of the film, perhaps making it in many ways a successor to the Gothic tales discussed by Elisabeth Bronfen, in which the truth of the self and its origin is often the mystery to which all other mysteries lead, and from which they spring.[7] This search, ironically, does not take him back to Hong Kong or China, but instead takes on a global dimension, as Chan pursues the mystery of his identity from Africa to Europe—from the colonies, that is, to the heart of empire. "Whoami" is revealed to be "Jackie," a Hong Kong–born CIA agent, associating him not so much with China as with America. However, once this is revealed, his decision is to reject this role too, deciding at the end of the film to return to Africa, which he calls (in one dub of the film, at least) "home." Africa, of course, is neither China nor the West, but introduces a third term into what might otherwise be a structuring binary of Hong Kong identity in order to symbolically resolve the conflict between the two. Through the very process of his search, his most authentic identity turns out ultimately not to be "Jackie," but "Whoami." This offers a different solution to the problems of belonging and identity, one that does not derive them from "roots" in the past, but instead emphasizes the "route" to the present. Such, perhaps, might be a hopeful image that the film offers us of Hong Kong itself: the burden of legacy and of history gives way to the possibility of choice and self-creation here and now. Chan's hysterical (and historical) amnesia becomes, in and of itself, the origin of a new identity, even though this is one that ultimately constitutes an impossible flight from reality in its primitivistic fantasy of a "return to nature."[8]

Legacy, Masculinity, and the Drunken Master Cycle

The comedies of the drunken master cycle, created at a somewhat earlier moment in Hong Kong's history, are no less concerned with problems of the legacy of the past, but offer different resources to address this. Rather than a present-day, transnational world, they are typically located in a somewhat indeterminate moment toward the end of the Qing or the start of the Republican era. Though specific historical events or conflicts seem to be erased from such a setting, as Siu Leung Li has noted in an influential essay on kung fu cinema, this is a moment lodged in the liminal zone between dynastic and modern history,[9] and such a setting already speaks to a condition of Hong Kong audiences similarly perched between the forces of tradition and modernity.

With clear reference to history and politics erased from such films, questions of legacy, however, become concentrated on problems of masculinity and its relation to paternity, and to the father's (and, by extension the "man's") possession of phallic power within patriarchy. The profusion of orphans in this genre—for example, Chien Fu in *Snake in the Eagle's Shadow,* Ah Chi in *Thundering Mantis,* or the brothers Taipao and Yipao in *Knockabout,* not to mention Sing Lung in *Fearless Hyena* (dir. Kenneth Tsang and Jackie Chan, 1979) or Dragon in *The Young Master* (dir. Jackie Chan, 1980)—might in itself signal to us the extent to which a crisis in heritage and the relation to the father are central within their structure.

In *Snake in the Eagle's Shadow,* Chien Fu's menial status—his lack of power in the world—is a result of his lack of parents to provide him with a legacy, and this is played out in terms of class privilege. *Gongfu* itself—something handed down from master to disciple or from father to son, and incorporated in the subject's body—can be understood as a cipher for such a question of heritage and for the fate of inheritance within a society approaching modernity. In the film's quasi-capitalist universe, *gongfu,* a product on the open market, is the preserve primarily of the privileged rich kids whose fathers pay for it, and it is also what affords them the power to bully their social inferiors—to bully, that is, someone like Chien Fu, who has no money and no *gongfu,* and so has to put up with their beatings. *Gongfu,* seen in this light, is no longer quite translatable as labor, as we viewed it in a previous chapter, but is here a kind of social power or capital that is handed down along with wealth.[10] Chien Fu escapes his fate as subservient to this form of power and violence only when he is adopted by a hidden martial arts master, becomes his disciple, and finally inherits that which gives him power and protection in the world.

It would certainly be possible to complicate this formulation, inasmuch as the hero of the kung fu comedy also often needs to add in a component of innovation to defeat the villain. Hence Chien Fu combines the snake style he has learned from his master with a leaping "cat" style he develops after watching a kitten fight a snake. Similarly, in *Drunken Master,* Wong Fei-hung fails to learn the full "eight drunken immortals" style, and with this element missing from his inheritance he is forced to improvise to replace it. Probably the most systematic auteurial thematization of such a tension between tradition or heritance and innovation in the martial arts is, however, in the works of Lau Kar-leung.[11] In these, starting with *Executioners from Shaolin* (1977), the passing down of *gongfu* from master to disciple or father to son is often a problematic process, and the hero's maturation as a martial artist usually involves either an element of invention or the intervention of a female figure. In *Executioners* itself, for example, the hero Hung Wen-ting has to reinvent his dead father's tiger style from a rat-eaten manual, which offers a striking visual image of a patrilineal culture in crisis or decay, and combine it with his mother's crane style.

In *Drunken Master,* however, the themes of class so prominent in *Snake in the Eagle's Shadow* are stripped away from the narrative, and what we have instead is a story much more clearly organized around the relation to fatherhood and to the authority or power of dominance that seems—within the film's patriarchal universe—to be implicit within paternity. With the removal of class questions, what comes to the fore more clearly in *Drunken Master* is the relation of *masculinity* to the heritability of *gongfu.* The film's hero, Wong Fei-hung, is not an orphan like Chien Fu, but rather the legitimate son and heir to a renowned martial arts master, Wong Kei-ying. Wong Fei-hung would furthermore have been a familiar icon to Hong Kong's cinema-going audience from the hundred-odd movies that had been made about him by *Drunken Master*'s release date, and stood precisely as the epitome of the Confucian patriarch and his upright morality.[12] The problem of the film, then, is one of how a boy grows into such a man, and of how he inherits his father's status and character in a world where such inheritance seems to be in crisis.

Fei-hung's relations with others, from the very start of the film, seem to be posited around the play of domination. As we first meet the rebellious Fei-hung, he is in a conflict with his father's arrogant and preening assistant instructor (played by Dean Shek), who is left in charge of the class. Undermining the assistant instructor's authority, Fei-hung, the son and heir, challenges him, easily outwits him and physically overpowers him, humiliating him in front of the rest of the class. Such is the pattern in the film of Fei-hung's relations with others—and in fact the general principle of relationships that pervades almost throughout.

In the next scene after his conflict with the instructor, for example, Fei-hung sexually harasses a young woman at the local marketplace, frightening her with a (phallic) eel to cause her to leap into his arms. However, his plans go awry when her mother arrives and turns out to be a kung fu adept, in her turn humiliating Fei-hung by beating him in a fight. Fei-hung, still in the marketplace, then meets a rich bully. This bully has himself been using his *gongfu* and his privilege to sadistically torment a local peasant who has been forced to sell his family heirloom, a piece of jade, to support his family. The bully smashes the jade and refuses to pay. We have, in essence, a man with inherited privilege humiliating one who is forced to sell his inheritance. Fei-hung intervenes and beats the bully—he has in his own martial arts abilities, after all, a superior inheritance to that of his foe. However, the scene remains ambiguous: is Fei-hung's response a matter of the heroism for which he would later be known in the many films and novels that recount and mythologize his life—as righteous protector of the weak against the strong—or is it simply a matter of imposing his own will as "top dog" and reversing the humiliation he has just received at the hands of a woman, in order to reassert his masculinity? The nature of what Fei-hung inherits from his father (i.e., *gongfu*) thus remains ambiguous: is it simply the power to bully others, or is it, in fact, righteousness itself, the power to defend others?

Fei-hung's ensuing encounters with a string of characters (for example, "Iron Head" or "The King of Sticks") continue to follow this pattern of Oedipal rivalry. In each fight scene, the question of masculinity, and of "who has the best *gongfu*," is articulated around a ritual contest in which each opponent seeks to overpower and humiliate the other. It is, perhaps, just this cynical brutality that seems to undermine the legitimacy of the logic of authority or power that is invested in the father and thus to place the beneficence of patrilineality itself in question. At the start of the film, Fei-hung's relationship with his father seems in many ways to follow this pattern of a will to power, too. Paternal authority is strict, and at each transgression Wong Kei-ying imposes ever harsher punishment upon his son—escalating from beating, through five hours of "horse stance," to hanging his son from the ceiling by hands tied behind the back, a heavy jar suspended from his neck. At one point, Kei-ying even seeks to kill his son, who has brought dishonor on his name (and thus on the family legacy), until Fei-hung's aunt intervenes to stay his hand. It is in such a guise as the tyrant with the power of life or death over his progeny that we first see Kei-ying.

Fei-hung, for his part, serves the role of the rebel, the *xiaozi* or "punk" kid who would become the typical kung fu comedy hero. Such a figure draws from the influence of the Western counterculture in Hong Kong and is in many ways an adaptation of conventions and characters developed in the "youth film" of the 1960s, in which, as Poshek Fu has described, the "delinquency problem" was explored.[13] This antiauthoritarian figure is a harbinger of both Westernization and modernization—of the disintegration of the hegemony of the Confucian and traditional values of patriarchy with which Wong Kei-ying (and the earlier filmic depictions of Wong Fei-hung) may be associated. Fei-hung's rebellion also fits into an Oedipal dynamic, where he resists the attempts of his father to hold power over him in order to assert his own autonomy—his "manhood"—in the world. The *xiaozi* in many ways, as harbinger of anti-Confucian trends, can be understood as the flip side of the instrumentality of human relations—properly that of capitalist social life itself[14]—that more fundamentally places the old order in a crisis of legitimation and characterizes the underlying logic of the film's world.

The exception to this logic of social relations in the film, however, arrives with the figure of the Drunken Master, Beggar So himself. At the outset, the

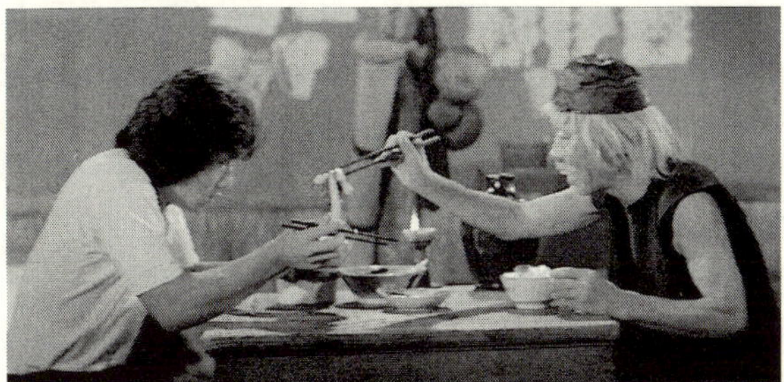

Fig. 5.1. A moment of authentic humanity and friendship between Beggar So and Wong Fei-hung, as the two eat together, and So places food in Chan's bowl. Video still from *Drunken Master.* © 1978/1985 Seasonal Film Corporation / 2017 Sony Pictures Home Entertainment / Eureka! Entertainment.

relation between So and Fei-hung appears to be of very much the same ilk as the other relations of the film. So (who is rumored to be brutal and to maim his students) sets out to impose his authority on Fei-hung, and the latter attempts at first to beat So in a battle of both wits and fists, and so to assert his own superiority. Then, when this fails, he tries to escape. The relationship between So and Fei-hung, however, transforms, with the two ultimately developing an affection that transcends the order of antagonism prevalent elsewhere in the film (fig. 5.1).

The turnabout, however, also comes with Fei-hung's meeting with and humiliation by the film's archvillain, Thunderfoot (Hwang Jang-lee). When Fei-hung attempts to assert his will on Thunderfoot as he does with other characters in the film, he is proved to be decisively the weaker of the two. As they start to fight, Thunderfoot insults Fei-hung's martial arts and questions the value of his paternal legacy. Indeed, what most enrages Fei-hung in their exchange is Thunderfoot laughing at his father's *gongfu*. However, when he exclaims "Nobody calls my father's kung fu shit!" Thunderfoot retorts, "Perhaps it's better you call me father." Beating Fei-hung so that he is forced to sit and stand on command, Thunderfoot laughs, "All my sons obey!" The equation here of fatherhood (and by extension masculinity) with naked domination brings the film's thematic correlation of the two to its most explicit articulation. At the end of the fight, utterly humiliated, Fei-hung is made to crawl, like a dog, through his opponent's legs, drawn down to the level of the animal and the abject, and ordered to "go and clean crud and piss-holes." In the image of menial labor as degrading, we are once again in the territory of class: what Fei-hung inherits from his father, along with his masculinity and his kung fu, is a form of social superiority and immunity from such work, and this is also conflated with his status as a "man."

If Man-Fung Yip argues, as we have seen, that the kung fu body serves to register aspects of the experience of physical labor in Hong Kong in this period when the body was blue-collar men's primary vehicle for social advancement,[15] Thunderfoot's insult might remind us that such an experience of work was also an experience of emasculation as much as it was one in which masculinity was defined and asserted.

Thunderfoot threatens to rob Fei-hung, then, of class and gender simultaneously, inasmuch as these are interlinked. Fei-hung is further symbolically castrated and feminized by the burning of his trousers and by his partial nakedness throughout the fight. Thunderfoot thus figuratively takes on the role of the Oedipus complex's tyrannical, castrating father figure, most fully personifying the logic of antagonistic masculinity and patriarchy that orders the film's world as the most ferocious, powerful martial artist of the film, and the one most driven by the sadistic desire to defeat, humiliate, and kill any competitor. As a hired assassin, he also most fully typifies a logic whereby such power is subject to a capitalistic logic of exchange.

The meeting with Thunderfoot introduces what Melanie Klein might have described as a "paranoid" splitting of the father figure in the film into the "good father" and the "bad father."[16] Thunderfoot takes on the guise of the evil and despotic aspects of the Oedipal father so Wong Kei-ying—and his other paternal substitute, Beggar So—can take on exclusively the "good" characteristics, becoming viable objects of affection, cleansed of the complicating feelings of Oedipal rage, hatred, competition, and rebellion that are now leveled at Thunderfoot. Kei-ying turns out to be a principled man, caring for his villagers' interests in the face of a plot to rob them of ancestral lands. Beggar So becomes the loving and mischievously human father figure with whom Fei-hung grows close.

It is in the wake of this castrating experience that Fei-hung accepts rather than battles the authority of Beggar So, thus becoming able to enter into discipleship, "inherit" drunken boxing, and return to defend his father against Thunderfoot as a filial son. The anarchic, rebellious Fei-hung, then, ultimately subjects himself to castration under the Law of the Father in order to gain power and masculinity—to become a "master"—and to take on his inheritance as such. If there seems something at first transgressive about recasting Wong Fei-hung the Confucian patriarch as a juvenile delinquent, the sting in this is neutralized by the conventional narrative in which a traditional, patriarchal order is restituted and revivified.

Such a conformity to dominant values is, however, precisely in the order of hysteria, and if the film undermines these at all, it is perhaps in the very exaggerated theatricality and the "hysterical abandon" of the embodied performance, in which narrative themes become, to a large extent, self-parodic. The roles played, furthermore, reach a near-Gothic instability, as different visions of masculinity waver before the viewer's eyes. The levity with which the narrative and its morals are treated and the stylization of its portrayal offer a way in which, as with the genre's relation to violence, an ideology is repeated, but nonetheless at the same time its hold on us is loosened as attention is drawn elsewhere. The anarchic physical excess of the film and its "wild" aesthetic pleasures, while they allow the film's narrative-ideological order to stand, nonetheless work against its closure and offer so many "hysteric" symptoms that can be enjoyed in its stead.

Masculine Anxiety and Feminine Excess in *Drunken Master*

The extent to which masculinity is at stake here is reinforced by the images of femininity within the film. Fei-hung's first encounter with the feminine, toward the start of the film, is in the threatening guise of his encounter with an older woman in the marketplace, who turns out to be his aunt. This is initiated by Fei-hung's attempt to sexually harass her daughter—an attempt to assert his "masculine" libido—which is foiled by her intervention. Fei-hung's belief in his superior strength is confounded by her "feminine" style of martial arts, which instead of strength relies on extreme flexibility, agility, and intelligence, often bringing the body horizontal to attack Fei-hung from surprising angles, while Fei-hung attempts to remain standing phallically upright. His defeat ultimately deals a strong blow to his self-assurance.

Perhaps there is in this an aspect inherent to the myth of the Asian martial arts that serves to problematize and threaten their use to establish "masculinity," certainly within the context of a globally hegemonic Western order of genders. Such, we have seen in this book's first chapter, was the intent of the rise of Chinese martial arts within the early twentieth-century physical culture movements, in the face of humiliation at the hands of foreign imperial aggression, the feminization of the "Orient," and the characterization of China as the "Sick Man of East Asia." Within this context, the reassertion of Chinese and Asian masculinity was a core part of the reconstruction of national identities that sought to offer viable forms of Chinese ethno-national identity within the modern world. I have also discussed how such a revirilized masculinity was key within the nationalist politics of the heroic martial arts film.

Such a project, however, is not without its contradictions. The martial arts are, as we know them from popular culture at least, a technique by which the weak can overcome the strong and escape the inevitable triumph of superior size.

In doing this, the martial arts offer a way to be powerful—and hence, within a phallocentric order, "masculine"—that is different from Western norms that associate masculinity with the sheer brawn that Yvonne Tasker, in her work on the body in Hollywood action cinema, punningly calls "musculinity."[17] I have already explored certain aspects of this dynamic as they played out in Chan's American career in the previous chapter. Such an alternative articulation of masculine strength as we have in the image of kung fu supports a differentiated identity that is not swallowed up into Western sameness but nonetheless remains a place of power. However, as Kwai-Cheung Lo argues, such a strategy brings with it a problem, in that, to be different from the Western vision, it must necessarily draw on aspects identified within this hegemonic order as different to the "masculine" norm, which are hence inherently marked within it as "feminine."[18] The soft and yielding strategies of kung fu, its use of technique over force and principles such as "one ounce can move a thousand pounds"—in other words, the very strategies that allow the defeat of the strong by the weak (and hence make it attractive to Asian nationalists encountering the imperial might of the West)—are marked precisely as a yin, feminine "excess" with regards to hegemonic masculinity. Precisely as Asian culture attempts to assert its special version of "masculine" identity through martial arts, it nonetheless contaminates itself with the feminine.

We perhaps see this already in Bruce Lee's films, where the logic of masculinity is stretched to an extreme in his steroid-pumped body. Lee's body, in this very excess of masculinity, slips into a kind of hysterical performance of maleness, and in its theatricality, its "to-be-looked-at-ness," it begins to become coded as feminine. In *Way of the Dragon* especially (not insignificantly the film from Lee's small oeuvre that goes furthest into the comic register), Lee's body becomes an eroticized spectacle, in much the way that Laura Mulvey has famously argued women's bodies are in classic Hollywood cinema.[19] As both Jachinson Chan and Paul Bowman have discussed, in one scene, performing a solo martial arts routine on a domestic balcony, Lee is all pose and glistening muscles, exhibited for the camera. Commentators have noted the knowing way in which he is positioned in this scene in front of an erotic print that focuses on a woman's body, hanging on the wall of the flat behind him. Lee draws further attention to the picture when he pauses his martial arts performance to look at it. Doing so, Lee seems to ask the audience complex questions about the differences and similarities between the erotic display of his muscular body and the soft, curvaceous, but equally bare flesh of the female figure in the image of the print.[20] As Chan and Bowman also note, the film also subjects Lee to the scrutiny not only of the heterosexual female gaze of the beautiful restaurateuse Chen Ching-hua (Nora Miao), but also the gay male gaze of Ho, a camp Chinese consigliere for the mafia gang with whom Lee is in conflict, who makes a number of comments about Lee's sexual desirability.[21] Though in many ways a clearly stigmatized position within the film's narrative, Ho's eroticizing, homosexual regard of Lee's physique remains a presence that seems to disturb the film's heteronormative order and adds—or at the very least signals the preexistence of—an element of queer destabilization to the viewer's subject position and the film's gendered gaze.

In the kung fu comedy, these perplexities in the formation of "masculinity" seem to multiply, and their presence is marked by the appearance of the repeated figure of the woman kung fu fighter, who, like Fei-hung's aunt in *Drunken Master,* is potentially superior to the male protagonist, throwing his virility into question. The extent to which the genre is posited around questions of masculinity is in fact perhaps most clearly signaled in the preponderance of female fighters within the norms of its fictional universe[22]—which suggests that the potential for violence or power is uncoupled from the biologically male body—and yet the peculiar paucity of strong women protagonists. While the heroic swordplay and kung fu genres gave us resonant images of powerful leading ladies such as Cheng Pei-pei, Hsu Feng, Angela Mao, or Polly Shangguan, it is hard to think of a prominent parallel in the comedy genre until Michelle Yeoh's performance in *Wing Chun* (dir. Yuen Woo-ping, 1994).[23]

Aside from the presence of Fei-hung's aunt, in *Drunken Master* the anxiety around gender is raised again when he is asked to learn "Eight Drunken Immortals" style. This involves martial arts routines based on the different characters and movements of legendary Daoist saints, one of whom is a woman, Miss Ho (He Xiangu). Fei-hung refuses to learn the movements for this section of the martial arts form, ashamed of their femininity. Fearing the contamination of his own masculinity, he instead mocks So's performance of them with a brief, caricatural dance and returns to spending his efforts on more "manly" versions of kung fu.

Nonetheless, within the film, embracing femininity turns out to be an essential source of power, inscribing the "feminine" at the very heart of a "masculinity" that is thus destabilized. Early on, Fei-hung's aunt, after punishing him for his assault on her daughter, turns out to be a useful ally in confronting the family of the bully he beats in the marketplace, who come to Fei-hung's home seeking recompense. She uses wile and intelligence to set up a situation where, instead of being punished by his father, he is met with a martial contest with an inferior opponent, and she even guides him on the techniques he should use to win. In her use of intelligence, rather than unyielding strength, Fei-hung's aunt echoes the characteristics that exemplify Beggar So. Drunken boxing itself is a "soft" martial art, and in the scene where Fei-hung and So meet, this is emphasized in So's use of a dishcloth, brandished like a whip, to beat a massively muscular opponent (played by former "Mr. Hong Kong" bodybuilding champion, Bolo Yeung). So's choice of weapon typifies the "feminine" kung fu principles of the weak beating the strong, pliability overcoming rigidity, softness beating strength. So also uses agile, yielding movement and allows his body to depart from the upright, making his kung fu more like Fei-hung's aunt's than the orthodox style (Hung Gar) that Wong Kei-ying teaches.

It is also, ultimately, by drawing on the feminine that Fei-hung is able to defeat Thunderfoot in the film's final battle. Though he has rejected learning the Miss Ho component of the Eight Drunken Immortals style, without this element of the feminine to complete it, he is unable to defeat his powerfully masculine enemy. Beggar So, cheering Fei-hung on from the sidelines, prompts him to invent Miss Ho, to channel her into his being in a form of cross-gender spirit possession (fig. 5.2). Chan's strange, unorthodox, improvised (or inspired) Miss Ho is played in a sort of camped-up operatic drag or masquerade, and the movements take on obscene names such as "Widow Seeing Her Lover Off" or "Woman Sitting on the Toilet Seat." Chan even uses the bumping of his hips and buttocks against his enemy as a form of attack. Though in the final moves Chan needs to fluidly and creatively combine all the different gods to defeat his enemy, it is Miss Ho who provides the key to doing this, as Chan integrates both yin and yang, masculine and feminine into his movement repertoire.

The device of cross-dressing is repeatedly reprieved in the films that Chan made in the following years, suggesting the popularity of the device and the extent to which it became a part of Chan's star image. In *Fearless Hyena* (dir. Jackie Chan and Kenneth Tsang, 1979), Chan's protagonist Sing Lung takes a job at a martial arts school. However, as he is forbidden by his grandfather to practice martial arts publicly, he disguises himself to do so—in one extended scene dressing in full drag as a woman to defeat a lecherous opponent who attempts to make advances on him. In *Young Master* (dir. Jackie Chan, 1980), Chan is defeated by a woman whose skirts disguise her footwork, allowing kicks to come seemingly from nowhere, and Chan, in a fight later in the film, picks up the device from her, grabbing a skirt from a market stall in order to defeat a powerful opponent. In *Once a Cop* (dir. Stanley Tong and Matthew Tang, 1993), a loose sequel to *Police Story 3: Supercop* (dir. Stanley Tong, 1992), Chan plays a cameo as a police inspector pursuing and arresting jewelry-heist suspects while in drag. *City Hunter* (dir. Wong Jing, 1993), includes a set-piece scene where Chan dresses as the female character Chun Li from the Streetfighter series of videogames.

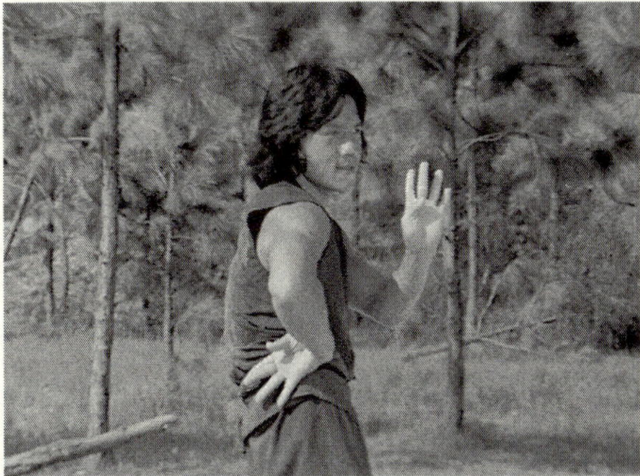

Fig. 5.2. Jackie Chan camps it up in a cross-gender performance as Miss Ho. Video still from *Drunken Master.* © 1978/1985 Seasonal Film Corporation / 2017 Sony Pictures Home Entertainment / Eureka! Entertainment.

This, of course, is far from making *Drunken Master* a feminist text. Chan's drag—as some feminists have argued regarding the wider phenomenon of comic female impersonation[24]—is deeply marked by misogyny. The male privilege of appropriating the image of the "feminine" may well hardly be liberating for women. Chan's masquerade of Miss Ho is ultimately in the service of the film's reimposition of a phallic, patriarchal, and patrilineal order of (kung fu) "mastery," handed down from father to son, with, perhaps, the help of outside agents such as the (bachelor) uncle and (female) aunt. Chan's Miss Ho might in this sense be read as entailing a form of male mastery over and possession of the feminine, making the disruptive power of its excess safe and reining it into harness for useful work.

However, even within this schema, Chan lifts both masculinity and femininity into the artificiality of what Judith Butler famously terms the "performative."[25] His assumption of gender becomes fragmentary, "overdone," unstable—that is to say, classically hysteric. The excess that Kwai-Cheung Lo associates with Asian masculinity here appears as the destabilizing lack that disorders the hysteric's universe and, if read in the most positive light, perhaps even carries a certain potential for placing our wider symbolic order in a certain degree of flux.

Once analyzed in this way, Chan's performance brings to my mind the image of the male "hysterics" treated in the nineteenth century by Charcot. Though many doctors had refused *a priori* to admit the existence of the male hysteric, seeing the disease as by definition a woman's one, Charcot campaigned against this idea and documented some ninety-odd case histories that he diagnosed as "*hystérie mâle*" (male hysteria). [26] While Charcot's women patients' symptoms often centered around a performance of their "femininity," Charcot's male patients' illnesses seem to have articulated themselves around images and tropes of masculinity.[27] Far from the stereotypically "effete" aristocrats or the oversensitive and bookish bourgeois, most of Charcot's male hysterics were working men, often from the new mass-mechanized industries, who had experienced a traumatic injury or a threat to their life.[28] As Julia Borossa has suggested, such experiences had dealt a powerful blow to the patients' self-images and threatened their sense of themselves as "men."[29] The resulting symptoms often involved particularly hyperathletic fits of the type that Charcot identified as "clownism," often presenting in pantomime form what appeared to be scenes of violence and aggression.

Can something of this blow to narcissistic, male self-image also be considered to be at work in the (post-)colonial situation, where the "native" body is feminized, marked as inferior, robbed of "legacy," and subjected to tough conditions of labor and insecurity, akin in many ways to those of Charcot's workers?[30] Something of this could certainly be read in the humiliation of China in the "unequal treaties" of the nineteenth century and the semicolonial status to which the nation was reduced. If nationalism—and the ethno-nationalist kung fu body of the start and middle of the twentieth century—sought to salvage an image of masculine strength, then the problematization of this project for Hongkongers in the wake of Maoism, the rivalry between the PRC on the mainland and the ROC in Taiwan, and the experience of exile and increasing de-identification with any nation-state may well be understood to have dealt a second, equally traumatic blow to that image. Such a narrative would explain the "hysterical" quality of images of masculinity in comedy films such as *Drunken Master* as continuing to articulate—and perhaps, even, in complex ways contest—continuing anxieties around masculinity, nationality, and ethnicity created by such traumatic conditions.

Inheritance, Masculinity, and the Blood-Sucking Patriarch in the Miracle Fighters Series

Such themes of the anxieties that surround inheritance and masculinity intensified in the Miracle Fighters series of films that the Yuen Brothers went on, after their success with the drunken master formula, to make in the early 1980s.[31] These films drew on elements and concerns of the drunken master genre (training sequences, master–pupil relationships, the figure of the alcoholic beggar-master, "low" and bodily comedy, etc.), developing these in new directions and raising kung fu comedy's surreal, hysterical tone to an almost hallucinatory intensity. Motifs from Gothic horror, swordplay, and even sexual farce genres were mixed into the kung fu comedy formula, with magic becoming commingled with martial artistry, so that it becomes uncertain to what extent the "*gongfu*" that is learned or performed by the film's characters is conjuring and trickery, feats of technology, martial skill, or actual sorcery. Scenes rapidly oscillate in them between the horrific, grotesque, or ultraviolent (with wires and undercranking of the cameras adding kinetic force to the fight scenes), the comedic (with the familiar blend of slapstick and scatological humor), and the fantastical (with special effects and cinematic trickery becoming a key pleasure in what often seems a return to what Tom Gunning has described as a "cinema of attractions").[32] The oscillation between the different tones of the film is often so rapid that the viewer is caught in a state of uncertainty with regard to how to respond, as recognition of the codes that would orient them lags behind the onrush of dramatic impressions.[33]

In the first film of the series, *Miracle Fighters,* the protagonist, Shu Gut (Yuen Yat-choh), another of the kung fu comedy genre's orphan-heroes, is involved in two different "legacies." In the film's early storyline—largely abandoned halfway through—he is brought up by a general who is on the run from the palace authorities and who now lives undercover as an umbrella salesman. He has taken Shu Gut on as an apprentice and given him a piece of jade that is in fact a royal heirloom. Once it is recognized by palace assassins sent to kill the general, they believe him to be a Royal Prince, so a number of imperial agents attempt to capture him and bring him back to the palace. However, in escaping these, he stumbles into the house of a pair of kung fu magicians, the disciples of a dead master who is depicted in a painting on their altar in the form of Simon Yuen, the real-life deceased patriarch of the Yuen clan, in his Beggar So garb.[34] Of these two disciples, one is a grotesque old man, played by Leung Kar-yan, the other a grotesque old woman, played by Yuen Cheung-yan in a comic drag performance that echoes and extends to a film-length performance Chan's earlier cross-dressing scenes. The two elderly disciples are locked in a constant struggle over who is the proper successor of their master's legacy. When Shu Gut arrives, they also squabble over whose disciple he is to be (and hence whose legacy he is to take on). He ends up taking on the status of a third disciple to the dead master and fights the evil Sorcerer Bat (Yuen Shun-yi)—the lead henchman of the imperial court—in a competition to become the leader of the magicians' association and hence to take on himself the mantle of the missing patriarch.

The motif of inheritance is made even more explicit as an issue of concern in *Taoism Drunkard,* which revolves around the conflict over another clan-leadership token. The rightful heir, Wu Shun-chiu (played by Yuen Yat-choh again) is being trained by his grandmother (played in drag again by Yuen

Cheung-yan) to take on the role. However, the villainous Starry Devil (Yuen Shun-yi, in a reprisal of his role as the evil, tyrannical patriarch-sorcerer from *Miracle Fighters*) also has designs on it. In *Taoism Drunkard,* however, the psychosexual aspects of inheritance are brought much closer to the surface than in most comedy kung fu films, where themes of love and/or sex are usually replaced by homosocial masculine bonding and antagonism. Throughout the film a series of relationships are played out on the level of farce, and as viewers we are never far from the field of sexual innuendo. The clan's token is—appropriately enough if we see it as a figure of the phallic power of the patriarch—guarded by the bizarre "banana addict" monster, a ball-shaped magical robot that attacks any male visitor to the ancestral hall, pursuing them at groin height with gnashing teeth, threatening a castration euphemistically figured as the monster's insatiable appetite to eat "bananas." Such figures of castration anxiety, though more subtly, are reiterated throughout the film series—in particular in the repeated image of trousers with a torn crotch indicating a "close escape," and protagonists who find themselves fighting in their underwear. To complicate the question of inheritance, Shun-chiu is also picked by a drunken Daoist priest (played by Yuen Cheung-yan, taking on a second role within the film) on a mission to find a successor to lead his monastery, who require a virgin boy born at the correct astrological moment. What one inherits becomes a matter of a "destiny" inscribed in the very moment of one's origination.

In *Shaolin Drunkard,* much the same themes and tropes prevail, and very much the same group of actors are cast in similar roles, allowing different permutations of their relationships: Yuen Cheung-yan doubles up again as both a drunken monk and clan matriarch, Yuen Yat-choh plays the hero (this time named Yau Pai-yuen), and Yuen Shun-yi reprises the evil magician. Once again the figure of the virgin boy, born at a particular astrological juncture, figures strongly, though this time it is the evil sorcerer who seeks such a person, aiming to suck his blood to gain supernatural powers.

As in *Taoism Drunkard,* the protagonist's family is ruled matriarchally by a grandmother, leaving any literal father figures absent and opening a space within the film for a series of good and evil paternal substitutes, including the drunken beggar and the despotic sorcerer. As well as fulfilling this sorcerer's criteria for a victim, Yau Pai-yuen is being sent by his grandmother into the world to find a wife to carry on a family line that has been cursed to have only a single male heir in each generation. The wife he finds—exhibiting all the ambivalence of the feminine within patriarchy—wavers for him between being a beautiful object of desire and an abject cause of horror and revulsion, as she has a large birthmark on one side of her otherwise attractive face. Her ambivalence is also linked, once again, to a threat to masculinity. To win her hand, Yau triumphs in a test of martial arts skills, but when, having won, he sees her marked face, he rejects her.

Angered by this rejection, she pursues and catches him, showing her equality to him as a martial artist, and, gripping his head like an ersatz phallus between her thighs to hold him still, threatens to castrate him. Though he manages to escape, she chases him throughout the film, hoping to force him to marry her. It is only at the end of the film that she fully adopts a submissive, "feminine" attitude toward her prospective husband and is then cured of the facial mark, becoming unambiguously an object of desire and opening up the possibility that Yau might fulfill his role in passing on the family legacy to a further generation. She and Yau must then defeat her father in battle, figuring another kind of Oedipal moment. On the wedding day, however, the evil sorcerer manages to substitute himself in the bridal chamber, drawing on a repeated trope in the kung fu comedy where fighting in the bedroom, heard from outside, is thought to be an act of sex. This confusion perhaps hints at the erotic dimension fantasied in the series' repeated images of a blood-sucking patriarch.

Capitalism, History, and Hong Kong Identity: Hopping Corpses in the Mr. Vampire Series

In such films as I have been discussing this far, these anxieties of legacy and the father seem primarily articulated around the individual psyche and around the vicissitudes of masculinity. However, I've been arguing more broadly that the horror of the "blood-sucking patriarch" (as he literally becomes in *Shaolin Drunkard*) articulates more than simply a crisis in generic, global masculinity; rather, it has a specific resonance within the Hong Kong context, which speaks of the complex and ambivalent relation to ethnicity, nationality, and the past as sources of identity, and of course the role of ideas of masculinity in valorizing such identities.

It is in the craze for the "hopping corpse" (*geongsi*) subgenre through the late 1980s and early 1990s, initiated largely by the success of *Mr. Vampire* (dir. Ricky Lau, 1985),[35] that the problem of legacy and paternity becomes most clearly articulated in terms of the relationship to a historical past and to the forms of identity that it might harbor. These films drew on the elements of Gothic horror and the supernatural that were also being introduced in the Miracle Fighters series, mixing these with kung fu and comedy. Tropes from the drunken master cycle—primarily the fundamental focus on master–disciple relationships—were continued into the *geongsi* genre, though "kung fu" became increasingly a matter of skills in Daoist magic, often performed by kung fu players to emphasize the continuity between martial dexterity and the performance of ritual.

The Cantonese word *geongsi* (*jiangshi* in Mandarin) is often translated into English as "Chinese vampire," though the equation is, perhaps, a little misleading as the *geongsi* is, as Stephanie Lam has elaborated, somewhat different to its Western counterpart.[36] It is more literally translated as "stiff corpse," and the *geongsi* is a form of undead being with as much in common with the zombie as with the vampire. As depicted in the Hong Kong cinema of the 1980s, the *geongsi* is characterized by its peculiar hopping gait. Its body having become stiff with rigor mortis, it moves—comically—in little leaps, legs together, arms outstretched in front of it. When weak, the *geongsi,* like a zombie, is prone to magical manipulation, and indeed a common trope has hopping corpses who have died far from home herded by Daoist priests back to their native villages for burial, led along the road at night to avoid the living. Alternatively, an evil sorcerer may reanimate such a corpse in order to send it out into the world to do their bidding. A strong *geongsi*—someone particularly evil, someone who has died unhappy or wronged and returns to life with business unfinished, or someone with a malicious curse upon them—is more like the Western vampire, attempting to suck the *qi* (life energy) from the living. Though still moving with the same comically stiff manner as its weaker relatives, such a *geongsi* becomes uncannily powerful and appears as driven by an inhuman desire that exceeds and negates the human purposes of the living.

In a recent book, David McNally has drawn on Marx's use of metaphors from Gothic fiction as figures for capitalism to explore the pervasiveness to this day, across global cultures, of images of the zombie and the vampire, arguing for their interrelation.[37] McNally traces the origin of the figure of the zombie in images of Caribbean slaves whose souls seemed to have been stolen, leaving only hopeless bodies without will, laboring beyond life as the walking dead. He argues for the continued interest in such an image as articulating the horror of capital's possession of the body of the laborer. He proposes that the vampire, as imagined by Marx as a metaphor for capital itself, provides us with the flip side of this image: a demonic will that sucks the life from living laborers to feed its own undead powers. Both figures offer uncanny images of exploitation under capitalist modernity, a theme I have explored at some length in earlier chapters. The *geongsi,* then, wavering between these two poles of vampire and zombie, and read in the light of McNally's argument, is legible as a trope made popular during Hong Kong's rise as hypercapitalist global city and as powerfully expressing the contradictions of this moment, serving, perhaps, to cathartically transform these into comic laughter.

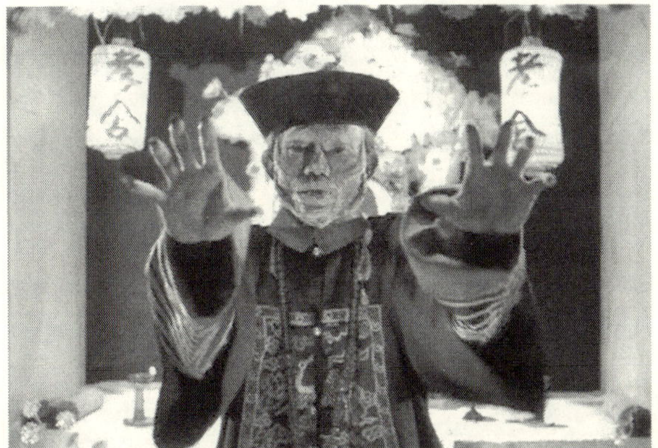

Fig. 5.3. The weight of the imperial past: a *geongsi*, dressed in the garb of a Mandarin returns to life, in *Mr. Vampire*. Video still. © 1985 Paragon Films / 1993 Star TV Filmed Entertainment.

However, the *geongsi*, stereotypically dressed—even in most modern-day settings—in the robes of a Qing-dynasty official (a "mandarin"), also seems to be a figure that has as much to do with the weight of history and tradition (fig. 5.3). In the guise of the *geongsi*, China's imperial past and the old order of things return in the present. Such a return takes on a particular valence in a Hong Kong where identity must be negotiated between on the one hand traditional, ethnic, and national narratives of "roots," and on the other an investment in the present (and future) world of modernity and the global flows of capital.[38]

Mr. Vampire itself—the ur-text of the genre—registers much of the ambivalence toward the past that is formed in such circumstances. It is set, like many kung fu comedies, in the Republican era, which, following Siu Leung Li, I have noted above forms a liminal moment between the worlds of "tradition" and "modernity." It is the moment, precisely, when a dead parent might have been buried in the dress of a dynastic official, but life would be continuing for his children in a modernizing and Westernizing society. The gap between two such generations would signify nothing less than a gulf between two worlds. Congruently with this, in *Mr. Vampire*, old burial traditions, magical practices, and traditional forms of dress coexist with department stores, Western fashion, uniformed police, colonial architecture, and firearms. *Mr. Vampire* begins with a series of comic sketches that locate its characters within this tension between tradition and modernity. In one of these, the film's Daoist master, "Uncle Kau" (Lam Ching-ying), and his disciple Man Choi (Ricky Hui) meet with a wealthy client, Mr. Yam, in a Western restaurant. Standing in many ways for tradition and the old ways, Kau is something of a bumpkin, and comedy is drawn from his attempts to negotiate the appropriate mores and manners of cosmopolitan dining. Unable to read the menu, he orders what his host does, swallows the strange drink of coffee black to discover it undrinkably bitter, and then (in an attempt to copy what Mr. Yam does with his coffee) adds milk and sugar to his egg tart, stirring them into its custard filling to make it unpalatably sweet.

With this gulf between tradition and modernity set up, issues more clearly of inheritance and paternity—in other words, of the relation between present and past—are introduced along with the figure of the vampire itself. Yam has asked for a reburial of his father, as he believes that his own prosperity depends on the proper rites having been performed, but his business has been going from bad to worse. In the process of exhumation, Kau notes that the burial seems to have been deliberately misperformed, so that its effects have been deleterious, in spite of the prime real estate that the burial site occupies. Quizzing Mr. Yam, Kau discovers that that the land was purchased—probably using "underhand" methods of persuasion—from the same fortune-teller who advised on the burial, and hence the bungled burial was a deliberate act of revenge and sabotage. During the exhumation, inauspicious omens appear, and once dug up, having been corrupted by its initial improper burial, the corpse transforms into a *geongsi,* ruthlessly pursuing its own descendants—killing first Mr. Yam and then coming for his daughter.

In relation to my reading of the film as negotiating experiences of identity, history, and legacy in Hong Kong, there are a number of understandings that can be teased out of this scenario, and ultimately my argument is that the figure of the *geongsi* offers a complex, ambivalent image in which a series of feelings are condensed. His return is, first off, a matter of legacy. This is most literally the legacy of Mr. Yam's millions, which he has inherited from his now-undead father, but as with the Miracle Fighters films it also involves questions of the fate, whether this be a blessing or not, that is handed down from the past. Mr. Yam inherits not only money from his father, but also a curse, leading to an early death and his becoming, like his father, a walking corpse.

It's also worth noting that in the film it is capitalist business—in which there exists, as Marx puts it, "no other nexus between man and man than naked self-interest"[39]—that has corrupted the bond between the present and the past, disturbing the proper rites that traditionally regulate the relationship with ancestors and the exchange, between the living and the dead, of piety for good fortune. The film thus articulates a set of anxieties about the nature of a rapidly modernizing and rapaciously mercantile Hong Kong society and the ways that its materialism may be altering older values, ways of life, and relations to tradition.

However, the vampire itself also figures this tradition itself in a negative light, turning the revered figure of the father into a tyrannical, Oedipal monster—very much the successor of the whole line of kung fu villains I have been presenting here—returning to feed off the blood of the living. This is the "tradition of all dead generations" that, as Marx put it in *The Eighteenth Brumaire of Louis Bonaparte,* "weighs like a nightmare on the brains of the living,"[40] appearing as a source of violence and fear rather than nurture, and registering, perhaps, something of the modern recognition of the authoritarian, restrictive nature of the older forms of patriarchy through which tradition—and the legacy of identity—was passed down. The *geongsi* is thus a profoundly ambivalent figure, articulating anxieties about both modernity and tradition, and registering guilt about an abandonment of the past that is then projected as the imaginary hostility of that past toward the present.

This ambivalence could only have taken on extra resonance in 1980s Hong Kong. As I have already argued in a previous chapter, over the previous decade Hong Kong identity had been increasingly defined as much in opposition to "Chineseness" as through identification with it, with Hongkongers defining themselves in terms of modernity, urbanity, Westernization, globalization, diaspora-orientation, the Cantonese language, and capitalism, in counterpoint to the mainland, which was imagined in terms of the traditional or backward, the peasant, the "Oriental," the national, an orientation to homeland, the Mandarin language, and, of course, communism. In this situation, and with the pervasive hostility to the PRC, to be a Hongkonger is to be only ambiguously or problematically Chinese and entails a certain rejection of the identity with, and consequently of the affective link to, the "ancestral country" (*zuguo*). Such ambivalences were intensified in the context of the 1984 Sino-British Joint Declaration on Hong Kong's 1997 return to Chinese rule, made the year before *Mr. Vampire*'s release. In such a context, the ancestral land could be imagined as devouring and monstrous (with widespread hostility to communism and fear about the threat to Hong Kong identities and ways of life), as well as a nurturing source of selfhood.

Allegorizing Hong Kong

In this chapter, then, I have drawn on my previous proposal that the body in kung fu comedies can productively be understood through the notion of hysteria to offer a series of readings of films, spanning from the mid-1970s to the mid-1980s. In this, I have explored the "legacy" of the drunken master cycle in new subgenres or film cycles. These borrowed its motifs and mixed comedy and kung fu with elements of horror, producing film texts that are often fragmentary and hyperactive and swing wildly from an atmosphere of darkness to one of levity. The aim has been to explore these films as structured around the themes of Hong Kong identity, masculinity, and patriarchy, which provide a pervasive thread of material within them, and which, I have suggested, are articulated in particular around the figure of the legacy, with its implications of a connection between the present and the past and its entwinement with patriarchal forms of inheritance, identity and property. In this, I have suggested, more recent films draw on and develop the concerns of the drunken master cycle. Such an engagement with a complex that revolves around the Oedipal relation to paternity and the phallus takes us close to the heart of the structures of bourgeois patriarchy, which, of course, define hysteria itself. Within such an analysis, we find ourselves concerned with the questions Elisabeth Bronfen has identified as lying at the heart of hysteria: questions about origins and how these define us; questions about the body and its vulnerability; and questions about (impossible) desire.

My mode of analysis has been primarily on the level of narrative, and—having started with the model of hysteria—it has drawn on the repertoire of psychoanalysis, though the aim has been to connect the "complexes" we might discover in this cinema back to the social and to questions that as well as being aesthetic are political in nature rather than a matter of individual pathology. I have proposed that we find in the figure of the legacy, as it occurs and recurs in the kung fu comedy, a concern with the ambivalences of Hong Kong's relation to both China and the West, to colonial rule and capitalism, and to the "nationalist" discourses through which resistance to the latter two had been previously articulated within modernity.

Rather than proposing that such films automatically "reflect" this situation, my aim has been to suggest that they are complex cultural responses to it. I have been proposing that such films *allegorize* their historical situation. But such a claim that the mode of allegory is at work seems to need more explanation: what might I *mean* by allegory here? This question of how films—both in general and in the specific case of Hong Kong cinema—might relate (allegorically or otherwise) to their historical context has been for some time a matter of discussion within film studies. My position, in the particular case of the kung fu comedy, draws on the understanding I have been developing over the last two chapters of these films as "hysterical" in their relation to social, political, and historical content.

As Tony Rayns has argued, discussing Hong Kong cinema in the 1990s, many of the only-too-obvious "resonances" between material in films and contemporaneous events—though picked up easily by cinema-going audiences—are "too flip and facetious to amount to a serious political comment."[41] Certainly, the films can be understood as indulging in the "strategic ambiguity" that David Bordwell proposed typifies Hollywood cinema and that undermines any reading of such films as deliberate political "statements."[42] Why alienate a section of your audience by too-clearly articulating a politics that they might not agree with? Bordwell suggests such films often deliberately echo topical concerns to make them look "contemporary" and "meaningful," but ultimately leave space for different interpretations by different audiences, who may well each want to see their own attitudes and understandings of the world reflected in the culture they consume.

However, while Rayns is certainly correct in warning us against reading the films he discusses as overtly political "statements," Julian Stringer has noted that this standpoint is nonetheless problematic—especially as articulated by a Western critic—in its ultimately trivializing treatment of Hong Kong cinema as a "camp" pleasure. Stringer argues Rayns' judgment fits neatly into a wider pattern of consumption, marketing, and criticism that pervaded the European and American response to Hong Kong cinema during the 1990s.[43] For Stringer, Hong Kong cinema is striking in the degree that it echoes a camp aesthetic, but he also recognizes the danger of the ironizing and exoticizing attitude of camp consumption, which often leaches historical specificity from its objects. This is so especially when camp is understood as no longer the preserve of minorities for whom it allows the articulation of their difference to a mainstream culture and serves instead as a means to appropriate the images of that larger culture for its own ends. Rather, camp has increasingly become a mainstream mode of cultural enjoyment, through which the production of marginalized "others" can be reappropriated and set to work within the hegemonic order, and through which they can be subjected to a "superior" and amused gaze that asserts the position of economic advantage of the consumer. Stringer draws a distinction between the forms of irony entailed in this "postmodern" consumer camp in the West and those that Hong Kong cinema inhabits. Western, mainstream consumer camp often involves the appropriation of symbols that no longer have power and can therefore be approached with amused detachment as artifacts from a primitive world that "we" have now surpassed. In contrast, argues Stringer, the material in Hong Kong cinema is "most definitely not spent"—it remains vital and traversed by still-vivid anxieties, affects, and social and cultural contradictions.[44]

In this regard, the notion of hysteria might be one that is more suited to thinking about this particular kind of ironic relation to history than camp. In his essay on "Hong Kong Hysteria," Sarkar, agreeing to some extent with Rayns, admits that we should not read "martial arts films as modernist texts, with self-conscious strategies for articulating social contradictions"[45]—they are not allegorical, this is to say, in the deliberate way that modernist art and literature often sought to be. Nonetheless, he suggests, Hong Kong martial arts cinema, enacting a "spirited engagement with the crucial questions facing Hong Kong," and "playing out . . . various anxieties" emerging from its historical nexus, might be understood as a film industry subject to a mode of "unruly allegory," already spinning vertiginously to a point of "overload" and "loss of control," and so ultimately hysterical and symptomatic (if not *sinthomatic*) in its nature.[46] We might, then, mark in the films we have examined here, and in their treatment of the anxieties of masculinity and national or ethnic identity as these are transformed under neocolonial and capitalist conditions and under the shadow of "1997," not the "statement" of the "protestant ethnic," but rather the performative theatricalization and the "bodily conversion" of the hysteric. As I have discussed it in the previous chapter, such a "hysterical" relation to politics involves not only forms of conformism (with these films, for example, reiterating narratives of phallic mastery, cultural or ethnic nationalism, and patrilineal inheritance) but also subtle dissent and evasion, in which the themes, becoming theatricalized, slip into a (comic) mode close to parody, unhinging affect from its "proper" aim, and distracting from narrative and ideological closure, precisely as performance outstrips what is performed.[47]

CHAPTER 6

Legacies

> We should not be deceived into thinking that this heritage is an acquisition, a possession that grows and solidifies; rather, it is an unstable assemblage of faults, fissures, and heterogeneous layers that threaten the fragile inheritor from within or from underneath.
>
> —*Michel Foucault*

This book so far has focused on tracing some immediate legacies around the event of Jackie Chan's *Drunken Master.* I have examined some of the properties of the explosion of kung fu comedies that followed in its wake, exploring their intensely corporeal, carnivalesque inversions, their utopias of the body, their aestheticized violence, and their hysterical playing out of gendered and postcolonial identities. Much of this work has located the "golden age" of kung fu comedy within the social, political, and economic context of Hong Kong during the 1970s and 1980s, although certainly I have traced such tendencies forward and outward, in, for example, Jackie Chan's crossover into the American market and in the "hopping corpse" movies of the late 1980s and early 1990s as the genre increasingly hybridized.

Given the title of the book—and my methodological interest in organizing the work around a temporality of the "legacy"—it seems apt to finish with a further exploration of the ways in which such legacies stretch toward the present, with all their "unstable assemblage of faults, fissures, and heterogeneous layers."

Where Are the Legacies of the Drunken Master?

This, of course, is not without complications. As Foucault notes, the passing of time is hardly conducive to a legacy becoming "a possession that grows and solidifies." As one moves further from the "event" around which the research is organized, the legacies become both more diffused and intermixed with other materials. We are faced with the problem of where we might stop looking.

As action cinema has become increasingly globalized, with aspects of Hong Kong style, motifs, and personnel increasingly integrated into transnational circuits of cinema, might not its legacies be traced almost *everywhere* in the global production of action comedies, especially where "martial arts" are represented? How useful would it be for this study, though, to find itself tracing such diverse offerings as *Beverly Hills Ninja* (USA, dir. Dennis Dugan, 1997), *Kung Pow: Enter the Fist* (USA, dir. Steve Oedekerk, 2002), *Who Killed Captain Alex?* (Uganda, dir. I. G. G. Nabwana, 2010), and *Chadni Chowk to China* (India, dir. Nikhil Advani, 2009)? The task, some forty years on, of enumerating and accounting for the legacy of the Drunken Master would seem an almost infinite one, made all the more unwieldy in that in each instantiation different legacies would appear to be activated for new purposes and circumstances, each of which themselves would require explanation and analysis.

In many ways, even in Hong Kong what we are dealing with, rather than the simple continuation of a genre, is precisely a *legacy.* For convenience this book has used the phrase "kung fu comedy" to name its object of study, but within the more historically grounded account I have given, it is not enough for a film to contain martial arts and to have comic elements in it to place it squarely within my remit: I have instead examined a much more narrow set of qualities, specific to their moment, which were brought to the fore in explosion of kung fu comedic production opened up by the formula pioneered by Jackie Chan and Yuen Wooping's collaborations in the late 1970s.

In my account, the body has taken a central place, and one reason many contemporary films may well involve something very different is that the highly corporeal performance styles of these original kung fu comedies have increasingly become an anachronism. The skills, comic repertoire, and artistic sensibility of the key directors, choreographers, and stars of the 1970s were built around their shared opera training. They emerged into cinema at a moment when film was eclipsing theater as a popular entertainment, just as the silent comedians of 1920s Hollywood were similarly displaced from the disappearing art of vaudeville into the new medium, bringing their particular comic craft with them from stage to screen.[1] The performing body as we meet it in films such as *Drunken Master* belongs to such a moment of displacement and could hardly exist at any other historical juncture.

In this light, even the work of Stephen Chow, who most clearly and successfully carries the flag of Hong Kong martial-arts-themed comedy into the present, involves something fundamentally different. Certainly, Chow's films share much of the grotesquely corporeal carnival laughter of those films, as well as the absurdism that pervades so much Hong Kong humor—a continuation, perhaps, of a hysterical attack on the cultural and linguistic logic of a (post-)colonial order—but this may well situate him as much in the interlinked tradition of the comedies of the Hui brothers, the Aces Go Places series, or the wider oeuvres of directors such as Jeffrey Lau or Wong Jing, who both went on to direct a number of Chow's films. Chow is, furthermore, primarily a comedian rather than a martial artist or acrobat, and the comic elements of his films are as much about witty linguistic play, slapstick falls, surreal sight gags, and well timed face-pulling[2] as they are about the rather different physical virtuosity of his predecessors, in which the comedy and performance style of the drunken master films was grounded.

If Chow's films are replete with devices and motifs from the kung fu comedy, this would, furthermore, need to be understood in terms of a prevailing comic mechanism (if not a condition of being) that constructs his films around a nostalgic but irreverent evocation and combination of seemingly incompatible genre tropes from the history of Hong Kong cinema and beyond. Chow's references are as much about Bruce Lee, 1960s swordplays, social dramas from the 1950s, and even Chow Yun-fat's New Wave gangster or gambler persona—not to mention Hollywood high-school teen dramas and James Bond—as they are about the kung fu comedy. Anything drawn from this last seems thus to arrive self-consciously in quotation marks, and it is sometimes hard to know whether to situate Chow's films "within" the tradition of kung fu comedy or merely to locate the devices that he draws from them as witty—even perhaps satirical—intertextual evocations within a meta-genre of comic eclecticism, conjuring an only-ironically loved history of local popular culture that he shares with his audience, and through which this audience comes to recognize itself.

The fusion of comedy and martial arts similarly remains pervasive in contemporary swordplay films—such as, for example, *Treasure Inn* (dir. Wong Jing and Corey Yuen, 2011), *My Own Swordsman* (dir. Jong Shan, 2011), *Call Me Nobody* (dir. Kevin Chu, 2010), or *Just Another Margin* (dir. Jeff Lau, 2014). Again, however, there is a very different formula at work to that established in the 1970s. Often, these films are vehicles not for martial artists but for the crossover actor-cum-singer heartthrobs who are so central to the Hong Kong star system, and it is these star bodies (as objects of desire) that are ultimately at stake in them, rather than the kung fu comedic body I have described here.

In both mainland and Hong Kong television drama, the swordplay remains a popular genre. Humor is again a prime ingredient (usually alongside romance, melodramatic tragedy, and wire-enhanced action), and this is often a matter of a tension in the characters between maturity and immaturity, with the leads frequently performing the role of lovable brats who need to find their heroic selves later in the story. In many ways, this, of course, follows the trajectory of classic "kung fu punks" such as Jackie Chan's Wong Fei-hung. However, rather than offering an image of adolescent high spirits, as Chan did, we are now offered a version of immaturity plunged much further into childhood, and into the culture of the "cute" (famously in Japanese, the *kawaii,* or in Mandarin *ke'ai*). A case in point might be Michelle Chen's performance in the series *Legend of Qin* (2015), in which, in certain scenes, she takes on to a startling degree the postures and expressions of an animated character from a manga serial. *Legend of Qin* was, in fact, a live-action reversioning of a successful animated series (*Qin's Moon,* 2007), which drew heavily on the Japanese *anime* style. Exaggerated, "comic-book" acting was a part of the kung fu comedic repertoire (drawn from opera as well as the graphic image), but if this is continued into contemporary *wuxia* comedy scenes, it is now also combined with another set of cultural reference points and comes to mean something new, drawing on a fusion of pan-Asian cultural tropes and speaking of the wider regional cross-pollination of popular cultures. In such circumstances, continuities may be as misleading as they are informative.

Changing Circumstances of Production

Such differences are in many ways hardly surprising, given the huge sociopolitical shifts that constitute Hong Kong cinema's changing context. In recent chapters, we have edged toward what seemed for many years the historical horizon of the 1997 handover, a horizon that has long since receded.

As the second decade of Chinese rule has drawn toward a close, political tensions within Hong Kong have grown increasingly visible. These were spectacularly manifest in the 2014 "Umbrella Revolution" of the Occupy Central with Love and Peace campaign, in which opposition to the CPC veto on candidates for local elections was opposed in massive street demonstrations that brought traffic in the financial heart of the island to a standstill, and which only ended after riot police attacked demonstrators with tear gas.[3] This pro-democracy campaign was itself built on youth and student movements such as Scholarism, whose base was developed in a set of 2012 protests against the introduction of the "Moral and National Education" program in schools, which they criticized as pro-Beijing propaganda.[4] Their aftermath has seen not only the entrenchment of a democratic movement (and the formation as part of this of the center-left party Demosisto, by prominent figures within the Umbrella Revolution), but also a more controversial separatist politics, characterized, for example, by the party Hong Kong Indigenous, which is highly critical of the ways that local customs and culture are being erased by the reintegration with China.[5] Although the Occupy movement was primarily a peaceful protest, riots broke out in Kowloon in 2016 after police attempted to close down the stalls of unlicensed street traders selling the traditional local snack of fishballs, an incident interpreted by localists as symptomatic of a wider attempt to crush indigenous culture by the authorities.[6] Such politics has divided Hong Kong, with a conservative older generation, who lived through the uncertainty of the Cultural Revolution and the Cold War, and for whom stability is a primary concern, often set against a younger generation whose experience has been largely—and for some now even wholly—formed within the wake of 1997, and who fear the loss of a Westernized way of life and its freedoms.[7]

Even more extensive unrest with regard to these issues broke out in June 2019 in the wake of attempts by Carrie Lam, Hong Kong's Chief Executive, to push through an extradition bill that many feared would leave Hong Kong citizens—and political dissidents in particular—vulnerable to forced removal to the PRC to face trial. Opponents of the law argued that the protections of the rule of law enjoyed in Hong Kong were not available in China, where the courts are under the CCP's political control, and that it therefore entailed a substantive end to the constitutional principle of "one country, two systems," whereby Hong Kong, though a part of China, would keep its legal and governmental systems, and so retain the liberal freedoms and the safeguards regarding human rights that had been introduced in the colony before 1997. Responding to such fears, a march through central Hong Kong on June 9 drew over a million participants, according to its organizers. The march exceeded in scale even the Umbrella Revolution protests of 2014, and in its inclusion of a much wider demographic seemed to mark a much broader consensus, too.[8] On June 12, the day the bill was due to be read, another large demonstration outside the Legislative Council broke into violent clashes with the police. The reading of the bill was delayed, and Lam announced that it would be suspended—though not abandoned. Anger over this refusal to fully withdraw the bill, as well as alleged police brutality during the demonstrations and increased opposition to Lam herself, drew out an even larger march on June 16, this time, according to its organizers, of 2 million protesters—over a quarter of the SAR's population.[9] Protests continued throughout the summer, with mounting tension: on July 1, the anniversary of the 1997 handover, the Legislative Council building was occupied and vandalized by protesters, and throughout July demonstrations were increasingly accompanied by clashes with the police, or with pro-Beijing groups. As this book passes through its final stages of editing, quite how the situation will end remains unclear, but it nonetheless seems certain that overall the decade of mounting mass protests evidences a growing hostility towards the PRC.

Of course, contemporary concerns with independence or the "local" in Hong Kong politics are in many ways themselves a product of the cultural histories that have been examined here already, in which Hong Kong identity in the wake of 1967 increasingly grew away from and became defined in opposition to the mainland. The protesters themselves seem to have aligned themselves with the image of Bruce Lee—the archetypal "protestant ethnic" of heroic kung fu cinema—carrying banners and wearing t-shirts reproducing his famous admonishment to "be like water," and adopting this as an explicit inspiration for their organizational strategy, replacing the fixed occupation of 2014 with a series of shifting, formless, flowing protests. Jackie Chan, the foremost exponent of kung fu comedy, is altogether less revered, due to the generally conservative and pro-Beijing personal politics he has expressed in recent years.[10] However, although it would stretch matters to claim that the growth of protest movements in Hong Kong is a "legacy of the kung fu comedy," this latter is, I've argued in earlier chapters, at least an element within the development of a distinct Hong Kong culture, and was one of the many popular-cultural sites in which the complexity of relations between China and the West, and the distinct, hybrid nature of identity in the enclave, were negotiated. Are the popular, carnival bodies and "stateless subjects" I discovered in kung fu comedies forebears of the more recent "fishball revolution" rioting of 2016? It doesn't seem coincidental, at least, that the kung fu comedian Stephen Chow celebrates precisely this culture of local street food in *God of Cookery* (1996), in which a Shaolin-trained chef makes his comeback from ruin by inventing and promoting "pissing beef balls," uniting the products of rival vendors in a Kowloon night market.

An irony, however, surrounds this movement in relation to cinematic culture. The articulation of Hong Kong identity in popular comedies in the 1970s and 1980s was marked precisely by the lack of a social movement in which such identities could become properly "political." However, just as a movement of political dissent arises, pitting local identities now against mainland China, Hong Kong's popular cinema itself seems increasingly weak in its ability to mediate or even register such dissonance. It might be argued, in fact, that increasingly "Hong Kong" cinema per se, as a popular phenomenon, is ceasing to exist, as it is absorbed, both in terms of production and consumption, into a larger Chinese entertainment economy.

Before the détente of the 1980s, the mainland market was impenetrable for cinema made outside the PRC, making it an irrelevance for filmmakers. However, the "opening up" of China since then has meant the emergence of a market for films that eclipses that of Hong Kong itself, or even of its traditional diasporic audiences in Southeast Asia and around the Pacific Rim. Increasingly, the economically rational thing to do is to make films that address the cultural references and needs of this vast new marketplace and that thus leave behind the specificities of the Hong Kong context.

Furthermore, access to such markets comes with a price. One aspect of this is the direct regulation placed on such films, which, to receive mainland release, need to pass tight political and moral censorship. The carnival laxity of the classic kung fu comedy, of course, would sit very uneasily within the straitlaced moral framework of the PRC's moral codes. In the wake of the 2003 Closer Economic Partnership Agreement, it is, moreover, advantageous with regards to distribution for a film to be a coproduction, and hence to include mainland stars and crew, allowing it to be treated as a domestic release rather than a foreign production subject to quotas.[11] Capital has flooded out of Hong Kong and into mainland studios, pursuing native Mandarin stars rather than Cantonese-speaking actors. Chinese entertainment behemoths such as the Huayi Brothers Media Corporation have eclipsed Hong Kong companies, drawing local talent away from the enclave and into PRC productions. While in the 1990s the Hong Kong industry was regularly making some 300 films a year, by 2007 this was reduced to only 51.[12]

Stephen Chow's career in the twenty-first century offers us a vivid example of such transformation. During the 1990s, Chow's "untranslatable" *mo lei tau* (nonsensical) humor made him a more bankable star at the Hong Kong box office even than Jackie Chan, but he was thought to be impossible to export elsewhere.[13] However, in the 2000s, Chow's films slowly attempted to reach out to a more international audience. *Shaolin Soccer* (dir. Stephen Chow, 2001) cast him opposite Vicki Zhao, who rose to stardom in mainland television dramas. Though the urban background is primarily nondescript, and could easily pass for Hong Kong, it is actually filmed in Shanghai, a fact perhaps not lost on Chinese viewers. Furthermore, in *Shaolin Soccer*—and even more so in *Kung Fu Hustle* (dir. Stephen Chow, 2004), a coproduction of Beijing Film Studio, Huayi Bros, and Hong Kong's Star Overseas (among others), initiated by Columbia Pictures Film Production Asia—Chow left behind his trademark *mo lei tau* banter and absurdism for more transnationally appealing modes of humor. Since then, Chow has increasingly retreated behind the camera, allowing him to further jettison his performance style itself, culturally rooted as this is in the local. In *Journey to the West* (2013) and *The Mermaid* (2016), Chow worked as director rather than star, and both of these films were essentially PRC productions, released in Mandarin.

Ghosts of the Drunken Master

The "legacy" of the Drunken Master in the present is thus something difficult to lay hold of. Diffuse, misleading, simultaneously everywhere and nowhere, it takes on the phenomenality of the ghost—a specter, perhaps, that haunts action cinema in the way Hamlet's dead father stalks the walls of Elsinore. Such ghosts—as Derrida has pointed out in *Specters of Marx*—are hardly things in the world, so need a different form of treatment to that which we take to simple positivities. Derrida terms the method that might deal with them "hauntology," punning on the notion of "ontology" (the study of the nature and order of beings and being), where hauntology must deal instead with something that is not a being as such.[14] Just as with Hamlet's relation to his father, such ghosts, of course, are a matter of the ways we are tied up, both with regard to what we owe the past and the future, with legacies.[15] If there is a legacy of the Drunken Master that we are interested in (and that I have been interested in throughout this work), this concerns the ways that such a figure might continue to "haunt" the world, now and in the future.

To lay hold—if only partially, provisionally, and for a brief moment—of the vanishing apparition of the kung fu comedy as a legacy, I propose in this chapter to narrow my examination to the transformation of the cinematic figure of the "Drunken Master" himself, So Chan ("Beggar So"—the *sifu,* played by Simon Yuen in *Drunken Master,* who teaches Jackie Chan's Wong Fei-hung the "drunken fist"), in the period from the early 1990s to the present. These changing representations, I will argue, evidence the developing relation of film production to its mainland audiences and backers, and the shifting politics of Hong Kong. Within the films this is evidenced in an increasing nationalism. However, I shall conclude by briefly looking at the way this nationalism is once again rendered problematic in some recent examples of transnational kung fu comedic coproductions.

The Drunken Master in the 1990s

During the early 1990s a flurry of films returned to the motif of "drunken boxing" and to revising or imagining anew the myths of Wong Fei-hung and "Beggar So," around whom the 1978 film *Drunken Master* was set. Gordon Chan's *King of Beggars* (1992), a vehicle for the then ascendant Stephen Chow, was followed by *Heroes Among Heroes* (dir. Yuen Woo-ping and Chan Chin-chung, 1993), which starred Donnie Yen, also coming into his own as a star at this point. Jackie Chan's own reprisal of the role of Wong Fei-hung in the rather loose *Drunken Master* sequel, *Drunken Master II* (dir. Lau Kar-leung, 1994) followed close on the heels of both, an attempt, perhaps, among all the new competition, to reclaim the myth and stamp his mark of ownership upon it once more.

As a group, these films in many respects established a continuation of the themes and motifs of the "drunken master" comedies of the late 1970s, and were made with many of the genre's instigators still at the creative helm. However, they were also involved in the reinvention of martial arts comedy for a new historical moment, both in terms of their incorporation of the newly dominant cinematic aesthetic of the period, and also in terms of their response to historical circumstances. By the 1990s, the kung fu comedy in its original guise already looked decidedly anachronistic, both in terms of cinematic style and of the social realities that had made it relevant. The same thing had happened to the kung fu comedy as I have argued happened to the "heroic" kung fu film of the early 1970s, which they in their turn had superseded.

The dominant figure of the new cinematic style of the 1990s was Tsui Hark, who had risen to prominence at the end of the 1970s with a series of provocative "New Wave" films, which were daringly flamboyant in style, taking on social realities in an often sensationalist manner.[16] In the 1980s, Tsui's output as a producer and director became increasingly commercial, known for its highly mobile camerawork and fast pacing. As producer of John Woo's *A Better Tomorrow* (1986), Tsui had a major hand in the rise of the gangster genre that characterized the end of that decade. At the start of the 1990s, Tsui turned his attention to swordplay films, and although the making of *wuxia* had certainly not ground to a halt in the meantime, it was, Stephen Teo argues, in particular the box-office success of Tsui's production of *Swordsman* (dir. King Hu,[17] 1990) that spawned a new cycle of production around the genre.[18]

We have already met these 1990s swordplay films in Sarkar's account of them as "hysterical." Mainland critics, irrespective of actual authorship, generically labeled these "Tsui Hark films," emphasizing his influence on the genre.[19] For Sarkar, as I have noted, they are typified by their dramatic lighting, rousing soundtrack, intense pace, hyperactive camerawork, bending or blending of gender and genre alike, uncertainty toward identity and ontology in general, and their "unruly" sense of historical and political allegory.[20] Working in particular with Beijing-opera-trained stunt coordinator (and director in his own right) Ching Siu-tung, Tsui's films established a choreographic style of gracefully soaring and spinning, weightless fighting bodies, suspended on wires, whose kinesthetic effect was enhanced by rapid cutting and the use of explosive charges to register the force of magical *qi* strikes.

Though far from its ruling principle, comedy was nonetheless a key ingredient in Tsui's new swordplay formula. The casting of Sam Hui, primarily known as a comedian rather than a heroic actor, as *Swordsman*'s leading man is indicative of this fact. Many of Tsui's films borrowed elements of humor from his earlier success, *Peking Opera Blues* (1986), which had spun together taut action scenes, romance, and elements of gender-bending farce within an intricately staged setting among the political reversals of the early Republic.

As Teo notes, Tsui's films—and their many imitations—tend to return obsessively to themes of Chinese history and the question of national identity, to the colonial setting of Hong Kong, and to mythological and supernatural scenarios.[21] In this, Tsui's films have thus been read as responses to the anxieties of "1997."[22] Returning to Chinese tradition and history, to the cinematic realm of mythical certainty beyond this, to the perplexities of Hong Kong's own, separate past, and to the encounter with Western imperialism enabled Tsui to produce complex, conflicted images that refigured a condition suspended between tradition and modernity, China and the West, and between capitalism and communism.

The particular film—not incidentally directed by Tsui himself—that is most clearly a spur for the 1990s re-engagement with the stories and characters of *Drunken Master* was *Once Upon a Time in China* (1991). This had returned to the figure of Wong Fei-hung for the first time since Lau Kar-leung's *Martial Club* (1981).[23] Jackie Chan's 1978 depiction of this folkloric character in *Drunken Master* had iconoclastically imagined Wong not as the embodiment of strict, upright, patrician, and Confucian values that Hong Kong popular culture during the preceding decades had made him, but as an undisciplined rebel and an anarchistic clown. Tsui's version, played by a similarly youthful Jet Li, took a different, if also controversial angle on him. While Wong Fei-hung had stood in the cinema of the 1950s and 1960s for the very essence of Chinese tradition, Tsui's version of the character is defined precisely by his need to compromise and adapt in a moment when tradition and modernity are in conflict. Rather than embodying the wholeness of a fantasied past to which the cinematic audience could return, Tsui offered in Wong a mirror of the audience's crisis of identity and their struggle to negotiate a world of historical flux and moral or political uncertainty. Wong encounters—and even comes ambivalently to embrace—the effects of alien technologies such as firearms, train travel, cameras, and Western dress. These are introduced in particular through the character of his young "Thirteenth Aunt" (Rosamund Kwan), who has been educated in Europe and carries with her a series of Western values and ideas. Wong comes to grapple with these, as the two tentatively begin—and develop through the series of sequels that ran through the early 1990s—an intergenerational romance that transgresses traditional proprieties.[24]

This historical ambivalence in Wong's character is also achieved through his location in relation to very particular historical referents and through the rich period detail with which turn-of-the-century Guangdong is depicted. In Tsui's Wong Fei-hung series, Wong is variously faced with the effects of the "unequal treaties," opium smuggling, people trafficking of Chinese citizens to the United States to work as coolies, the attempted Republican uprisings of Sun Yat-sen (who even turns up as a character in the second film), heterodox White Lotus/Boxer unrest, the palace intrigues of the Dowager Empress Cixi, and much else besides. This emphatic return of history and of historical events to the series bucked the pattern not only of the initial series of Wong Fei-hung films, but also Yuen Woo-ping's *Drunken Master,* which, as I argued in previous chapters, seemed primarily designed to escape the historical tumult evoked by, for example, the Shaolin films of the preceding era. Tsui's return to such history, without the moral certainties of these earlier films, seems to be calculated to respond to new and urgent sociopolitical realities.

King of Beggars

Once Upon a Time in China ran for two months and grossed HK$29,672,278 in Hong Kong,[25] and it was in the wake of this success that Gordon Chan's *King of Beggars* was released. This starred Stephen Chow, who over the previous two years had made a string of successful comic films, primarily with contemporary settings. 1992 marked a new departure for Chow, as he resituated his comedic performances within the period universe of the new "Tsui Hark" style of swordplays. Chow followed the success of his costume-drama comedy *Justice My Foot* (dir. Johnnie To, 1992) with *Royal Tramp* (dir. Wong Jing, 1992) and its sequel *Royal Tramp II* (dir. Wong Jing, 1992), adapting between them Jin Yong's satirical *wuxia* novel, *The Deer and the Cauldron.* All three out-grossed even Tsui Hark's *Once Upon a Time in China II* (1992), which in turn took more than the film of which it was a sequel.[26]

Following closely on the heels of these films, *King of Beggars* allowed Chow, under the direction of Gordon Chan, to revisit the mythology surrounding Wong Fei-hung. However, rather than competing directly with Tsui's vision of Wong himself, Chan and Chow turned to the character of So Chan, who had appeared as Wong's mentor in *Drunken Master.* As Po Fung has noted, Beggar So, in fact, already had a long history within the Wong Fei-hung films, offering moments of comic relief within the original 1950s movie series and even taking the lead role in three spinoffs released in 1953. In 1982, drawing on the success of *Drunken Master* and its many imitations, a TV series starring Chow Yun-fat, *The Legend of Master So,* had broken new ground in imagining the character, casting So not as an elderly teacher but as a young and handsome hero, offering him for the first time a backstory where he masters the drunken fist and becomes a beggar.[27] It is this backstory that Gordon Chan took on with his filmic retelling and that has also provided the basis for a number of further versions.

So is depicted in Chan's film as a young, rich playboy from the Qing era who falls in love with Yu-shang, the daughter of the leader of the Beggar Clan. When she tells him she will only marry the number-one kung fu scholar, he enters the national martial arts examinations. Though an excellent martial artist, So is illiterate and cheats in the written aspect of the examinations. This is revealed by his nemesis, an evil sorcerer with designs on the royal throne, and he is crippled and condemned by the Emperor to a life of beggary. To triumph, So learns the martial art not of drunken boxing, but of the "sleeping fist," and takes over the Beggar Clan in order to rescue his beloved—and the Emperor—from the evil sorcerer. So, however, is finally uninterested in resuming his wealthy lifestyle and his family's traditional official position, instead opting to become "King of Beggars" and live happily ever after with Yu-shang.

In telling this story, Chan reversed the decision in *Drunken Master* to lift Beggar So and Wong Fei-hung out of the political history of the Qing period. This was a world to which they were, in the early 1970s, firmly attached as auxiliary figures within the larger Cantonese popular-cultural and martial arts mythologies surrounding the burning of the Southern Shaolin Temple, whose survivors are depicted resisting the Manchurian rule of China. This mythology had cast Wong and So—the martial inheritors of the Shaolin survivors—as patriotic heroes. This is seen, for example, in the late entry to the Shaw Brothers cycle of Shaolin films, *Ten Tigers of Kwantung* (dir. Chang Cheh, 1979), in which Beggar So figures as one of a group of Cantonese heroes aiding escapees from the Shaolin Temple and their collaborators to evade and resist the Qing authorities.

However, if the re-emergence of the historical in a period film made in the wake of *Once Upon a Time in China* would seem unsurprising, Chan added a spin on this, one perhaps no less transgressive with regards to the canons of martial arts mythology and their politics than that which had been provided in *Drunken Master.* Rather than a patriotic Cantonese rebel, So is envisioned as the spoiled son of a Manchurian military official—a fact that would seem otherwise to mark him as a prime candidate for a villain rather than a hero in the Shaolin films. If history returns (and with it the political), it is thus in a transformed guise. Far from attempting to overthrow the Qing dynasty, at the end of the film So even saves the Emperor's life and rescues him from an attempted coup. So's reward is an accommodation with the Qing state: in the final images of the film, he is awarded a royal seal for his begging, which requires citizens to give him whatever he asks of them.

So's attitude is nonetheless more complicated than a simple embrace of the state. So's rescue of the Emperor is more a by-product of the desire to save the woman he loves than a direct aim in and of itself, and when So is offered an official post at the end of the film, he rejects it. Gordon Chan, in fact, in interview has talked of the conception of his film emerging from a traditional saying that having been a beggar one would not wish to be an official.[28] So Chan's beggary thus seems to enact a willful indifference to government, rather than either opposition or embrace, and, if it is not simply to be read as an expression of Hong Kong's famous political apathy at a moment of saturation with the discourse around "1997," it may well bring us back to the territory of Petrus Liu's "stateless subjects" and the longstanding utopian desire in *wuxia* fiction for a basis of human relations beyond state politics entirely. The motif of the Beggars' Clan—drawn from Jin Yong's seminal *wuxia* novels, along with the character of "Northern Beggar" Hong Qigong, who teaches So in a dream, and the martial arts of the "Dog Beating Stick" and the "Eighteen Dragon-Subduing Palms"—may, as an organization of those living outside the law, stand in for this realm beyond the state and its troubles.

This attitude to the state and its politics is mirrored in the treatment of the performing body. When we first see Chow (and his doubles) perform, in a fight in a brothel, we are treated to a display of graceful, athletic *wushu*-type movements, emphasizing youth and strength, and the aim seems more to establish Chow's handsome, charismatic, and heroic star persona than to deliver comedy. However, such an ideal body is increasingly satirized and subjected to carnival inversion. In a lengthy set piece in the middle of the film, depicting the Qing military examinations, the martial body is anachronistically imagined through the guise of Western sporting culture. The examinations are depicted as taking the form of a series of Olympic events, including running, high jump, and weight lifting, complete with judges holding up scorecards (fig. 6.1). At the end of performing a spinning, wire-and-trampoline-enhanced leap in the high jump, cut together in the *wuxia* style of weightless, aerial flight, Chow imitates the landing and finishing pose of a gymnast, waving to the audience and flouncing off screen. When Chow fights, it is to perform a pastiche of his modern-day hero, Bruce Lee, complete with impromptu nunchaku. The viability of reading such parody of the corporeal ideal and its technologies (both martial and sporting) as an inversionary carnival strategy continuous with the kung fu comedy tradition is reinforced by the film's insistence (evident throughout Chow's oeuvre) on gross-out and toilet humor.[29]

The heroic body presented by Chow in the first section of the film is increasingly rejected as the narrative progresses. Unable to defeat his nemesis, So is crippled and is forbidden to work, and so is condemned to a life of beggary. He spends the middle part of the film in a state of misery and abjection, so incompetent, depressed and physically disabled he is unable even to actually beg successfully. However, Chow's defeat is transcended when he learns "sleeping kung fu," a martial art paradoxically based in sloth. Although it seems to derive in part from the "stumbling," "falling," out-of-control aspects of drunken boxing, the choreography for this, put together by Yuen Woo-ping's brother Yuen Cheung-yan, seems to involve a deliberately parodic reversal of the hyperathletic and gymnastic style his family established with the original *Drunken Master* cycle.

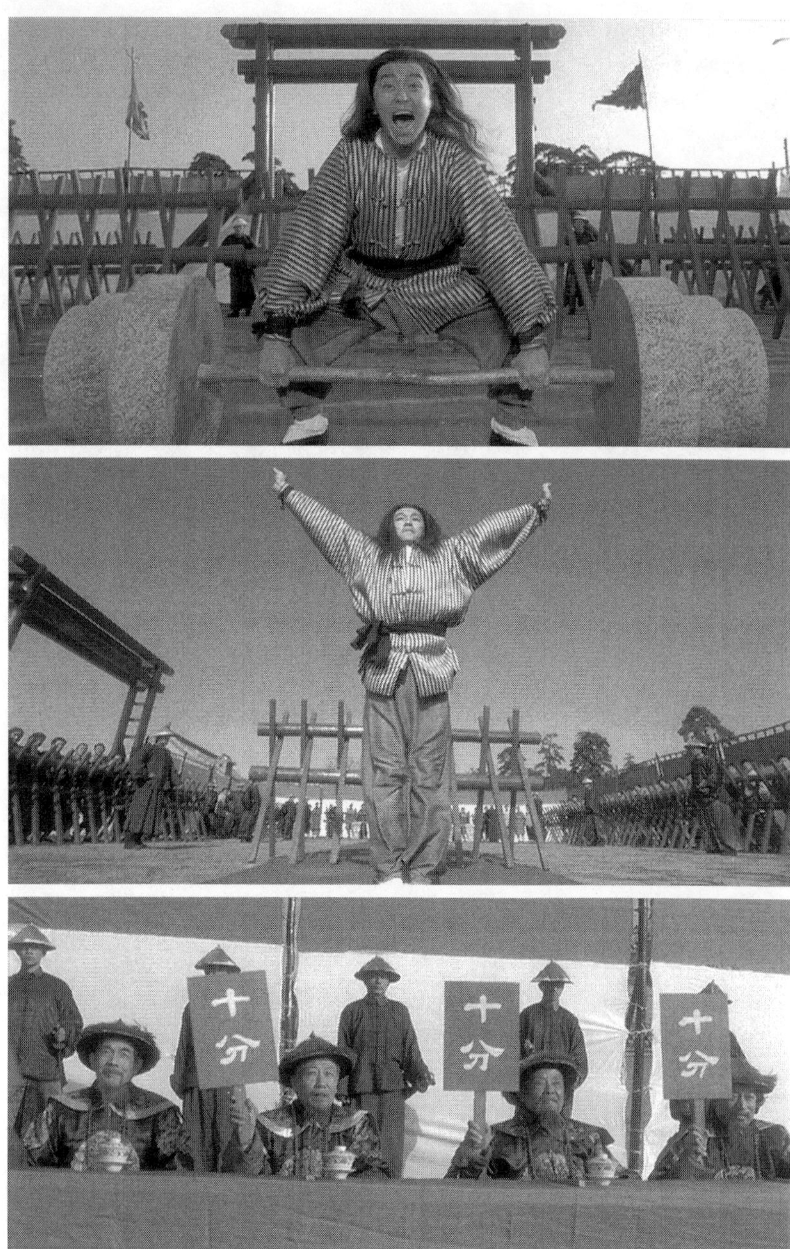

Fig. 6.1. The martial contest in *King of Beggars*. Video stills. © 2010 Fortune Star Media.

Chow's performance is in fact a virtuoso display of physical inactivity. His body remains relaxed, nerveless, and prone as wires hoist him limply around. When, for example, lying on the floor, he dodges a standing opponent's attack by sliding through their legs, this is clearly an effect of his being hauled by cables, and there is no pretense made that it is an effect of any physical effort on his part. Where the athletic body (associated historically, as we have seen, with nationalist discourse and modernity) is inadequate, it is passivity and apathy that win out in this film. Chow's performance of "sleeping kung fu" is in stark contrast to that of Leung Kar-yan in *Sleeping Fist* (dir. Teddy Yip, 1979), a *Drunken Master* clone that also starred Simon Yuen in his usual role of an old beggar-master. While Chow offers us a descent into slumber in the "sleeping fist," Leung performed it with his trademark muscularity and manic energy, making it resemble nothing so much as a convulsive and sudden awakening.

Just as it rejects the athleticism of drunken kung fu, *King of Beggars* also reverses the "training sequence" convention. In contrast to the grueling routines Jackie Chan and Gordon Liu were put through in the 1970s, Chow's Beggar So learns his secret art not through hard work but entirely without effort, having it revealed in a dream—literally, that is, by sleeping. In keeping with the film's reversal of the usual narrative of physical transformation, starting with a gymnastic body and ending with an abject one, the structural place of the training montage is replaced with So's plunge into despair and inaction, and it is through this emotional ordeal, rather than through physical training, that he emerges victorious.

It is tempting to read this all as an allegory—however tongue in cheek—of a (post-)colonial situation, and of a response to a power that is at once that of the Chinese mainland and the British colonial government at a time when negotiations were going on between these authorities with little direct input from the Hong Kong population. It offers an excessive, absurd caricature of stereotypically "Oriental" passivity (instantiated as politics most famously in Gandhi's *satyagraha*), taking the mystique of a kung fu that beats strength through softness to the point of *reductio ad absurdum*. However, such a reading would at the very least have to recognize this as a deeply hysterical allegory, layered with irony and marking the film's politics themselves as akin to the narcoleptic fit of "sleeping kung fu."

King of Beggars also seems to extend the thematics of inheritance and of the relation to patriarchy I traced in previous chapters, and this, too, can help us understand the film's treatment of the body. The opening shot of the film, in fact, emphasizes that legacy is a theme, as it pans down a painted scroll on an altar, showing the past patriarchs (all officials) who constitute the ancestral line of the

So family. Beneath the painting, So Chan and his father (played by Chow's eternal sidekick, Ng Man-tat) are squandering their inheritance, as they do in spectacular style throughout the first section of the film.

The motifs of literacy and of the written word seem key in untangling the significance of this motif of inheritance in the film. The initial scene, just described, appears immediately after a title sequence entirely consisting of the calligraphic mark, and has So Chan showing off his "calligraphy" to his father. However, So Chan, in fact, cannot write his own name, and his father cannot tell this because he, too, is illiterate. It is this cultural heritage—writing, and through it the Chinese language, identity itself, the name—that their family has failed to carry. It is, furthermore, precisely this illiteracy that becomes the reason for So's fall into beggary, when he is caught cheating in the written section of the imperial examinations.

My earlier reading of what might take the place of the training montage in the middle section of *King of Beggars*, then, can be nuanced by further identifying it with So's acquisition of literacy, which he masters by tracing the melancholic words on tombstones as an expression of his despair. This seems to play along the dichotomy in Chinese thought between the martial (*wu*) and the civil or scholarly (*wen*), with So's transformation happening in the latter rather than the former realm. It is through acquisition of civil rather than martial skills that he is able to read the kung fu manuals bequeathed to him by Hong Qigong and to acquire the martial arts (and healing) contained within them.

Petrus Liu has argued that the common motif of the secret manual in *wuxia* novels serves to mark "kung fu" as cultural heritage and place literature itself at the heart of its transmission.[30] In this regard, we can interpret the film as concerning itself (like the "hopping corpse" movies discussed earlier) with the conflicted relation of Hongkongers to the culture of the ancestral land, at once prized and yet abandoned as oppressive.

As with films previously analyzed, this theme of inheritance seems to intersect with a crisis in masculinity, a term also, according to Kam Louie and Louise Edwards, articulated around the poles of *wen* and *wu*.[31] At the start of the film, So is cocksure and virile, but with his failure in the martial arts contest he undergoes not only a loss of wealth and status but also a further symbolic castration when he is crippled by his nemesis, who breaks his bones and severs his tendons, leaving him physically limp and unable to perform the athletic masculinity he embodies at the start of the film. In this regard the Sleeping Kung Fu he acquires might well be regarded as a fantasy image of compensated castration. So's masculinity returns only via this passage through castration, and through the acquisition of literature as the source of the Name of the Father; it is the masculinity of the scholar, not the warrior, that he has been missing. Writing—ownership of culture—is thus figured as a decisively phallic technology of inheritance.

This all suggests that the politics of the film are ultimately nationalist in their embrace of inherited "Chineseness" as masculine fullness. This reading would be reinforced by the choice to shoot many of the film's outdoor scenes in historic and iconic locations on the mainland, embracing the landscape as an emotive national signifier. So Chan and the Beggar Clan, for example, rush to the rescue of Yu-shang at the end of the film along a section of the Great Wall. However, much also seems to go against such a reading. Although So Chan is a Manchu, the film resurrects a series of tropes that seem to emphasize his Cantoneseness and thus express instead a localist sensibility. So refuses, for example, to plait his hair in the Manchurian style, and the film's language is, of course, Cantonese, with plenty of Chow's trademark wordplay. The villain, furthermore, is emphatically Manchurian in a way that distinguishes him from So, and the military exam takes the familiar form of a competition between North and South. (However, with the Mongolian enemy So faces, this might alternatively be understood as constituting a wider Han ethnic nationalism.) Beggar So's ultimate distrust of the official world of the court and authority, and his embrace of a vagabond existence, might also seem to provide an image of life—as in Hong Kong—somewhat beyond the arm of the Chinese state, and an image of local autonomy that expresses a distrust of the future authority of Beijing. This might be reinforced through the film's insistent evocation of Hong Kong popular-cultural references from Jin Yong to Bruce Lee. Thus a final reading would have to recognize what seems a strategy of maximal contradiction, where familiar codes and iconographies, and all their ideological baggage, are deliberately muddled and entangled.

Heroes Among Heroes

In contrast to *King of Beggars,* the encoding of the "politics" of *Heroes Among Heroes,* which reprised the story of the young So Chan the following year (1993), seems altogether simpler. Based on a premise that, rather than imagining them as master and student, teams up So Chan and Wong Fei-hung as young men in rivalry with each other, the film revisits the familiar iconographies of the *Once Upon a Time in China* film series, and it shares this latter's insistent concern with political history. We have, for example, opium smuggling, corrupt Manchurian nobility, rapacious foreigners, and sinister "White Lotus" acolytes. Tying us further to the *Once Upon a Time in China* series, So's love interest in the film (played by Fennie Yuen), toting a camera and wearing Western clothes, could hardly but evoke Rosamund Kwan's performance as Wong's Thirteenth Aunt. Donnie Yen himself, who takes up the heroic role of Beggar So, of course, had also played the villain in the second installment of that series. However, whereas *Once Upon a Time in China* was primarily dramatic, with performances by supporting actors such as Yuen Biao adding comic relief, the balance shifts in *Heroes Among Heroes,* with the protagonist, So himself, getting into a series of scrapes and misadventures throughout the first part of the film.

The politics of the film are, in fact, much less ambiguous or entangled not just than *King of Beggars,* but also than the *Once Upon a Time in China* series. The film imagines So and Wong as accomplices of Lin Zexu, the famous historical Viceroy of Guangdong and Guangxi, whose staunch campaign against the illegal opium trade by the British in China sparked the first Opium War of 1839–1842. The film starts with patriotic speeches and the seizing of opium, and ends with another grand scene of the seizure and destruction of opium in a British warehouse. So himself is tricked into taking opium by a plotting Manchurian prince in the film and must pass through and overcome the "weakness" of addiction in order to become a hero and join the struggle against the imposition of the drug on the Chinese people. Such images of opium had long been shorthand in Hong Kong cinema for the reduction of China to semicolonial status and for all the themes of the "Sick Man of East Asia" with which the heroic era of kung fu cinema was concerned.[32] It seems in this regard to offer an unproblematically ethnonationalist story harking back to the cinema of the early 1970s with which the kung fu comedy so starkly broke. Such a reading is only belied by the levity with which all this material is treated in its comic rehash.

The physical performance within the film also seems to mark a shift from the earlier comedies. The choreography—although again by Yuen Woo-ping and his brothers—is much more akin to the work that they did on *Once Upon a Time in China* itself. It is played as "straight" fighting, enhanced by wires, undercranking, and slow motion, given impact with rapid cuts and dramatic camera angles. When Donnie Yen performs "drunken boxing," his *wushu*-influenced version of this is much more elegant, graceful, and even classical than Jackie Chan's, involving flowing movements, agile leaps and spins, rapid high kicks, and dramatic poses. In this regard the action and the comedy are far more divorced from each other than in earlier films, with much of the laughter provided by the portrayal of a farcical romantic and familial relationship between So Chan's ineffectual, widowed father and his sexually repressed sister-in-law, played by Ng Man-tat (reprising his role from *King of Beggars*) and Sheila Chan.

Drunken Master II

The straightforward nationalism and anti-imperialism of *Heroes Among Heroes* (tinged as it is with a specifically "local" Cantonese setting) was taken up and extended in Jackie Chan's return to the *Drunken Master* mythology, with the release in 1994 of *Drunken Master II,* produced in collaboration with veteran martial arts director and choreographer Lau Kar-leung.[33] This cast Chan not as Beggar So, but in the role of Wong Fei-hung, whom he had played in the original 1978 *Drunken Master* film. In contrast to Jet Li's recently influential depiction of Wong, which had imagined him once more in the mold of the upright and sober character made famous by Kwan Tak-hing throughout the 1950s and 1960s, Chan drew on the recent interest in the Beggar So films to reassert the more anarchic image of the character he had invented in *Drunken Master.* Chan's sequel (if such it is) replaced *Heroes Among Heroes*'s Qing setting with the early Republic, and rather than involving Wong with the defense against the opium trade, it set him at loggerheads with a plot by British diplomats to spirit Chinese antiquities out of the country and into European museums. This was supplemented with a side-plot where the same foreign dignitaries are exploiting Chinese workers in the local steel factory.

This concern with the theft of antiquities, of course, engages with the questions of cultural legacy and identity at stake in *King of Beggars.* The political form that this takes is made further explicit when Wong comes into possession of an article that the British are particularly interested in appropriating: the former regime's imperial jade seal. The jade seal is an image of the authority of the Emperor, used to stamp and authenticate his commands, and the symbolic ceding of this authority to the British—and the struggle to keep this within China—introduces a metaphorics of national autonomy or self-rule, conceived as something handed down from the past, but nonetheless alienable.

In conjunction with this theme, it seems significant that Beggar So, Wong's mentor and teacher in the original *Drunken Master* film, is notable by his absence in the film, not only in appearance, but even in mention. Wong's father, the inflexibly Confucian Kei-ying (Ti Lung), is now also given a much more humane side as purveyor of wisdom (primarily about moderation in drinking), taking on something of So's role in the first film. So is further replaced by the figure of the elderly Master Fu Wen-chi (Lau Kar-leung), who appears in order to test Wong's kung fu and guide him onto a righteous path, drawing him into the fight against the British. Rather than a disreputable beggar living beyond the margins of both the state and the Confucian order, Fu is a highly decorated military officer of the preceding dynasty, standing for staunch national service and continuity with the past.

Although this is a "sequel," then, in this return to patriotic themes much of the signification of the original *Drunken Master* film is reversed. This is also echoed in Wong's character and his relation to paternal authority. Wong remains a figure tied to disorder, but in *Drunken Master II,* this is linked to the introduction of a new stepmother character, Ling, played by Anita Mui, who replaces the "aunt" Wong meets in the original film. A martial artist in her own right, Ling is independent, gambles her days away with her friends, colludes with Fei-hung in his mischief, and even encourages him to drink and fight. Overall, she presents an element of unruly "feminine" chaos, disrupting the order of the Wong household and Fei-hung's moral upbringing.

In the early part of the film, Fei-hung thus creates a series of comic misadventures through his impetuous high spirits, and through his new mother's instigation, and this may well seem to mark continuities with the hero of the original *Drunken Master.* However, a series of parallels to scenes in this earlier film only underline the differences between the two. For example, when Fei-hung—just as in the first film—visits the market, he encounters a girl. This time, however, it is clearly the girl who is smitten with him, rather than vice versa, and it is she who drops a (phallic) snake, rather than he. She is in fact a snake-vendor, and instead of leaping away in horror, as Fei-hung's cousin does in the first film, she calmly steps on it, laughing at the men in the market who are frightened. When Fei-hung is then drawn into a fight in the market, rather than beating and humiliating his opponent, he nobly claims the fight is a draw, although it is clear that he easily outclasses his adversary. By doing so, instead of making a dangerous enemy, he builds an alliance that he will draw on later in the film. All this seems to remove much of the moral ambiguity in his character in the earlier film, inscribing him more squarely, from the start, within an order that is both bourgeois and Confucian, and that dovetails with the nationalism of the script.

The choreography that accompanies such a narrative seems on the one hand to hark back to the earlier comedic style that had largely been jettisoned by both *King of Beggars* and *Heroes Among Heroes.* Such a style is, of course, Chan's trademark, and its resurrection was in large part possible thanks to the new market for martial arts films, whether comedic or serious, pioneered by Tsui Hark. However, Chan's decision to place the sustained depiction of martial arts central within the film's performance, rather than the grand stunt-and-chase scenes that had come to typify his output over the preceding years, certainly entails a reversal and marks a return to an image of the body more emphatically marked by the ethno-national connotations of "kung fu." The placement of these extended action scenes within the detailed historical Republican "period" universe of the "Tsui Hark films," and in the context of the new forms of choreography that typified these films, also, however, seems to have required a revision of the earlier style. The depiction of drunken boxing retains the original film's fantastical comic inventiveness in its play on the possibilities of bodily movement—often rising to the level of the marvelous—but it rejects the clown-like jerkiness and staccato rhythms of the choreography of the 1970s, opting instead for a breathtaking fluidity of motion that perhaps has more affiliation with the dominant *wushu* aesthetics of the 1990s martial arts genres. Wires were also used, but not to allow the fantastical somersaults of the swordplay film; rather, they blur the lines between balance and unbalance and subtly add moments of weightlessness into leaps, emphasizing the dizzy qualities of Chan's "drunken style." Even as the carnivalesque play of bodies is resurrected in the film's acrobatic displays, it, too, seems to be held increasingly within the limits of a "classicist" aesthetic.

These three films of the early 1990s, then, marked a certain revival of the mythology of the Drunken Master, and did so by reimagining So Chan and Wong Fei-hung anew for a turbulent moment when Hong Kong was overshadowed by the impending reunification with China. In them, the sense of national rather than local identity appears increasingly (if nonetheless ambivalently) resurgent, and this mirrored the overall transformation of martial arts genres, which, under the sway especially of Tsui Hark, had returned to period detail in order to re-engage (often critically) with themes of national and colonial history. Although they reiterated a series of tropes of the 1970s kung fu comedies, they nonetheless often reversed many of the ways that these signified a relationship to local and national identity, and to the very idea of the nation-state. Ultimately, the films, taken together, return not only to the comic material of the late 1970s, but also to the motifs and the themes of the "heroic" films from earlier in that decade, with their very different politics and their very different vision of the body. Amalgamated together, these perhaps contradictory aesthetics served to articulate the complex, ambivalent experiences of identity of their producers and primary consumers—creating a playground in which what it is to be from Hong Kong could be explored.

True Legend—Beggar So Sobers Up

It is only after a decade and a half—and thus well into the period in which Hong Kong film production has been reoriented toward a mainland market—that Beggar So makes his next cinematic appearance, in Yuen Woo-ping's *True Legend* (2010). Directed by a Hong Kong director, the film's cast was clearly calculated for its international appeal, including iconic Hong Kong veterans such as Michelle Yeoh, Gordon Liu, and Leung Kar-yan alongside Taiwanese Mandopop star Jay Chou and mainland actors, including Zhou Xun, who, playing So's wife, takes the female lead. David Carradine appears in a minor villainous role, and the film's primary antagonist is Andy On, who was also born in America. The lead role, So Chan himself, is taken by Vincent Zhao, who was born in China and gained his initial success in national *wushu* competitions, but who also went on to develop a career in Hong Kong, rising to stardom when he took over the role of Wong Fei-hung from Jet Li in the fourth installment of the *Once Upon a Time in China* series (1994), and in a spinoff TV series produced by Tsui Hark. Belying this international cast, however, *True Legend* was primarily shot on location amidst iconic scenery in mainland China and in Beijing studios; the production credits include the state-owned China Film Group Corporation, Beijing Forbidden City Film Co. Ltd., and Edko Beijing; and it was released in Mandarin. It is thus a clear example of the kind of coproduction, aimed at a mainland market, described toward the start of this chapter.

When Beggar So does reappear, then, in this renationalized form, it is in a singularly humorless guise, in a film reiterating the comedic stories of the 1990s in the register of tragedy. The choreography leaves behind the dance-like formalism of the comedy film and its ethical distance on the violence it depicts. The fighting is often acrobatic, with fluid, intricate, spinning, airborne wirework, but the emphasis is continually on visceral impact and on depicting the force that is unleashed in martial arts, sinking us through technical mediation into the "real" of the body. Repeatedly, a strike will be shown, followed by a slow-motion, reverse-angle close-up of the impact of the blow, or of a weapon slicing through flesh. The film is replete with gruesome beheadings, severed limbs, and blood splatter. Furniture and walls shatter and explode as bodies collide with them—though these are no longer the rubbery, cartoon bodies of Jackie Chan's stunt team in *Project A;* they are hard, invulnerable, powerful, and ultimately phallic.

True Legend is set, just as the previous films, in the late Qing dynasty and, also like those films, attempts to recount the story of how So Chan develops "drunken boxing" and becomes "Beggar So," pursuing his path through defeat, drunkenness, and despair toward spiritual and martial insight. This time, however, So is not a spoiled rich playboy living in Cantonese civil society, but rather an already-heroic—and married—general. Gone, that is to say, is the anarchic *xiaozi* of the earlier films. The tragedy is initiated when his venomous adopted brother, Yuan Lie, kills So's father and kidnaps his son. Defeated, So retires to the mountains, drinks, goes mad, and learns martial arts by fighting his alcohol-and-grief-induced hallucinations of the "God of Wushu." He returns to defeat and exact vengeance on Yuan, but not before the latter has buried So's wife alive. This second tragedy, rather than providing the closure of an ending, however unhappy, propels the film onto a new trajectory, initiating a second "chapter" of the movie where So, broken by his grief, has taken to wandering the country as an alcoholic vagrant and arrives in a northern border town. His private despair is projected against the background of the collapse of the Qing dynasty and the growing humiliation of China at the hand of foreign imperialism in the wake of the opium wars.

Along the fault lines of this two-chapter structure, a shift in style—and kung fu subgenre—occurs. The initial chapter is set in a fantastical past, with wire-enhanced, aerial armed combat and esoteric kung fu styles such as Yuan's "five venoms fist," trained by absorbing insect poisons. This then gives way to something more like the rich period detail of Tsui Hark's historical films. At the same time, the tragic revenge plot gives way to a narrative based around a death-match tournament, organized by a Caucasian impresario who mounts the spectacle of hulking, drug-fueled, muscle-bound Western fighters ("Killer Anton's Invincible Wrestlers") defeating and humiliating Chinese martial artists. As with so many films before, the protagonist must avenge the defeat of his compatriots in order to symbolically restore the honor and dignity of China, and of *wushu* itself.

The film's strange splicing of these two different sections into a single film—with their different plotlines, visual styles, and even choreography—serves to cast So in the archetypal model of the real-life hero Huo Yuanjia, famous for his public fights (and victories) against Western and Japanese opponents, and also the subject of many filmic representations.[34] Huo is, of course, the teacher who has just died at the start of Bruce Lee's *Fist of Fury,* discussed at the very start of this book, and significant as the figurehead of the Jingwu Athletic Federation, which pioneered the modernization of Chinese martial arts at the start of the twentieth century, setting out to tie them to a nationalist agenda.

Huo had, in fact, acquired a new topicality in the years preceding the production of *True Legend,* after the release of a biopic telling his life, *Fearless* (dir. Ronny Yu, 2006), which starred Jet Li—and was also choreographed by Yuen Woo-ping. This film started and finished with Huo's fights against a series of foreign martial artists, on a raised *lei tai* stage,[35] just before his death by poisoning. It seems to be from a pattern established by this film and its box-office success that *True Legend* draws its blueprint.

Finishing at the moment of Huo's death, *Fearless* leaves off where *Fist of Fury* begins, and in many ways, it serves as a belated prequel to it, evoking Bruce Lee himself as another "modernizing" figure in Chinese martial arts history and suggesting his kinship, as such a modernizer, to Huo Yuanjia. The very format of the arena or tournament, where a smaller, lithe, intelligent Chinese body is pitted against an overmuscular and monstrously powerful Caucasian foe is itself redolent of Lee's confrontations with Bob Wall in *Enter the Dragon* or Chuck Norris in *Way of the Dragon.* The link to Lee was, perhaps, hammered home soon after in Wilson Yip's *Ip Man* (2008), which applied *Fearless*'s biopic format to Lee's real-life teacher, Ip Man, resurrecting along the way many of the tropes of *Fist of Fury.* Like *Fearless* (and *True Legend*), *Ip Man* ends with a grand public fight on a *lei tai* stage, where Chinese national honor is at stake against a foreign opponent.

True Legend thus also evokes Bruce Lee by taking up this format and aligns the So Chan mythology not to the history of the comedy film but rather once more to the earlier moment of heroic kung fu with which this book started, and to the longer history of the perfected body of the modernist and nationalist martial arts movement, which this in turn echoed. The fictional So is presented as an ancestor of modern Chinese martial arts alongside the squarely historical characters of Huo Yuanjia and Ip Man.

Within its nationalist framework, of course, So's passage through weakness and alcoholism appears clearly as an allegory of the nineteenth-century decay of Chinese power. This reading makes much sense of the awkward splicing of the film's two sections: with its nationalist subtext, the narrative cannot be resolved at the level of the personal. Only when individual tragedy is sublimated back onto the level of the nation-state and of politics can a final redemption and resolution be offered. Unlike in earlier films, drunkenness no longer entails an ecstatic state of freedom or the transgressive disorder of grotesquery; it is no longer something to celebrate in and for itself. It is, rather, primarily a malaise or a madness to recover or wake from; far from carnivalesque, the drunken body is now above all else abject.

This nationalism is given a very particular spin by the framing of the story in the film's opening images. Through the device of an opening book, the narrative is presented as a chapter within an unfolding story of "The Chronicles of Wushu Masters." The use of the term *wushu* here—different in its connotations to *kung fu* or other possible terms for the martial arts—ties the Chinese martial arts to their particular state-sponsored instantiation in the PRC, which it serves properly to name. Taken in the light of my analyses so far of the theme of heritage, this, too, is a film about cultural legacies. It makes a claim about the sport of *wushu* as the proper inheritor of China's martial traditions and about its value for the production of a strong, modern body politic.

Though repeating an old cinematic trope, the images of the *lei tai* platform as the site of the final showdown lend this nationalism a very particular, new context, making new sense from familiar images. As depicted in the twenty-first century, these *lei tai* stages are clearly meant to echo the cages and rings of the MMA ("Mixed Martial Arts") phenomenon. MMA, growing from America in the 1990s in the wake of its promotion by the UFC (Ultimate Fighting Championship), offered the televisual spectacle of brutal "realistic" fighting competitions, amidst claims to supersede through synthesis and science the various "traditional" styles of martial art from around the world. In doing so, it resurrected once more the shades of early twentieth-century discourses that set up the modernity of Western techniques of the body against those of "primitive" and irrational

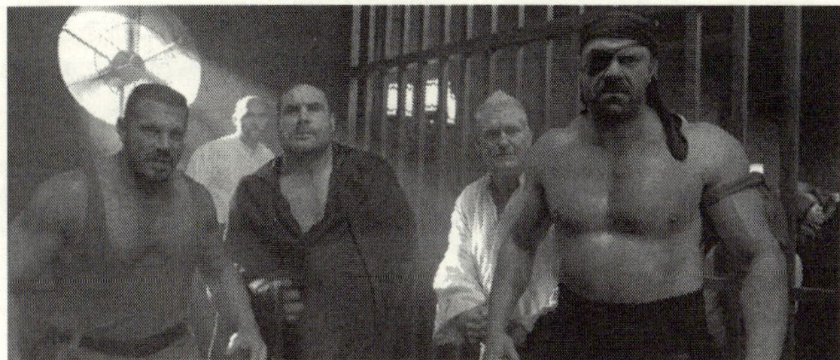

Fig. 6.2. The monstrous body of the West. Beggar So's muscle-bound opponents in *True Legend*. Video still. © 2014 StudioCanal VOD.

"others," and such claims once again seemed to place the Chinese martial arts, and hence Chinese tradition more generally, in doubt as offering a valid source of strength and self-affirmation. In this context, the cinematic image of Beggar So lined up against huge, muscular, and drug-fueled (so technologically enhanced) Western fighters seems to evoke the contrast between the *wushu* body and the hypermuscular physiques on display in MMA. The opponents chosen for Vincent Zhao included figures who had in fact moved between competitive wrestling, MMA, and "pro wrestling" careers (fig. 6.2). His cinematic victory over them reasserts national superiority.

What the film needs to conjure within its depictions of the martial arts, then, are the oppositions between tradition and modernity. *Wushu* must be represented as at the same time ancient "intangible cultural heritage" and yet also modern and rational. Its paradoxical "authenticity" rides on both of these seemingly contradictory ideas at once. It is significant in this regard that Vincent Zhao was asked by Yuen Woo-ping to undertake an intensive study of breakdancing before taking up his role, to allow the creation of a fusion of "traditional" and "modern" styles, combining the whippy fluidity of *wushu* with the broken, "contemporary" rhythms of American hip-hop culture.

While in *King of Beggars* So Chan has his martial arts revealed by a magical ancestor in a dream, in *True Legend* the divine intercessor can only be framed as unreal, an effect of madness, presented as it were "under erasure," but nonetheless there, present, and effective. In this regard, we are certainly dealing with something "spectral" (and spectrally operative) in the way discussed in the early part of this chapter. We have, precisely, not the Drunken Master, but his ghost. The film's vision of the martial arts needs at once to conjure the specter of the folkish, "superstitious" irrationality that in the wake of the Boxer Rebellion gave the martial arts such a bad image in the eyes of the intellectual elite, drawing on it for its cultural power, but at the same time, as a part of the same modernizing project those early twentieth-century intellectuals had embarked on, it needs to deny and exorcise this. The film seems to suggest that, like drunkenness, the mythical or dream world of the martial arts as heritage—the world we find in *wuxia* cinema—is at once a dangerous form of psychosis, but also a nurturing and enabling spring of meaning, power, consolation, and truth without which the modernizing project cannot function.

It is the pressure of such a narrative around the nationalist *wushu* body that seems to motivate—as a kind of neurotic symptom—the split of the film into its two heterogeneous chapters, in an awkward suturing together of the temporalities of the "ancient" and the "modern" themselves, and the various film genres and styles that might suit these. However, although speaking as such a splitting does of Freudian processes of disavowal, what seems to a large degree to slip away in *True Legend* is the "hysterical" mode of allegory that the comic films of the 1970s, 1980s, and 1990s alike took up. Instead, contradiction is resolved much more clearly into straightforward propaganda.

This remains true in the most recent Beggar So film at the time of writing, *Master of the Drunken Fist: Beggar So* (dir. Guo Jianying, 2016). This was made for TV by HBO Asia, as one of two martial arts films that served as their first foray into Chinese-language production. Pitching the films primarily at a Mandarin-speaking rather than English-speaking audience and aiming to extend their presence in the PRC market—and to gain grace with the Chinese authorities who hold sway over foreign presence there—HBO aimed to avoid these films becoming an "awkward East–West mashup" by assigning Asian writers and crew to the project and aiming for "authenticity."[36] *Master of the Drunken Fist* sported a director and cast from the PRC, with Jun Cao, a popular mainland television actor, starring, and choreography by Jackie Chan's classmate Corey Yuen. Its plot reiterates—largely without the humor—the basic story of *King of Beggars.* So Chan has just become the top martial scholar in the national examinations, but his family's enemies plot against him at court and have him expelled from the Forbidden City and crippled, while his family home is burned down. So returns from tragedy with the help of the Beggar Sect, and he confronts the evil eunuch Song Fok-hai, who is attempting to take over the Imperial Court in order to dominate and exploit the country. However, although the plot resembles *King of Beggars,* all the ambivalence and contradiction of the Chow film—and its Canton-centric vision—are leached from it, in a celebration of uncomplicated martial arts, filial piety, and patriotic heroism, with the North–South themes of the earlier films resolved into a wider Han ethnic nationalism. The film's drunken boxing is performed as something resembling its standard *wushu* forms more than even *True Legend*'s play between the traditional and the contemporary, mixing in—instead of breakdance—what seem to be elements of the archetypally Chinese martial arts of *taijiquan* and *baguazhang*.

From National to Transnational

Such films, then, offer suggestive examples of the effects of the pressure of the development of national markets and audiences around Hong Kong and Chinese martial arts cinema on the legacies of the kung fu comedy, in spite of growing localist sentiment in Hong Kong. These pressures, however, are balanced by countervailing forces toward the development of transnational markets. Already the international cast of *True Legend*—and its final credits, with their reference to the global spread of *wushu* and "drunken boxing" into not a national but a worldwide phenomenon—signal this, as does the fact that *Master of the Drunken Fist* is in fact an experiment funded by the Asian arm of an American media conglomerate. It is thus also in a global rather than just a national arena that the "legacy" of the kung fu comedy might today be played out. In action cinema, the economy of scale that allows the production of high-tech cinematic spectacles that compete with Hollywood only adds further pressure toward the capture of markets beyond the national scale.

Even if it doesn't suit so well the ideological imperatives of a Chinese nation–centered martial arts cinema, within such a transnational context, kung fu comedy constitutes a recognizable national "brand" through which filmmakers can sell an identifiable product in a marketplace that often fetishizes identity, and through which the films' funders and governmental backers, often on behalf of local, regional, and national cinemas, can pursue soft power and economic advantage alike.

Perhaps the clearest example of this in terms of the continuing viability of the kung fu comedy is in the star persona of Jackie Chan, who continues (in spite of having entered his sixties) making films with a global box-office showing. As a studio executive of the American backers of his recent American-oriented film, *Skiptrace* (dir. Renny Harlin, 2016), put it, Chan is "one of the few actors who has proven ability to appeal to audiences worldwide and over and over again does not disappoint at the box office."[37]

Skiptrace was a joint endeavor between the LA-based Exclusive Media and Beijing's Talent International, approved as an official coproduction by the PRC's State Administration of Radio, Film, and Television. It followed the well-trodden buddy-movie formula of the Rush Hour series or *Shanghai Noon,* casting Chan, in his familiar role of the dutiful and straitlaced cop, alongside the usual fast-talking, anarchic American comedian, this time Johnny Knoxville. For added

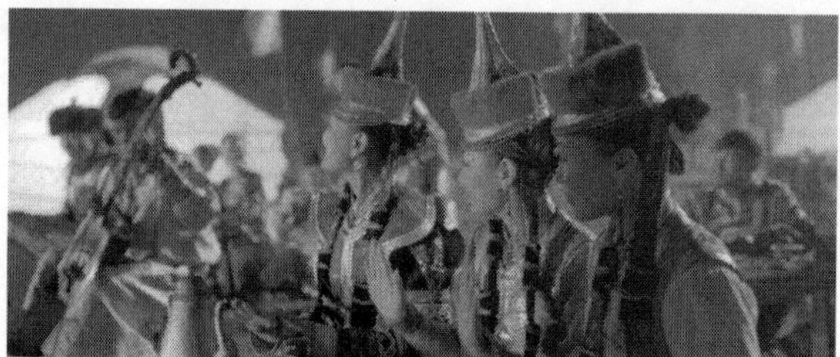

Fig. 6.3. Orientalizing images of regional minorities abound in *Skiptrace*—here an exoticized vision of Mongolian culture. Video Still. © 2015 Talent International Film / Dasym Entertainment.

appeal to the market in the PRC, Fan Bingbing (who had topped the Forbes "China Celebrity 100" list for the previous three years) was added to the cast. Backed by the Chinese authorities, the film is structured primarily as a road movie, taking the mismatched heroes across a spectacularly filmed Chinese landscape as they travel from Russia to Hong Kong.

Though to an extent relying on Orientalizing representations, presenting a parade of exotic local customs and costumes as the film moves from Mongolia to Southeast China, the film did as well at the Chinese box office as in America[38]—perhaps because the stereotyping of the film could easily be displaced into a sort of internal exoticization of the various ethnic minorities who are presented for a primitivizing urban Chinese (or Hong Kong) gaze in much the same way as they are for a Western viewer (fig. 6.3).

However, even in its success, *Skiptrace* seems to highlight some of the structural contradictions that place crossover projects such as this in jeopardy. Such projects, produced through international collaboration and in fact also often thematizing the same (as a means to integrate the different stars into a coherent narrative) are caught within the mutual gazes of the different consuming populations and their desires for self-affirmation in representation, with regard to an "other."

It is perhaps for such reasons that *Skiptrace*'s cross-cultural box-office success—and even the smooth running of its relations of commercial collaboration—were not replicated in Chan's even more recent attempt to cross the boundaries of regional or national audience, this time with an excursion into the Bollywood market, with *Kung Fu Yoga* (dir. Stanley Tong, 2017). This was significant as the first of three flagship joint productions agreed during Xi Jinping's diplomatic visit to India in 2014. In it, Chan stars alongside Sonu Sood, Disha Patani, Amyra Dastur, and Korean pop idol Lay. Chan reprises his role as an archaeologist from the Armour of God films, this time pursuing an Indian lost treasure alongside an Indian colleague.

However, the coproduction disintegrated when the Indian backer, Viacom 18, pulled out as filming was commencing, leaving the Chinese companies Taihe Entertainment and Shinework financing and managing the film.

Reflecting the Chinese origins of its script and its production, the film did unsurprisingly well when released in China.[39] However, it crashed in India, with regard to both critics' responses and audience turnout.[40] Poor attendance may well have been due to the audience's unwillingness to see themselves exoticized through the eyes of an alien culture, with Indian mythology and culture in the film ultimately serving as a spectacular backdrop for Chinese heroism. Critics complained that if the stereotypes of Indian culture in the film had been presented in a Hollywood production, the result would have been outrage.[41]

In an article in the Indian media, S. V. Srinivas argued that although regional cinemas desire to push beyond their native markets, the failure of *Kung Fu Yoga* to transfer to the Indian context, remaining an essentially Chinese film, targeted at a Chinese audience and expressing a Chinese worldview, shows the difficulties in actually making this kind of coproduction work to cross the boundaries of different cinema markets—difficulties both practical in terms of the maintenance of cross-cultural partnerships, and artistic in terms of the stories, images, filmmaking styles, and messages that can cross the divides of culture.[42] However, it also points to the internal contradictions inherent in the leveraging of cinematic culture within "soft power" national agendas, as cinema is expected to express ideas about national identity—and to market itself on the basis of these—while also appealing beyond national boundaries. Where the meeting with "otherness" seems to inevitably end up as a thematic concern as well as an outcome of the production process, the maintenance of multiple positions from which different audiences might experience the film's narrative with satisfaction remains a difficult task.

In such transnational productions, the comedic body, in all its carnival plurality, which encompasses a collectivity both in audience and production that transcends national boundaries, offers a potential movement beyond the ethnic particularity of the kung fu comedies of the late 1970s. However, if there seems in this a seed of the utopian figure of a global popular body, this remains in tension with the fact that it is the national stereotype that remains the stock-in-trade of the transnational comedy.

This chapter, then, has examined the ways that the "legacies" of the kung fu comedy, approaching the present, have been molded by a series of factors. The changing relations between Hong Kong and China have impacted in profound ways on Hong Kong film production. During the 1990s, the horizon of "reunification" provoked a new flurry of interest in martial arts cinema, in kung fu comedy, and in the Wong Fei-hung / Beggar So myth in particular, as a means to reimagine and renegotiate Hong Kong and Chinese identities. After reunification, Hong Kong film production—and its cinematic imaginary—has increasingly been absorbed within a mainland industry, drawing it back more and more to the heroic mode that was consistently associated during the twentieth century with nationalist projects. Thus, although we meet familiar characters in recent films—and even where they are made by familiar auteurs such as Yuen Woo-ping or Corey Yuen—the narrative register and mode of performance is one very different to that of the kung fu comedy in its classic stage. Rather than producing an ideological closure, however, the impetus to nationalism is also balanced by the impetus within an increasingly global film market to compete by capturing audiences on the transnational scale, drawing filmmakers into often fraught and complex international collaborations, which are shot through with the contradictions inherent to the market for national identities in our globalized, neoliberal era.

CONCLUSION

Inheritors

> What of the future? The future can only be for ghosts. And the past.
>
> —*Jacques Derrida*

The Politics of the Kung Fu Comedic Body

Throughout this book, I have been exploring the politics of the kung fu comedic body. Certainly, this task has been carried out with the aim of revalorizing a genre that is often critically dismissed. However, rather than positing these politics as unproblematically "progressive," I have attempted to draw out their complexity and contradictoriness, with the kung fu comedy marking not so much a militant discourse as a field of contestation within which politics continues to take place. Popular culture, after all, as I have understood it here, and as classically described within cultural studies, is a "compromise formation" between the interests of those who control its production and those who consume it. This contradictoriness is only exacerbated by the complex of tensions that defined Hong Kong society during (and after) the golden age of the kung fu comedy in the 1970s and 1980s. Hong Kong subjectivity, as we have met it here, was constituted within the opposing pull of forces—to name just a few of the antinomies encountered—between the experience of the colonized and the discourse of the colonizer; between simultaneous diasporic attraction and repulsion toward the ancestral land of China; between investment in tradition and desire for modernity; between desire for decolonization and fear of Cultural Revolution–era Communism; and between the pleasures of consumer society and the hardships of labor within a "sweatshop of the world."

On the positive side, the kung fu comedy's carnival, drawing precisely on the "doubleness" of consciousness inherent in the contradictory experiences just discussed, refigures a dominant order of discourse in inverted and parodic form and in terms of a utopian ontology of flux that undermines the totalitarian drive to fixity. Such carnival images of the transformable body and cosmos, I suggested, can also be read through the work of Walter Benjamin as containing an emancipatory drive beyond the alienating conditions of capitalism and colonialism. Through the combination of artisanal modes of physical performance and the industrial production of the cinematic image, kung fu comedies envision a future reconciliation of body and technology in the register of human liberation.

However, the equation of the kung fu comedy with Bakhtin's "grotesque body" should also remind us of the function of medieval European carnival in reinforcing the very order it parodies and providing a safety valve for otherwise dangerous desires. Furthermore, although the carnival qualities that typified the kung fu comedy of the 1970s are very different from the much more straitlaced martial arts cinema of today, they nonetheless seem to have fostered within their vision of a collective carnival body a more pervasive (if unstable) ethno-nationalism that is now arguably taking on an increasingly imperial rather than anticolonial appearance.

Such ambivalences also stalk representations of violence in the genre. Violence, by definition, remains at the heart of the kung fu comedy, and I have argued that it reflects the fundamental cruelty that pervades the experience of both colonial and capitalist exploitation. The genre's cinematic images of violence may involve aspects of Benjaminian "survival" for the subaltern, extending their "capacity to resist" in the face of domination. They may also be read as entailing a "positive barbarism" that refuses—and imagines a path beyond—the actually barbarous nature of a supposedly civilized bourgeois humanism and its platitudes. However, these images can also be read as normalizing the routine brutality of capitalist life. The kung fu comedy inculcates through its masochistic pleasures the resilience, flexibility, and instrumentalizing worldview demanded by capital's present-day neoliberal form. In this much, there is certainly some degree of truth in the critiques leveled at these films as being accommodated to the new socioeconomic conditions of globalization in the 1970s.

However, if the formalizing and aestheticizing aspects of the genre—its very treatment of violence as comic rather than "real"—seem trivializing in nature, it is nonetheless through these very properties that the kung fu comedy evades the sadistic closure of narrative realism, which may contribute—so Leo Bersani's analysis suggests—to destructive, fascistic historical manifestations. If this also seems to involve a "detour" from the more "revolutionary" forms of historical violence that might in a radical (if not a liberal) account be required for meaningful social change, the kung fu comedy's techniques of deferral—tarrying with the violent—may in any case make plenty of sense in unpropitious times for revolt.

The kung fu comedy, then, is far from being a "radical" phenomenon, and my argument has been that it differs profoundly in nature from the more "militant" films of the politically heady period that had preceded its appearance. Instead of what M. T. Kato has referred to, in writing about Bruce Lee, as the "popular cultural revolution,"[1] the kung fu comedy offers something much more akin to "hysterical resistance," with all the limitations that this may entail. The notion of hysteria—compliant while it resists, and paradoxically resistant even in its compliance—serves to makes sense of the continuation of "resistance" at a moment when "radical" discourse has been foreclosed, as it seemed so very much to have been in the years during which the kung fu comedy was at its height.

The Kung Fu Comedy, Then and Now

In setting out these arguments in the preceding chapters, much of my analysis has been rooted in attention to the context of production, understanding films as responses to the society from which they emerged. However, I have also attempted throughout to consider the meaning such films might bear for the present in which I am writing. There is little point, after all, in writing or reading about something without such relevance. It is to this present—and what the films might mean for me and others here and now (and elsewhere and in the future)—that I wish to turn more emphatically in these final pages. If in the last chapter I traced the "legacy" of the kung fu comedy into the present on the level of film production, it is on the level of their consumption that I wish now to discuss them. After all, audiences, too, are "inheritors" of the legacies of the kung fu comedy.

Such a conception of culture as offering (and itself already responding to) a "legacy"—with all that this implies in terms of the Nietzschean-Foucauldian genealogical processes I discussed in the introduction to this book—has been central as an organizing premise throughout this work, and central, too, to the temporality within which I have attempted to trace and analyze the kung fu comedy. It has become a critical commonplace in the wake of poststructuralism and deconstruction that culture does not have a single, "proper" destination essential to it, but is open to take on new meanings in new contexts. However, this insight is especially useful in understanding popular culture, with its "strategic ambiguity," its maximal openness to plural audiences, and the contradictions that transect it due to its nature as commodity. This is also exacerbated by the nature of contemporary media, which record and relay their content elsewhere, and in the context of the increasingly global circulations within which such media are caught up.[2] Given this openness, my interest in particular is what the legacy of these films might be for a progressive or even radical imagination.

As well as finding their place in the present, then, as the origin (or retransmitter) of tropes or themes that are taken up in new contemporary cinema, the kung fu comedies of the 1970s are thus themselves also transnationally available for viewing as never before, not only though television reruns and cinema festival screenings, but also through DVD rereleases, streaming services, and even illegal downloads, dispersing their legacy into emphatically multiple forms and across wide geographical regions. There is undeniably something problematic in a white, European author such as me, writing from within the privileged realm of academia, asserting my "inheritance" of a popular, (post-)colonial cinema from East Asia. However, this is at least ameliorated by the extent to which the kung fu comedy has become a part of an emphatically *global* popular culture—and in many ways was designed with the ambition to be so from the very start. I hope here to explore some of the ways in which such a claim may be at least a little less problematic than it first seems.

There are two primary ways that such films seem to speak to the present (and that I have at various moments evoked in my reading of them): first, in terms of the ways that they address us through shared experience and in relation to historical continuities; and second, in terms of elements of heterogeneity that they bring into the present from what already seems in many respects—some forty years on—like an alien world.

The first aspect of continuity I have drawn on throughout my analysis is the shared experience of the conditions of late capitalism. The kung fu comedy was pioneered at the very moment in which the neoliberal order of "flexible accumulation" and "globalization" was being instantiated, and in a location that was serving as one of the laboratories for the new forms of life that still fundamentally organize our world: flexible and precarious labor, consumerism, lack of political opposition, uprooted and hybrid identities, a veritable barrage of images submerging lived reality, the global circulation of culture, chronic instability and confusion, liquidity of all things. These experiences have been "rolled out" across the planet now, even in the first world. The kung fu comedy was made at a moment in which these were still new, vivid experiences, rather than striking us with the familiarity of "the way things have always been." It was also a time at which the neoliberal order still bore the nakedness and clumsiness of the prototype—and was instantiated through the bare force that could be applied only in the colony, rather than through stealth and the mediatizing power of what the Situationists termed "Spectacle."[3] All this makes the kung fu comedy, perhaps, express the experience of our world order with particular vividness and force.

The colonial context of Hong Kong might seem to mark out a difference rather than a similarity to the present and to pose the problem of why it is that culture made in such a context (which I have read as important in decoding its meanings) might resonate with the present. Applying the notion of the colonial is, at least, as Ackbar Abbas has argued, always complex in the Hong Kong context,[4] and certainly we have a very different experience here to that which was described so vividly and shockingly by, for example, Frantz Fanon.[5] It may well also have been in many ways Hong Kong's rapid transformation away from anything like the traditional colony in the late twentieth century, as it became a futuristic model of advanced globalization, that made its cinema such a source of fascination for European and American moviegoers.

However, certainly as I have presented it here, the "colonial" aspects of Hong Kong life and culture might entail as much what we share with such a place as they mark a difference. Within the discourse on martial arts cinema, M. T. Kato, for one, drawing on the work of Fredric Jameson and Arif Dirlik, argues that globalization, in any case, should be seen as the "latest stage of colonization," in which the latter reaches more intensively into culture and spreads into the heartlands of empire as well as the former colonies.[6] As Paul Gilroy has argued of the "Black Atlantic," it is in many ways on the margins of empire that modernity has been pioneered rather than at its center. Rather than constituting a primitive world separate from ours, the lives of slaves became experiments in modes of exploitation—ultimately reducing the life of the poor to an economic calculation for the elite—that were then applied in modified guise to the working classes in the heartlands of empire. Modernity, in Gilroy's model, spreads not outwards from the center, but seeps in from the margins.[7] Hong Kong's double existence as colonial outpost and hub of global trade—and its role as a pioneer of neoliberal accumulation—might alert us to the fact that this same logic was being reiterated in the late twentieth century. Just as Hong Kong's economy was being transformed, European intellectuals were starting to discuss the "colonization of everyday life" in the West. In spite of such uses of the term, colonialism, of course, involves a more nakedly brutal and direct form of domination and rule than the more consensual or ideological forms of control typical of the "advanced" West, but in the latter, too, the truth remains one of exploitation. While people remain unfree, I have argued, the astonishing utopian images of corporeal emancipation we find in the kung fu comedy will continue to reverberate with desires for liberation that are either more or less literal and physical or metaphorical and political. It is precisely the starkness of the "confinement" of colonial life that allows such haunting images to emerge with such force.

In terms of such continuity, it is ironically precisely the notorious weakness of opposition and the political conformity in Hong Kong during this period that makes the kung fu comedy most interesting for me as a case study. The West today also seems to mark a moment of the eclipse of viable radical leftist or emancipatory movements under the conformism of a culture in which, as Slavoj Žižek has remarked, it is "easier to imagine the end of the world than the end of capitalism."[8] Can cultural "opposition" survive such moments in any way? I have tried to argue that the "hysterical" register of kung fu comedy constitutes a moment when in fact it has, and in fact if there is a "legacy" that such films hand down to an impotent and apathetic audience in the twenty-first century, this is both directly in terms of the images of freedom or subversion it harbors, and also a model to consider with regards to our own contemporary culture. Certainly, this is far from being a "radical" culture of revolution or even revolt, but it is certainly one of (qualified) resistance, and also of utopian longing. The problem of what is handed down to us by it, or how we might understand this resistance as being of continued relevance, is one to which I shall return. However, I might already note here that perhaps the capacities to resist and the vision of life and identity beyond the nation-state fostered in these films during an unpropitious period for revolt played a small role in preparing the ground for the resurgence over the last decade of Hong Kong's protest movements.

The Kung Fu Comedy Then, but Not Now

In spite of continuities or resonances between the time in which the kung fu comedy was made and our own, the kung fu comedy does, however, certainly speak to us in terms of difference, too. This book emerges from my own experience of being struck by the shock and excitement of the heterologous in watching such films. It is an experience of being haunted—and thus of the ghosts that Derrida, in this chapter's epigraph, suggests inevitably haunt any future.

It furthermore emerges from a powerful nostalgia that pervades my own relation to kung fu comedies—this book is ultimately, perhaps, a work of mourning. A part of this nostalgia is personal. I was born in the early 1970s, and the kung fu comedy sprang from the historical moment in which my earliest memories were formed, binding it up for me with the mystery of my own origins. Stemming from this lost time, the kung fu comedy perhaps has a lot in common aesthetically with the most striking "postmodern" visual culture that typified the transition from the 1970s into the 1980s, such as for example Charles Moore's Piazza d'Italia in New Orleans (1978), the furniture of Memphis (founded in 1981), or April Greiman's cover for issue 20 of *WET* magazine (1979). These works, like the kung fu comedy with which they were so closely contemporary, displayed a tendency to excess and fragmentation, refusing good form, totality, or classical balance; they emphasized sensory saturation, playfulness, populism, insistence on pleasure, and an overall anarchic sensibility. Under the influence of a cultural homesickness such as my own, the present can easily seem blandly corporate, authoritarian, homogenized, and conformist in contrast to these earlier instantiations of the "cultural logic of late capitalism," displaying instead the properties of what Alan Kirby has (if in somewhat reactionary guise) typified as the "pseudo-modern."[9]

Perhaps the core difference between then and now is the extent to which the kung fu comedy and postmodernist design—though certainly both already marking the "sellout" moment in which political opposition dissolved and culture was subject to thoroughgoing integration into the economic and ideological circuits of capitalism—nonetheless still carry into themselves something of the rebellious and utopian energies of the 1960s countercultures, so still contain a spark of the utopian spirit of "modernity" within them. To the extent that they strike us with the effect of an exciting, strange image of an alien past, what they seem to present to us today is the extent to which the neoliberal order, having since become all the more efficient in its ideological work, has now closed over even such heterologous material. Discussing Hong Kong, Abbas argues that "a very efficient colonial administration . . . provides almost no outlet for political idealism."[10] The same might be said for the efficient functioning of Spectacle under the administration of the "colonization of everyday life."

However, perhaps another way of thinking about this shift between then and now—the shift that turns the kung fu comedy in the present into a heterologous image at once nostalgic and utopian—is to conceive this in terms of the changing nature of the "popular" itself. Richard Burt, for example, has proposed that culture has increasingly become "post-popular," as atomized, individualistic, and private consumption erodes the sense of a "people" to which a commodified culture addresses itself.[11] In this regard the very collectivity of the grotesque body I highlighted in earlier chapters may have been eroded, and there is something inherently odd about engaging with this carnival body from the screen of a laptop or tablet rather than in the festival atmosphere of a Kowloon cinema or a 42nd Street double bill, or even within the shared ritual of Saturday-afternoon viewing of "Black Belt Theater" on cable TV that many American fans look back on so fondly today in their comments on bulletin boards and YouTube clips. Certainly, however, it is as emphatically popular and populist that Hong Kong cinema strikes us in contrast to an increasingly globally dominant Hollywood aesthetic—as argued so persuasively by David Bordwell[12]—and the "popular" character of the kung fu comedy in particular (perhaps the apotheosis of Hong Kong popular entertainment) resides strongly in this collective "all-people's" body (as Bakhtin termed it) that remains at its heart.

The sense of the popular I have in mind here is also that which is explored in T. J. Clark's account of the Montmartre nightspots that the Impressionists loved to haunt and document. For Clark, these "painters of modern life" sought in such places the frisson of a popular culture of the songs, dance, cabaret, and fashion of the subaltern that conjured (and revolved around) an image of "the people." The nightclub or the bar presented spaces in which the collective body of such a people might be staged, and even joined. The authorities both sought to manipulate this staging of the popular for purposes of propaganda, filling the image of the people with officially sanctioned content, and also went to great lengths to guard against its unstable, potentially revolutionary potential.[13]

Rooting the notion of the popular in the figure of the "people" as I have done over the last couple of pages has also entailed drawing on the discussion of Bakhtin's "grotesque body." This, however, should already raise some questions about the notion of the popular, which is generally separated from "folk culture" by the intervention of industrialized commodity production. The Bakhtinian carnival is obviously a matter of the former, rather than the latter. What I'm suggesting in drawing Clark, Bakhtin, and Bordwell together to account for the character of the kung fu comedic body is that the "popular" of popular culture itself may involve a kind of anachronistic temporality in which folkloric elements of a popular consciousness far older than the modern are preserved within—and come to haunt, like Derrida's ghosts—a commodified cultural production that seeks both to utilize and control its material. Popular culture in this regard preserves the legacy of a counter-memory much older than itself, even as it represses it. The "heterologous" material carried into the present by the kung fu comedy may well be a matter of this more fundamental historical shift, on an altogether broader timescale than the mere transition from the 1970s to the present might suggest. To introduce such an idea is also to turn the notion of "legacy" around. We are no longer examining something that we simply inherit from a cinema initiated a few decades back, but rather something that this cinema itself inherits from a much longer cultural past, and passes on to us.

In its stories, characters, and modes of performance, the kung fu comedy draws from the long histories of popular theater, teahouse storytelling, and street performance, as well as from the narrative traditions that accompany the teaching of the martial arts themselves, filtered as these have been through late nineteenth- and early twentieth-century popular novels, newspaper serializations, radio programs, cinema, and television. If in an earlier chapter I have discussed Jackie Chan's repeated play with the chair as a prop, it is also worth considering that the two objects—still very much at the heart of the discipline of the kung fu comedian—that sit on the sparsely furnished traditional Beijing opera stage are a table and a chair, which are transformed imaginatively through performance into the variety of objects or environments that the stories' characters encounter.

Similarly, narrative content itself reaches back into this longer past. The protagonist of *Drunken Master,* Wong Fei-hung, started out as a real-life, turn-of-the-century martial artist, his legend appended to the genealogical narrative of practitioners of his style of Hung Gar boxing, before being taken up in 1930s popular "Guangdong-school" *wuxia* literature and making his way thence to film.[14] The comic and youthful form of this usually stern, patriarchal, and upright character introduced in *Drunken Master* seems to draw instead on the earlier character Fong Sai-yuk, who was also prominent within the same body of early twentieth-century Guangdong-school literature, and linked to him by martial genealogy.[15] Stretching further back into the historical past, the classics of Chinese epic literature both document and feed into a wider folkloric stock of tales, archetypes, and narrative models—with the episodes of comic characters such as, for example, Sun Wukong ("Monkey") in *Journey to the West,* Nezha in *Investiture of the Gods,* or Li Kui in *Outlaws of the Marsh* offering patterns for the tricksters of the kung fu comedies. Mark Meulenbeld has suggested that such novels played the role for Imperial-era official culture of capturing and absorbing into the canon of sanctioned worship the dangerous excesses of the cultic figures of local folk religion who stood outside this, often telling stories that have them work for a celestial hierarchy represented by the state and its liturgical forms.[16] Such an attempt at absorption—which nonetheless seems to preserve and tap the very dangerous energies that it seeks to make tame—serves as an example of the more general logic by which a culture managed by an elite treats the "low." This writes the political ambivalence of the kung fu comedy into a much longer history in which popular cultures record and manifest the dialectical tension between ruler and ruled.

Understanding the "popular" character of the kung fu comedy as stemming from what it draws into the present from such long durations of folkloric heterology opens a reading of the genre as exciting precisely because of the especially close relation Hong Kong's cultures of the martial arts have to this pre- (or extra-) capitalist realm. Hong Kong itself grew dramatically during the postwar period, with mass immigration in the face of the turbulence of modern Chinese history from a largely rural and underdeveloped Guangdong. It was such a newly proletarianized audience that Hong Kong popular culture of the time—by means of already well-developed technologies—was manufactured to serve. In doing so it was forced to play on the familiar stories and cultural forms of the colony's population, transforming them to address the new conditions and experiences of a (post)colonial, urban working class under the sway of rapid development and globalization.[17] The intervening decades have only produced an increasing distance between us and the resources of such a world.

Though formed through historical specificities, such broader experiences—both of a pre-capitalist peasantry and a colonial proletariat under conditions of globalizing capitalism—speak strongly to the shared histories of ordinary people across the planet and legitimate taking this up not in the name of an ethnonationalist subject, but rather as a heritage of a *global* popular culture. Vijay Prashad has at the very least attempted to do something similar with Bruce Lee in his book *Everybody Was Kung Fu Fighting,* which locates martial arts cinema in a shared, "polycultural" space of those on the wrong side of the histories of colonialism and globalization, stressing in the face of "the myth of cultural purity" a set of interconnections, resonances, and exchanges between African and Asian (and Afro- and Asian-American, and otherwise diasporic) cultures, which connect struggle rather than divide it.[18] Prashad's notion of polyculturalism, drawing on the work of Robin Kelley (who first coined the term), looks beyond the fixed identities of a "multiculturalism" he would like to leave behind and instead—like Nietzschean genealogy—foregrounds culture as being always complex, impure, and in process. Drawing on a vocabulary of the legacy that closely echoes Nietzsche's and Foucault's concerns, Kelley in fact argued that "so-called 'mixed-race' children are not the only ones with a claim on multiple heritages. All of us, and I mean ALL of us, are the inheritors of European, African, Native American, and even Asian pasts, even if we can't exactly trace our bloodlines to all of these continents."[19]

Within a world fundamentally structured by both the socioeconomic exploitation of neoliberalism and the racism of neocolonialism, such a polycultural experience is centrally a popular one. As Prashad puts it, "Polycuturalism exists most vividly among the poor and working class, among people who are forced to live among one another, and who ultimately work together toward freedom."[20] It is in the spirit of such arguments, rather than in the name of an implicitly white, supposedly global, undifferentiated, and universal "humanity," that I would like to wrest the kung fu comedy away from its original context and locate it in the present as a resource (however compromised) for the continuing struggle toward emancipation.

With its genealogy leading us back and beyond the modern, and a redemption that can only be properly manifested in a future that is far from inevitable, the legacy of the kung fu comedy described here may well be a matter of the "*weak* messianic power" that Walter Benjamin, in his "Theses on the Philosophy of History," suggests structures the relation between the future, the present, and the historical past.[21] In Benjamin's "Theses," this messianic power of the past is associated with a "tradition of the oppressed" that is always in opposition to the dominance of history's winners, the oppressive elites who, one after the other, seek to control the present by taking possession of the past, robbing it of the explosive power of memory. These ruling classes seek to turn culture into mere "treasure" to be paraded in a "triumphal procession in which the present victors step over those who are lying prostrate."[22]

For Benjamin, however, the folkloric culture of storytelling—which, as we have seen in earlier chapters, he sees popular cinema as extending into the present—embodies the radical aspect of his "messianic" temporal structure, inasmuch as it stores and transmits across time the experience (*Erfahrung*), the wisdom and the resources of the subjugated ("courage, humour, cunning, and fortitude"—precisely the qualities of the kung fu comedic hero), ready to provide an image that may "flash up" in a "moment of danger," filled with what Benjamin calls *Jetztzeit* (the "time of the here and now"), "blasting" open the historical continuity of the dominant order and its vision of history. Such an irruption into the present—which I am, in the register of utopian hope, associating with the heterologies of the kung fu comedy—promises (however weak the promise) in such a moment to "call into question every victory, past and present, of the rulers."[23] In "The Storyteller," Benjamin thus presents the nature of the traditionally told tale—due to an openness that it perhaps shares with popular culture more generally—as being in opposition to mere information in that it is never used up in its originary moment. It is thus capable of carrying "counsel" into the world for other times and places. Such culture, according to Benjamin, "resembles the seeds of grain which have lain for centuries in the chambers of the pyramids shut up air-tight and have retained their germinative power to this day."[24]

This, then, might be one power of resistance held within contemporary popular culture more generally. I have been wagering here that it is the true legacy handed down to us by the Drunken Master.

Notes

Introduction

Epigraph. Bakhtin, *Rabelais and His World,* 4.

1. Yip, *Martial Arts Cinema,* 109–110.

2. Sarkar, "Hong Kong Hysteria," 159–176.

3. Mandle, "Jackie Chan in Second Place." Mandle cites Grady Hendrix, a cofounder of the New York Asian Film Festival, who goes as far as to describe Chan as "the Mickey Mouse of Chinese culture, a celebrity who is so omnipresent that his name has become shorthand." The comparison between Chan and Mickey Mouse is one that I will take up later on in this book.

4. Bowman, *Theorizing Bruce Lee;* Bowman, *Beyond Bruce Lee;* Kato, *From Kung Fu to Hip Hop;* Russo, *Striking Distance.*

5. Chan has, of course, elicited a certain body of fan-oriented literature. This includes a (ghostwritten) autobiography, *I Am Jackie Chan;* Le Blanc and Odell's *Jackie Chan;* Gentry's, *Jackie Chan: Inside the Dragon;* Rovin and Tracy's, *The Essential Jackie Chan Sourcebook;* and Corcoran's *Unauthorized Jackie Chan Encyclopedia.* Though a significant body of fan literature, it does, of course, dwindle in relation to the body of work published on Bruce Lee. As of September 29, 2016, the British Library catalog lists 400 books under a keyword search for Bruce Lee, and just 31 for Jackie Chan.

6. A vivid image of the status of laughter in the longer duration of Western culture is provided in Umberto Eco's novel *The Name of the Rose,* which revolves around an attempt by the medieval church to repress the existence of Aristotle's (now lost) theory of comedy, which is feared as potentially sinful and disruptive. Laughter has often had this ambivalent status in Chinese culture, too. As Ashley Thorpe argues, though comedy was a key ingredient of the operatic stage, much of its traditional theatrical theory was concerned with keeping its excesses in check. Thorpe, *The Role of the* Chou, 77–83.

7. Teo, *Chinese Martial Arts Cinema,* 28–31.

8. For more on the Boxer Rebellion, see Esherick, *Origins of the Boxer Uprising.* For more on the impact of the Boxer Rebellion on intellectuals' attitudes to the martial arts at the start of the twentieth century, see Morris, *Marrow of the Nation,* 188–195.

9. Review of *Deep Thrust / Lady Whirlwind* (dir. Feng Huang, 1972), *Variety* (May 23, 1973), cited in Desser, "Kung Fu Craze," 23.

10. Kaminsky, "Italian Westerns," 47–68.

11. Kaminsky, "Italian Westerns," 60.

12. Desser, "Kung Fu Craze," 25.

13. See, e.g., Prashad, *Everybody Was Kung Fu Fighting;* Kato, *From Kung Fu to Hip Hop;* White, "Narrow World," 79–98.

14. See e.g., Fiske, *Reading Popular Culture,* 1–11; Storey, *Cultural Theory and Popular Culture: An Introduction,* 1–16; Hall, "Notes on Deconstructing the 'Popular,'" 442–453.

15. See, e.g., Fiske, *Reading Popular Culture,* 2.

16. See, e.g., Li, "Kung Fu," 515–542; Chan, "Bruce Lee's Fictional Modes," 371–387; Lo, "Muscles and Subjectivity," 105–125; Sarkar, "Hong Kong Hysteria," 159–176.

17. Teo, *Hong Kong Cinema,* 110–121.

18. Kato, *From Kung Fu to Hip Hop;* Prashad, *Everybody Was Kung Fu Fighting.*

19. Gateward, "Wong Fei Hung in da House," 51–67.

20. E.g., Hunt, *Kung Fu Cult Masters,* 99–116; Anderson, "Asian Martial Arts Cinema," 190–202; Bloom, "Chopsocky Slapstick"; Gallagher, "Masculinity in Translation," 23–41; Jayamanne, "Let's Miscegenate," 151–162.

21. Bordwell, *Planet Hong Kong.* Admittedly, Bordwell does discuss Jackie Chan at some length, 33–37. Bordwell, however, also lacks cultural studies' understanding of the popular as a category constituted by the commodity form, or of its historical emergence as a category in the class transformations of the modern world, as discussed by T.J. Clark in his exploration of the nineteenth-century spaces of leisure and consumption explored by the impressionists in *The Painting of Modern Life,* 205–258. As a result, he tends to make the popular a universalizing category, and so dehistoricizes it.

22. See Bordwell, *Planet Hong Kong,* esp. 4–9, 114–126.

23. Morris, "What Can a *Gwei por* Do?" 570.

24. Morris, "What Can a *Gwei por* Do?" 570.

25. Cheung, *Watershed;* Hung, "Uncertainty," 55–77.

26. In addition to Cheung, *Watershed* and Hung, "Uncertainty," cited above, for more on Hong Kong's social conditions, see Fu, "The 1960s," 73–74.

27. Hung, "Uncertainty," 58.

28. Abbas, *Hong Kong,* 5.

29. Freidman, cited in Bordwell, *Planet Hong Kong,* 19.

30. See, for example Chang Cheh's pronouncements in Chang, "Creating the Martial Arts Film," 21–22, and Chang, *Chang Cheh: A Memoir,* 87.

31. Chan "Knockabout," 149–150; Ng, "Kung Fu Comedies," 42–46.

32. Chan, "Knockabout," 149.

33. Ng, "Kung Fu Comedies," 43.

34. Lau, "Conflict and Desire," 33.

35. Hunt, *Kung Fu Cult Masters,* 102.

36. Yip, *Martial Arts Cinema,* 109.

37. Shu, "Reading the Kung Fu Film," 50.

38. Chow, *Protestant Ethnic.*

39. Chow, *Protestant Ethnic,* 47.

40. See Chow, *Protestant Ethnic,* esp. 47–49.

41. Chow's argument is also discussed, with reference to Bruce Lee, in Nitta, "Equivocal Space," 377–392; and in Bowman, *Beyond Bruce Lee,* 132–141.

42. Bordwell, *Planet Hong Kong,* 32.

43. Bordwell, "Aesthetics in Action," 73, 93.

44. Hunt, *Kung Fu Cult Masters,* 2, citing Shaviro, *The Cinematic Body,* and Williams, "Film Bodies," 140–157.

45. Shaviro, *The Cinematic Body,* 59.

46. This theme of the body as site of power's manifestation threads throughout Michel Foucault's work, from *Discipline and Punish* through to his *History of Sexuality,* and to his late work on "biopower" and "biopolitics": *Security, Territory, Population* and *The Birth of Biopolitics.*

47. Fanon, *Wretched of the Earth,* 29; White, "Narrow World," 79–98.

48. Fanon, *Wretched of the Earth,* 40.

49. White, "Toward an Aesthetic of Weightlessness," 60.

50. Leon Hunt's *Kung Fu Cult Masters,* 99–116, stands out as offering a chapter that provides a substantial and scholarly overview of the development of the genre. Teo's *Chinese Martial Arts Cinema,* 155–159, and Yip's *Martial Arts Cinema,* 109–114, both offer briefer accounts, but also provide a sense of how the comedy might fit into wider histories of Hong Kong martial arts cinema. Of note amongst more general books on Hong Kong Cinema are Stokes and Hoover's *City on Fire* and Bordwell's *Planet Hong Kong,* both of which are useful in particular in charting Jackie Chan's career. Bey Logan's *Hong Kong Action Cinema* is more fan-oriented in tone but offers an informative account of Hong Kong martial arts cinema, including extensive attention to comedies over a number of chapters. Also at the populist end of the spectrum is Hammond and Wilkins's *Sex and Zen and a Bullet in the Head,* which also offers some good overall coverage of kung fu comedy films amongst its exploration of Hong Kong's "extreme" cinema. Dannen and Long's *Hong Kong Babylon* sets out to be a "guidebook" to Hong Kong film, and offers some three hundred plot summaries for various films from 1976–1996, but this kind of work is perhaps superseded by more fully comprehensive online film databases such as hkmdb.com or hkcinemagic.com, both of which offer specialist versions of the more general, and better known, imdb.com, focusing on Hong Kong cinema. Though sites and blogs dedicated to reviewing Hong Kong or martial arts films from a fan perspective often come and go rapidly, there are also a number of these with extensive coverage, such as kungfumovieguide.com, kungfucinema.com, illuminatedlantern.com, cityonfire.com, fareastfilms.com, and many others.

51. For an introduction to this field, see Farrer and Whalen-Bridge, *Martial Arts as Embodied Knowledge,* and Bowman, *Martial Arts Studies.*

52. The core work in which these positions were elaborated is Bordwell and Carroll, *Post-Theory.*

53. Leon Hunt, in *Kung Fu Cult Masters,* 103, notes the inclusion of comic characters, for example, within the Wong Fei-hung films of the 1950s, which are often taken as pioneering the kung fu genre. The martial arts novels of Louis Cha, written under the pen name of Jin Yong between 1955 and 1972, also usually included comic elements and characters, and the young heroes, for example of his "Condor Heroes" trilogy, anticipate the cheeky and anarchic protagonists of the kung fu comedy. This comic mode was taken further and made central with Wei Xiaobao, the lovable but amoral antihero of his final novel, *Lu Ding Ji* (translated as by John Minford as *The Deer and the Cauldron*), first serialized between 1969 and 1972, in the run-up to Hong Kong cinema's own turn towards comedy. The inclusion of comedy is prominent in much of China's longer history of martial arts–related literature, as embodied, for example, in the tricksterish figure of Sun Wukong ("Monkey") in Wu Cheng'en's Ming-era classic *Journey to the West* (translated and abridged by Arthur Waley as *Monkey*), or by the

unpredictable Li Kui in Shi Nai'an and Luo Guanzhong's *Outlaws of the Marsh*. Stories such as those of Monkey and the Outlaws of the Marsh were of course mainstays of even longer traditions of popular theatrical performance, with all its inclusion of the acrobatic spectacle that forms the basis of the performance style and skills of the kung fu comedy. Commenting on the sensibility underpinning this longer theatrical and performance tradition, Colin Mackerras and Elizabeth Wichmann have proposed that "the Chinese audience has little patience with unrelieved solemnity." (See Mackerras and Wichmann, "Introduction," 2.)

54. For a summary of Badiou's ideas, see Pluth, *Badiou*, 60–65.

55. "Kung fu" itself is often imagined within such films as a kind of heritage handed down from master to student, and the often-gruelling task of learning it further allegorises the process of inheritance. Legacies are also thematised through the secret manuals and treasured weapons that often motivate plots. Above all, however, the various debts and obligations to the past—especially to parents and masters—that are often inherited as the flip side of the legacy of kung fu motivate its ubiquitous stories of revenge. It is, then, the motif of legacy, rather than revenge, that holds the real key to the kung fu film's thematics. The essay that takes this centrality of the notion of "legacy" in the kung fu genre most seriously—even if it develops this insight in a different direction from my own account—is Morris, "A Question of Legacy," 59–75.

56. Hunt, *Kung Fu Cult Masters*, 103.

57. Benjamin, *Illuminations*, 253.

58. Benjamin, *Illuminations*, 90.

59. Michel Foucault, "Nietzsche," 76–100.

60. Foucault, "Nietzsche," 79–81.

61. Foucault, "Nietzsche," 78.

62. Foucault, "Nietzsche," 81.

63. Foucault, "Nietzsche," 84.

64. For a history of the Shaw Bros. Studio, see Poshek Fu, ed. *China Forever,* and Hong Kong Film Archive, *The Shaw Screen.*

65. Shaw's aesthetically significant martial arts comedies, aside from Lau's films, include, for example, *Crippled Avengers* (dir. Chang Cheh, 1978), *Boxer from the Temple* (dir. Law Ma, 1979), *The Fighting Fool* (dir. Yuen Ho-chuen, 1980), *Kid from Kwangtung* (dir. Hsu Hsia, 1982), and *My Rebellious Son* (dir. Sun Cha, 1982).

Chapter 1: Carnival

Epigraph. Bakhtin, *Rabelais and His World,* 26.

1. Hunt, *Kung Fu Cult Masters,* 105; Gallagher, "Masculinity in Translation," 31–32.

2. For the complexity of "reading" Lee as a cultural icon, see Bowman, *Theorizing Bruce Lee* and *Beyond Bruce Lee.*

3. Teo, *Hong Kong Cinema,* 110–121. I have discussed Teo's reading in the introduction to this book.

4. See Tasker, *Spectacular Bodies.*

5. See Teo, *Hong Kong Cinema,* 113. The notion of the "sick man of East Asia" is in fact explicitly referenced in *Fist of Fury* itself, when a group of Japanese martial artists turn up at Huo Yuanjia's funeral to taunt his students and their national pride with the "gift" of a sign that, precisely, reiterates that phrase.

6. See Morris, *Marrow of the Nation.*

7. Jingwu is discussed at length in Morris, *Marrow of the Nation,* 186–203; see also Kennedy and Guo, *Jingwu.*

8. Morris, *Marrow of the Nation,* 1–10, and Joseph P. Alter's foreword to the same book, xv–xx.

9. For notions of biopolitics, see especially Michel Foucault, *Security, Territory, Population* and *The Birth of Biopolitics.*

10. Kuan-hsing Chen discusses the ambivalence of nationalist politics within the Asian context, in relation to liberation, colonialism, and imperialism, in *Asia as Method,* 82–83.

11. Bordwell, *Planet Hong Kong,* 7.

12. Mackerras and Wichmann, "Introduction," 2.

13. Ninth Hong Kong International Film Festival, *Tradition of Hong Kong Comedy,* 36, claims that around one-quarter of Cantonese films produced between 1950 and 1970 were comedies.

14. White, "Narrow World," 79–98.

15. See for example Chang Cheh in "Creating the Martial Arts Film," 21–22 and in *Chang Cheh: A Memoir,* 87.

16. Yip, *Martial Arts Cinema,* 30.

17. Anderson, *Imagined Communities,* 35. Also, see Lau, "Besides Fists and Blood," 163, where she notes that many of the TVB dramas and variety shows focused on "issues directly related to Hong Kong." Gary Ka-wai Cheung's *Hong Kong's Watershed,* 5–6, also proposes that this was a moment in which the government—in response to unrest—increasingly promoted the development of a sense of civic community and identity, and saw an important role for the media within this.

18. Teo, in "The 1970s," 95, notes that they were drawn in particular from the enormously popular variety show *Enjoy Yourself Tonight.*

19. My argument regarding the positioning of the audience by the film's address is made slightly more complex when we take the history of its script into account. The story is originally drawn from a well-known 1945 stage play—which had recently been rerun successfully in Hong Kong—set (like *Fist of Fury*) in Shanghai, and this fact would probably have been known to the audience. However, the play had also already been adapted within Cantonese cinema in a version by Wang Wei-yi in 1963, and the remake may have carried nostalgia for this cinematic moment with its more clearly local address, before the dominance of Mandarin filmmaking. In such a context, perhaps, Chor's decision to relocate the story may only serve the more to signal to its audience an embrace of a specifically Hong Kong identity. See Fang, *Arresting Cinemas,* p. 172, notes 20–21.

20. See Linda Lai Chiu-han, "Film and Enigmatization," 232.

21. Lau, "Beyond Fists and Blood," 165–166. Teo (in "The 1970s," 96) notes that it was Michael Hui's directorial debut for Golden Harvest, *Games Gamblers Play* (1974), that broke *House of 72 Tenants'* box office record, and Lau, 165, notes that in fact this film took in over three times as much as its nearest competitor that year.

22. Teo, "The 1970s," 96.

23. hkmdb.com lists him as the stunt director for *Games Gamblers Play* (1974) and *The Private Eyes* (1976). A number of the Hui brothers' films are not listed here with credited action directors, though there are certainly some brilliant sequences of choreography within them.

24. See Lau, "Beyond Fists and Blood," 167.

25. Lau, "Beyond Fists and Blood," 159.

26. Lau himself claimed the film as a "first" for the genre in an interview with *Cahiers du cinéma*. See Assayas and Tesson, "Interview."

27. See Hong Kong Cinemagic's biography of Fung Hak On, http://www.hkcinemagic.com/en/people.asp?id=797 (accessed November 2016).

28. One episode recounted in Jackie Chan's autobiography *I Am Jackie Chan*, 221, implies that, factoring in Southeast Asian markets, *Snake* at one point looked like it made more money for its producers than any of Bruce Lee's films had. However, even if Chan's account is not entirely reliable—the Hong Kong Film Archive database cites a box-office take for *Snake in the Eagle's Shadow* of HK$2,708,748, as compared with HK$4,431,423 for *Fist of Fury*—*Snake* was nonetheless a substantial hit. *Fist of Fury* was outperformed in any case by *Drunken Master*, which quickly reunited much of the cast of *Snake* in order to exploit its obviously winning formula, and was rewarded with an astonishing HK$6,763,793 box-office take.

29. See Chan, *I Am Jackie Chan*, 200–225.

30. Yuen, according to his son, was in fact a pivotal influence in transforming the fight choreography of both Cantonese opera and Hong Kong cinema, brought in from the more sophisticated Beijing schools of fight performance. Yuen, as both a martial artist and an opera performer, worked in particular on the Wong Fei-hung series of films that in their approach to depictions of stylistically "authentic" empty handed fighting paved the way for the "kung fu" genre of the 1970s. See Burr, "Kungfu Genius." Simon Yuen and his family also seem to have already had a close relationship with Yu Jim-yuen's opera school, with Woo-ping at one point attending as a day student. Jackie Chan's autobiography also remarks on Simon Yuen as having at one point been a martial arts instructor there (Chan, *I Am Jackie Chan*, 220). For more on Yuen's career as a fight choreographer, see also Yung, "Moving Body," 21–34.

31. Lo, "Muscles and Subjectivity," 115–126.

32. This gag is repeated, for example, in *Of Cooks and Kung Fu* (1979).

33. Becoming iconic in the role—and to martial arts movie fans synonymous with it—Simon Yuen plays this same basic character, or some variant of him, in *Snake in the Eagle's Shadow* (1978), *Drunken Master* (1978), *Story of Drunken Master* (1979), *The Mystery of Chessboxing* (1979), *Drunken Arts and Crippled Fist* (1979), *Sleeping Fist* (1979), and *Dance of the Drunk Mantis* (1979). Yuen was also lined up to reprise the role yet again in *Magnificent Butcher* (1979), but died during the early stages of filming and was replaced by stalwart martial arts character actor Fan Mei Sheng. Fan Mei Sheng continued to act in similar roles in, for example, *36 Deadly Styles* (1979), *The Buddhist Fist* (1980), and *Hitman in the Hand of Buddha* (1981).

34. See for example Lau Tai-muk, "Conflict and Desire," 32. Describing the impression we get from Lee's films, Lau writes, "The kung fu of Bruce Lee has not been improved through the exercises but are demonstrations of a perfect body."

35. *Enter the Fat Dragon*, dir. Sammo Hung, 1978.

36. Abbas, *Hong Kong*, 5.

37. Chan, "Knockabout," 149, cited in Hunt, *Kung Fu Cult Masters*, 102.

38. Bakhtin, *Rabelais*, 10.

39. Bakhtin, *Rabelais*, 9.

40. Bakhtin, *Rabelais*, 21.

41. However, it's worth noting that the medieval carnival was also strongly interested in sex in a way that remains largely repressed or ignored in Hong Kong kung fu comedies, which, if liberal in their treatment of the body's digestive processes, remain somewhat sexually puritan.

42. Bakhtin, *Rabelais*, 49.

43. For a set of applications of ideas of the Bakhtinian carnivalesque to reading a dizzying array of film texts, see, for example, Stam, *Subversive Pleasures*, 108–121. Stallybrass and White also track the rapid rise of the notion of carnival in theoretical writing in *Politics and Poetics*, 6–7.

44. Stallybrass and White, *Politics and Poetics*, 13–14.

45. Stam, *Subversive Pleasures*, 96.

46. Bakhtin, *Rabelais*, 7.

47. See, for example, Leon Hunt's descriptions of participatory crowds at London double bills vocally cheering or deriding the "wicked shapes" of screen stars (Hunt, *Kung-fu Cult Masters*, 28), or the often-riotous reception of films in Hong Kong described by Kato in *From Kung Fu to Hip Hop*, 12–13. In such cases, there was certainly slippage of the carnival atmosphere from one side of the screen to another. This slippage is also evidenced in the adoption of the most spectacular martial arts moves into breakdancing repertoires—see Gateward, "Wong Fei Hung," 51–67.

48. See Wills, "Upsetting the Public," 131.

49. Stam, *Subversive Pleasures*, 96.

50. Stallybrass and White, *Politics and Poetics*, 14.

51. Stallybrass and White, *Politics and Poetics*, 19, 53–57.

52. Stallybrass and White, *Politics and Poetics*, 10.

53. Stallybrass and White, *Politics and Poetics*, 6.

54. For more on the history of its publication, see for example Holquist, *Dialogism*, xxv.

55. See, for example, Ken Hirschkop, "Introduction," 34; Stam, *Subversive Pleasures*, 158; Stallybrass and White, *Politics and Poetics*, 11; Terry Eagleton, *Walter Benjamin*, 144.

56. Stallybrass and White, *Politics and Poetics*, 7.

57. See Deleuze, "Postscript," 3–7. Deleuze argues that the strict regimen of the factory was, for example, being replaced by the open structure of the corporation, where casualized work becomes a kind of an obligatory pleasure, and where we are managed, tracked, and controlled not through prohibition, but precisely through the calculability of our desires.

58. See, for example, Brian Massumi's interpretation of the logic of Deleuze and Guattari's Capitalism and Schizophrenia books, which he applies to contemporary capitalism, noting that it creates "deterritorializations" of desire in order to provide the dynamism required for a capitalist society, but also sets necessary limits to these deterritorializations, in that it needs to ensure the social order that facilitates the orderly accumulation of capital from them—and so still requires the "reterritorialization" of these desires to produce a named, legally accountable, Oedipalized individual who is accountable for debts and turns up to work at the appropriate time. Massumi, *User's Guide*, 136.

59. See Yip, *Martial Arts Cinema*, 24, 31, 52–55.

60. Bakhtin, *Rabelais*, 32.

61. Bakhtin, *Rabelais*, 32.

62. Bakhtin, Rabelais, 29.

63. Stam, *Subversive Pleasures*, 159.

64. See, respectively, *Drunken Master* (dir. Yuen Woo-ping, 1978), *Drunken Arts and Crippled Fist* (dir. Tang Ti, 1979), *Dance of the Drunk Mantis* (dir. Yuen Woo-ping, 1979).

65. For Western critics' contemptuous response to the first widespread release of Hong Kong martial arts cinema, see Desser, "Kung Fu Craze," 23.

66. Thompson, "Concept of Cinematic Excess," 54.

67. Heath, "Film and System," 10.

68. I draw the term—loosely—from Gilles Deleuze and Félix Guattari, and their discussion of "becoming-animal," which is articulated primarily in *A Thousand Plateaus,* 232–309. The details of this well-known theoretical concept are, however, largely irrelevant to my use. Perhaps, however, it is worth noting that for Deleuze and Guattari, "becoming" something is not literal: it doesn't so much involve an imitation of that thing, or a straightforward transformation into it. Rather, in such becomings the becomer enters into a new relationship with the thing it "becomes," ultimately blurring boundaries between the two. Deleuze and Guattari note that though the animal one becomes is not real, the "becoming" instantiated and its transformative effects certainly are (238–239).

69. Hunt, *Kung Fu Cult Masters,* 104.

70. Marx and Engels, *Manifesto.*

71. See Stallybrass and White, *Politics and Poetics,* 11. However, it's also worth noting that the most successful and most-discussed of these, including Roberto DaMatta's *Carnivals, Rogues and Heroes,* are often also based in Latin American cultures where a direct link of descent from European carnival traditions can also be traced. For more on DaMatta and Brazilian postcolonial critique through the carnivalesque, see Robert Stam, *Subversive Pleasures,* 122–156.

72. Stam, *Subversive Pleasures,* 123.

73. For an extended treatment of the character of Wong Fei-hung, see Po and Lau, *Mastering Virtue.*

74. Hunt, *Kung Fu Cult Masters,* 111.

75. Lo, "Muscles and Subjectivity," 115–126.

76. Bakhtin, *Rabelais,* 19.

77. Liu, *Stateless Subjects.*

Chapter 2: Utopia

Epigraph. Benjamin, "Work of Art [Second Version]," 37.

1. Logan, *Hong Kong Action Cinema,* 81.

2. See, for example, Duncan, "Traditional Thing," 353–367; Teo, *Hong Kong Cinema,* 127; Lo, *Chinese Face/Off,* 96; Stokes and Hoover, *City on Fire,* 122; Gallagher, "Masculinity in Translation," 30; Maslin, "Kicks, Swivels and Wisecracks"; Logan, *Hong Kong Action Cinema,* 67.

3. See, for example, Strauss, "Faster Than a Speeding Bullet."

4. For a discussion of the biographical factors that may have drawn Chan to the work of performers like Keaton or Chaplin, see Duncan, "The Traditional Thing."

5. The essay is available in its original German text in Benjamin, *Gesammelte Schriften,* vol. 6, 144–145, and in English translation as "On Mickey Mouse" in Kaes, Baer and Cowan, *The Promise of Cinema,* 403.

6. See, for example, Ward, *Mouse Morality;* Wasko, *Understanding Disney;* Byrne and McQuillan, *Deconstructing Disney.*

7. Leslie, *Hollywood Flatlands,* 80.

8. Benjamin, "On Mickey Mouse," 403.

9. Leslie, *Hollywood Flatlands,* 81.

10. Benjamin, "On Mickey Mouse," 403.

11. Benjamin, "On Mickey Mouse," 403.

12. Benjamin, *Illuminations,* 83–84, 156–162, 170–173.

13. See, for example, the analyses in Clayton, *The Body in Hollywood Slapstick,* 91–102. Clayton (25) cites James Agee's description of Keaton in a 1948 *Life* magazine article, which discusses the "sudden, machine-like angles" of Keaton's body, his "semaphore-like" arms, his "piston-like sprint," and his physical control as smooth as an "automatic gear shift."

14. Benjamin, "Experience and Poverty," 734–735.

15. The notion of "flexible accumulation" was most famously and influentially discussed in Jameson's *Postmodernism.*

16. In the last chapter, I noted briefly how the Hui Brothers films—providing the blueprint for the kung fu comedy—often depict these conditions of Hong Kong society in a more obviously serious and satirical manner. During the opening credits of *Private Eyes,* for example, we see Sam Hui quitting his job on a Chaplinesque production line in a bottling factory to pursue the glamorous life of a detective. The lyrics of the theme tune—sung by Sam Hui himself, who was a highly successful rock star as well as an actor—also refer to the dog-eat-dog world of the contemporary Hong Kong economy and the demeaning nature of factory work. In the Hui Brothers films, the alternative to such a world of work is participating in a tricky entrepreneurialism at the margins of the Hong Kong business world, with the films generally celebrating (as well as ridiculing) the basically hopeless efforts of a series of chancers to "make it big" within a system that stacks all the odds of privilege, wealth, and power against them. Set implicitly against the background of poorly paid work that offers little in terms of a "future" aside from the struggle to survive, such entrepreneurialism offers a critical image of the harsh capitalism of the day. Such tricksters, living on their wits, are often to be found projected into the peasant past in the kung fu comedy—they are especially clear, for example, in *Knockabout* (dir. Sammo Hung, 1979) or *Dirty Tiger, Crazy Frog!* (dir. Karl Maka, 1978), but they also, in many ways, inform the character of the drunken master himself, who drifts on the edge of society, surviving on his wile and his "tricky" kung fu . . .

17. Yip, *Martial Arts Cinema,* 24.

18. Yip, *Martial Arts Cinema,* 31.

19. Although labour is a theme to some extent avoided, Chien Fu is far from an outlying character in the kung fu comedy. For example, Leung Kar-yan's character, Ah Chi, in *Thundering Mantis* (dir. Yeh Yung-Cha, 1980), is an assistant to a fish seller; in *Dreadnaught* (dir. Yuen Woo-ping, 1981), "Mousy" (Yuen Biao) struggles to collect money for his sister's laundry business; in *Shaolin Rescuers* (dir. Chang Cheh, 1979) Chun Ah-chin and Ying Cha-po are a bean curd seller and a waiter, respectively, who dream of lives of heroism beyond the drudgery of their menial jobs.

20. Within accounts of Jackie Chan's life, often presented by Chan himself as well as by critics as the source for his depictions of martial arts training, it is often noted that he was in fact signed over contractually by his parents to the Beijing opera school where he learned his physical art, with a contract that legitimated his master disciplining him even to the point of death. The films thus have at their root a literal experience of having one's body and even one's life made into another's property. See Chan, *I Am Jackie Chan,* e.g. 1–2, 28–29.

21. Yip, *Martial Arts Cinema,* 31, 54.

22. This is, of course, precisely, the shift from the "disciplinary society" of Foucault to the Deleuzian "society of control" mentioned in the last chapter.

23. Chan's Cantonese stage name is Sing Lung—literally "Becoming Dragon."

24. The cycle of films, discussed in further length in Chapter 5, includes *Miracle Fighters* (dir. Yuen Woo-ping, 1982), *Shaolin Drunkard* (dir. Yuen Woo-ping, 1983), *Taoism Drunkard* (dir. Yuen Cheung-yan, 1984), and *Young Taoism Fighter* (dir. Chen Chi-hwa, 1986).

25. Benjamin, "Work of Art [First Version]," 30–31.

26. See Benjamin "Work of Art [Second Version]," 26–27.

27. Benjamin, "Work of Art [Second Version]," 26.

28. Benjamin, "Work of Art [Second Version]," 41–42.

29. Hansen, "Benjamin and Cinema: Not a One-way Street," 51–52.

30. Hansen, "Benjamin and Cinema: Not a One-way Street," 53.

31. Kennedy and Guo, *Chinese Martial Arts Training Manuals,* 34–60.

32. Abbas, *Hong Kong,* 3–4.

33. Clayton, *The Body in Hollywood Slapstick,* 32–33.

34. See Leslie, *Hollywood Flatlands,* 119.

35. Benjamin, "Experience and Poverty," 735.

36. Fanon, *Wretched of the Earth,* 29. See also my discussion of Fanon in the introduction to this book.

37. The overcrowded conditions of the colony are described vividly in Yip, *Martial Arts Cinema,* 59–60.

38. *Rediff India Abroad,* "What Scares Jackie," citing an interview with Chan on the television show *Rendezvous with Simi Garewal,* September 3, 2006.

Chapter 3: Violence

Epigraph. Kaminsky, "Italian Westerns," 60.

1. Kaminsky, "Italian Westerns," 67.

2. See Kendrick, *Film Violence,* 1–4; 21–24.

3. *Variety* (May 23, 1973), cited in David Desser, "The Kung Fu Craze," 23. Desser goes on to note how not only critics, but studios themselves—as reflected in their marketing strategies and the geographical patterns of cinematic release—assumed a primarily lower-class and African American audience as the main targets of their sensationalizing campaigns around the films.

4. Benjamin, "On Mickey Mouse," 403.

5. Benjamin, "On Mickey Mouse," 403.

6. Benjamin, "Experience and Poverty," 731–736.

7. Benjamin, "These Surfaces for Rent," 173.

8. Clayton, *The Body in Hollywood Slapstick,* 12.

9. Kaminsky, "Italian Westerns," 57.

10. Kaminsky, "Italian Westerns," 61.

11. Kaminsky, "Italian Westerns," 59.

12. Hunt, *Kung Fu Cult Masters,* 111.

13. Yip, *Martial Arts Cinema,* 110.

14. Thorpe, *The Role of the* Chou, see esp. 138–140, 209–246. Meulenbeld, in *Demonic Warfare,* has similarly discussed how, in the Ming-era novel and in the liturgical practices it draws on, dangerous martial deities or spirits who embody forces of potential disruption are symbolically drawn into a canon and hierarchy, making them "safe" and even useful.

15. Thorpe, *The Role of the* Chou, 5.

16. Benjamin "Work of Art [First Version]," 31. This might chime with Man-fung Yip's exploration of the René Girard's notion of "sacrificial violence" in martial arts cinema. Yip, *Martial Arts Cinema*, 37.

17. See Leslie, *Hollywood Flatlands*, 116.

18. Leslie, *Hollywood Flatlands*, 118.

19. Benjamin, "Work of Art [Second Version]," 51–52.

20. Adorno and Horkheimer, *Dialectic of Enlightenment*, 138.

21. Leslie, *Hollywood Flatlands*, 138.

22. See Hunt's taxonomy of forms of "authenticity" in kung fu cinema in *Kung Fu Cult Masters*, 21–47.

23. Chan, *I Am Jackie Chan*, esp. 34–57.

24. Hunt, *Kung Fu Cult Masters*, 29–41.

25. For example, *Just for Kicks: The Making of the Karate Kid* (2010); *The Karate Kid: Production Diaries* (2010); *Jackie Chan: Stunt Master and Mentor* (2010); *Making of Forbidden Kingdom* (2009); *Making Rush Hour 3* (2007); *Jackie Chan: The Inside Story* (2004); *Jackie Chan: My Stunts* (1999); *A Piece of the Action: Behind the Scenes in Rush Hour* (1999); *Jackie Chan: My Story* (1998); *The Making of Jackie Chan's Mr Nice Guy* (1997).

26. Neocleous, "Resisting Resilience," 2–7.

27. Caygill, "Also Sprach Zapata," 22 (Caygill's emphasis).

28. Caygill, "Also Sprach Zapata," 23–24.

29. I draw this particular use of the notion of "antinomy" from Battersby, *The Sublime*, 136–137. Battersby draws her definition, in turn, from Kant, who defines antinomy as involving equally rational but nonetheless opposing positions on the nature of reality that seem to offer us irresolvable contradiction, but only until we grasp that the very conditions we assume to be transcendental to the self are a product of the subject itself. Exploring "antinomies of the female," Battersby treats Kant's subject in a less abstract, more historicized manner in order to interrogate what particular (seemingly) irresolvable contradictions stem from the condition of being a "woman" in contemporary society, and the ways that such contradictoriness lodges itself within the embodied experience and cultural expression of twentieth-century women artists. In a similar move, I wish here to posit "antinomies of (capitalist) modernity," which register the ways that the contradictions of capitalism lodge themselves at the heart of the modern subject and of modern culture. Such antinomies cannot be resolved within capitalist modernity itself as they are structural to it.

30. See Kendrick, *Film Violence*, 7. Kendrick argues it is problematic to think of cinematic violence as a coherent object of study, and the notion of "violence" can too easily gather together things that may well be quite heterogeneous. By obscuring the difference between these it may serve to confound rather than clarify.

31. White, "Narrow World," 79–98.

32. See, for example, Gateward, "Wong Fei Hung," 51–67; Prashad, 126–149; Kato, *From Kung Fu to Hip Hop*.

33. White, "Narrow World," 82–83.

34. See, for example, Phillips, *Possible Origins;* Bowman, *Martial Arts Studies*, 109–135.

35. Donald Westlake, for example, puts it: "Jackie Chan is Fred Astaire and the world is Ginger Rogers." Cited in Corliss, "Go West, Hong Kong," 67.

36. Chan, in interview on the *Jackie-Chan-a-thon* presented on the Chicago Turner Network Television station, Oct 9–11, 1998, cited in Anderson, "Asian Martial Arts Cinema," 192. Chan also discusses the importance of this aestheticization to him in *I Am Jackie Chan*, 302.

37. Excellent examples of this style are in *Dirty Tiger, Crazy Frog!* (dir. Karl Maka, 1978) and *The Magnificent Butcher* (dir. Yuen Woo-ping, 1979).

38. Bersani, *Freudian Body,* 54–78.

39. Bersani, *Freudian Body,* 70.

40. Bersani, *Freudian Body,* 67–68.

41. Bersani, *Freudian Body,* 68–70.

42. Bersani, *Freudian Body,* 54. Bersani's emphasis.

43. For more on the ways that Western narrative conventions are frequently undermined in Hong Kong martial arts cinema, see, for example, Bordwell, *Planet Hong Kong,* 114–126.

44. Benjamin, *Illuminations,* 234–235. Philippe Lacoue-Labarthe has extended Benjamin's analysis in *Heidegger, Art and Politics,* 61–76.

45. Fanon, *Wretched of the Earth,* 44.

Chapter 4: Hysteria

Epigraph. Gentry, *Jackie Chan,* 22–23.
Epigraph. George Sand, cited in Bronfen, *Knotted Subject,* 139.

1. White, *Carnival, Hysteria, and Writing.*

2. White, "Hysteria and the End of Carnival," 157.

3. White, "Hysteria and the End of Carnival," 159.

4. For a parallel, see Fredric Jameson's use of schizophrenia as a metaphor for postmodern culture, which, rather than offering a "culture-personality diagnosis," offers a "suggestive aesthetic model." Jameson, *Postmodernism,* 26.

5. Cited in Bronfen, *Knotted Subject,* 174.

6. Wajeman, "The Hysteric's Discourse," 11, cited in Bronfen, *Knotted Subject,* 204.

7. Gentry, *Jackie Chan,* 23.

8. The choice to make a film centering around the style of "drunken boxing" is perhaps also significant here—drunken boxing depends precisely on the appearance of loss of control, on the qualities of hysteria.

9. Bordwell, "Aesthetics in Action," 93. This is discussed further in my introduction to this book.

10. Micale, *Approaching,* 200; Borossa, *Hysteria,* 3.

11. Bronfen, *Knotted Subject,* 105–106. Julia Borossa discusses Plato's discussion of the same understanding in his *Timaeus.* Borossa, *Hysteria,* 10.

12. Bronfen, *Knotted Subject,* 106; Borossa, *Hysteria,* 11.

13. See Bronfen, *Knotted Subject,* 108–114.

14. Borossa, *Hysteria,* 16–18.

15. Borossa, *Hysteria,* 6.

16. Bronfen, *Knotted Subject,* xii. Bronfen argues Freud was too quick to reject a traumatic etiology of the symptoms of his hysteric patients and to affirm their origin in sexual fantasy. For Bronfen, underpinning any such sexual content of the hysteric's fantasies is an anxiety about mortality, corporeal vulnerability and mutability, and the inability to know or master reality. Bronfen, *Knotted Subject,* xii–xiii. Considering the application of a concept of hysteria to the martial arts comedy, and the extent to which death, physical vulnerability, and fantasies of mastery are at stake in these, Bronfen's arguments seem useful, and I return to them in Chapter 5.

17. Two prominent counter-examples to medicine's rejection of the term from the recent psychological literature are Bollas, *Hysteria* and Mitchell, *Mad Men and Medusas.* Showalter's *Hystories* has also been influential in making the term current again. These examples appeared in tandem with a wider interest within feminist discourse since the 1970s in reassessing the nature of the highly gendered notion of hysteria, and in reappropriating and revalorizing the image of the hysteric.

18. For the gendering of the term, it's worth considering, for example, the invention of the disease of "shell shock," introduced during the First World War. The symptoms that the soldiers presented were often in line with those of hysteria, but the new name avoided feminizing them and afforded their trauma a seriousness and reality that was denied in women "hysterics." See Borossa, *Hysteria*, 59–61.

19. Borossa, *Hysteria*, 20; Didi-Huberman, *Invention of Hysteria.*

20. See for example Borossa's accounts of Freud's and Breuer's complex tussles with their patients, and a number of feminist responses to these, in Borossa, *Hysteria*, 34–50.

21. Borossa discusses the example of "Anna O." one of Freud's and Breuer's case studies, in their *Studies on Hysteria* (1895) whose real name was Bertha Pappenheim. Pappenheim went on to become a pioneering figure in the women's movement—but only after her "cure," and Borossa argues that it was only leaving behind "hysteria" that allowed her to become a strong, independent-minded activist. Borossa, *Hysteria*, 51.

22. See Bronfen, *Knotted Subject*, 182–183.

23. See for example Gallop, *The Daughter's Seduction*, 132–150.

24. Borossa, *Hysteria*, 38.

25. Hélène Cixous, in *La jeune née*, cited in Jane Gallup *The Daughter's Seduction*, 135, 134.

26. Smith-Rosenberg, *Disorderly Conduct*, 208.

27. Borossa, *Hysteria*, 7.

28. Hélène Cixous, *La jeune née*, cited in Jane Gallup, *The Daughter's Seduction*, 133.

29. Cheung, *Hong Kong's Watershed*, 5–6, 137–139.

30. Abbas, *Hong Kong*, 4–5.

31. For an analysis of Chang Cheh's film *The Assassin* (1967) in terms of a desire for historical agency and subjecthood see White, "Narrow World."

32. Sarkar, "Hong Kong Hysteria," 159–162.

33. The conflation of schizophrenia and hysteria seems a conscious tactic in Sarkar's essay. He draws the notion of postmodern schizophrenia from Jameson's essay on "the cultural logic of late capitalism" (Jameson, *Postmodernism*, 26), along with Baudrillard's proposal that under the spell of the postmodern, "alienation" and "repression," and hence the ground of hysteria, have been replaced by an absolute presence that produces instead the schizophrenic overload of the "ecstasy of communication" (Baudrillard, "Ecstasy of Communication," 130–131, cited in Sarkar, "Hong Kong Hysteria," 172–173). However, Sarkar questions the extent that the new schizophrenic collapse of reality into the present entails the end of alienation, and hence gives an account of postmodern, postcolonial conditions in which schizophrenic and hysterical formations seem to bleed into one another.

34. Baudrillard, "Ecstasy of Communication," 132, cited in Sarkar, "Hong Kong Hysteria," 173.

35. Sarkar, "Hong Kong Hysteria," 160, 170.

36. Sarkar, "Hong Kong Hysteria," 160.

37. Sarkar, "Hong Kong Hysteria," 159–160. For Sarkar such a notion of the shared "transnational Asian" condition explains the regional popularity of Hong Kong film, and it also explains, for example, a series of parallels with the "masala" films of the Mumbai cinema industry. Sarkar, "Hong Kong Hysteria," 163–164.

38. This wider relevance of the term signals a relation to the absurdist, nonsense comedy pioneered by the Hui Brothers, which fed into the kung fu genre and also saw its successor in the *mo lei tau* comedy of Stephen Chow. Chow's comedy—typified by nonsensical parody, a wild and jumbled profusion of intertextual references, deliberate anachronism, sudden juxtapositions, and surprises in both dialogue and action—is as fractured and hyped up as the 1990s swordplay genre, which it rose alongside. The term *mo lei tau* itself—usually translated as "makes no sense"—is a shortening of the phrase *mo lei tau gau*, which would be more literally translated as "can't tell head from tail"—an image of carnival inversion. The emphasis on the lower body would only be emphasized by the retention of the word *gau*, which is usually omitted from the phrase because it sounds too much like a vulgar Cantonese term for penis. The bodily imagery of the genre name signals the extent to which hysterical symptoms may be at stake.

39. Bronfen defines hysteria as a "somatic voicing of traces of a psychically traumatic impact—be this sexual or melancholic—whose origin is unknown or repressed. . . . Body symptoms *stand in for* a disorder that cannot be located in the body." Bronfen, *Knotted Subject*, 117 (Bronfen's emphasis).

40. Bronfen, *Knotted Subject*, 180–181.

41. Bronfen, *Knotted Subject*, 181.

42. The fit-like quality of movement is extended even further in the final confrontation in *Thundering Mantis*, discussed in Chapter 3.

43. The Police Story films are: *Police Story* (dir. Jackie Chan, 1985), *Police Story, Part II* (dir. Jackie Chan, 1988), *Police Story III: Supercop* (dir. Stanley Tong, 1992), and *Police Story IV: First Strike* (dir. Stanley Tong, 1996). Chan's dutiful cop roles in the Lucky Stars series are in *Winners and Sinners* (dir. Sammo Hung, 1983), *My Lucky Stars* (dir. Sammo Hung, 1985), and *Twinkle, Twinkle Lucky Stars* (dir. Sammo Hung, 1987).

44. Žižek, "Symptom," 424, cited in Bronfen, *Knotted Subject*, 151.

45. Žižek. "Symptom," 425, cited in Bronfen, *Knotted Subject*, 151.

46. White, "Hysteria and the End of Carnival," 157–158.

47. White, "Hysteria and the End of Carnival," 158.

48. White, "Hysteria and the End of Carnival," 164.

49. In fact, in Chan's other best-known Hollywood-made films, *Shanghai Noon* (dir. Tom Dey, 2000) and *Shanghai Knights* (dir. David Dobkin, 2003), he reprieves a very similar role, projected back into the past where instead of a cop he is an Imperial Guard.

50. Mark Gallagher, "Masculinity in Translation," 23–41.

51. Gallagher, "Masculinity in Translation," 29–31.

52. Gallagher, "Masculinity in Translation," 35–41.

53. Smith, *Clint Eastwood*, 173–180.

54. See Lo, *Excess and Masculinity*, 83–84. In making his argument about women warriors, Lo is drawing on Halberstam's account of the "female masculinity" that emerges in certain lesbian subcultures. In turn, the key reference point with regard to gender being "performed" rather than simply given by biology is Butler, *Gender Trouble*.

55. Lo, *Excess and Masculinity*, 96.

56. Lo, *Excess and Masculinity*, 100.

57. Within Lo's terms, women, too, are of course not excluded from such a pleasure of identification. Within Lo's account, masculinity, like the phallus, functions in our society as a position of power, so its possession is desirable. To achieve masculinity—whether one is a man or a woman—is to achieve a position of social power and self-valorization. A part of the pleasure of female audiences, too, in watching action films, comes from taking up the position of the "male gaze," and from identification with the male hero, bearer of phallic power. To some extent, the "achievement" of masculinity is also a task for women in our society, though one taken up in less favorable terms and made complicated by society's counterposing demands for "femininity." The logic of Lo's argument would seem to suggest that women kung fu stars and heroes from ethnic minorities alike perhaps speak especially strongly to a female audience.

58. Lo, *Excess and Masculinity*, 109.

59. Lo, *Excess and Masculinity*, 83–84.

60. Lo, *Excess and Masculinity*, 89.

61. Lo, *Excess and Masculinity*, 99–100.

Chapter 5: Masculinity

Epigraph. Bronfen, *Knotted Subject*, 188, citing Micale, "Charcot and the Idea," 406.

1. Bronfen, *Knotted Subject*, 158.
2. Yip, *Martial Arts Cinema*, 24.
3. Bronfen, *Knotted Subject*, xiii.
4. Bronfen, *Knotted Subject*, 156–157. For this notion of "encryption," Bronfen draws on Abraham and Torok, *The Shell and the Kernel*.
5. Lacan, cited in Bronfen, *Knotted Subject*, 204.
6. *Who Am I?* (dir. Jackie Chan and Benny Chan, 1998).
7. It is a search in which it is not only the individual's identity that is uncertain and obscure, but the very texture of the social and economic reality in which they exist. In *Who Am I?* "Jackie's" identity is already obscured from the outset in a transnational military special ops unit, where troops are asked to forget their past and referred to by a number rather than a name. As the film unfolds it becomes clear that whom the unit actually worked for and what interests they served was never known to them. As in other paranoid-identity-loss movies, it is not only Whoami whose identity is unclear—the pretty "journalist" he meets turns out to be spying on him with secret microphones and a camera that doubles as a gun. The figures at the top of the CIA and the military—who seem at first to be his allies—turn out to be running a double game, and are precisely the people trying to kill him . . .
8. The film's narrative has its analogue in the level of production. The film was produced by the Hong Kong film company Golden Harvest, with sponsorship from Mitsubishi, and filmed in South Africa, Holland, and Malaysia. The film cast Chan alongside Japanese actresses Mirai Yamamoto and Michelle Ferre, the latter of whom is of mixed French-Japanese heritage, and whose career as a journalist for CNN was built on her English-Japanese bilingualism; riffing on her life, she plays a CIA agent with the cover of being a South African journalist in the film.
9. Li, "Kung Fu," 519.
10. That one might shift in definition from seeing *gongfu* as (unalienated) labor to seeing it as capital itself draws feasibility from one of Marx's definitions, in which capital itself is

"dead labour, that, vampire-like, only lives by sucking living labour, and lives the more, the more labour it sucks." Marx and Engels, *Capital,* 1:163.

11. Yip, in *Martial Arts Cinema,* 105, proposes that the thematic of master–disciple relationships and martial training, so central to the kung fu comedy, developed from Lau's more "serious" collaborations with Chang Cheh on the Shaolin cycle of films from earlier in the 1970s.

12. For more on the history of Wong Fei-hung as one of Hong Kong cinema's most enduring icons, see Po and Lau, *Mastering Virtue. Drunken Master* is listed here as the 92nd film in Lau Yam's chronological filmography of Wong Fei-hung–related works (135).

13. Fu, "The 1960s," 71–89.

14. See, for example, Marx on the way capital strips away traditional ways of life—"all feudal, patriarchal, idyllic relations" and "the motley ties that bound man to his 'natural superiors'"—leaving "no other nexus between man and man than naked self-interest, callous 'cash payment.'" Rather than exploitation hidden under the guise of religion or custom, it leaves "naked, shameless, direct, brutal exploitation." Marx and Engels, *Manifesto,* chap. 1.

15. Yip, *Martial Arts Cinema,* 24.

16. See, for example, Klein, *Envy and Gratitude,* 61–93.

17. Tasker, *Spectacular Bodies,* 3.

18. Lo, *Excess and Masculinity,* xxi–xxiv.

19. Mulvey, "Visual Pleasure."

20. Chan, "Bruce Lee's Fictional Modes," 484–485; Bowman, *Beyond Bruce Lee,* 126–128.

21. Chan, "Bruce Lee's Fictional Modes," 379; Bowman, *Beyond Bruce Lee,* 128–129.

22. See Sasha Vojković, *Wing Chun,* 4.

23. Perhaps the star who came close was Kara Hui, who took up a central role within a number of Lau Kar-leung's comedies—in particular *My Young Auntie* (dir. Lau Kar-leung, 1981) and *Lady Is the Boss* (dir. Lau Kar-leung, 1983). However, even in these, where she often serves as a driver for narrative, Hui remains in many respects a secondary character with regard to the male characters through whose eyes we tend to see her. She plays the role of injecting disorder—though perhaps a fertile, exciting variety of disorder—into what may be otherwise a closed and decaying patriarchal world, which she helps revivify. In Lau's films, from *Executioners from Shaolin* (dir. Lau Kar-leung, 1977) on, women tend to symbolize the upending, potentially creative effects of modernity and change, in contradistinction to the patrilineal, traditional culture of the films' men. She is ultimately, however, seen from the perspective of that culture, within whose world her disruptive but enlivening energies are to be reabsorbed. Another actress who significantly breaks this mold is Cynthia Rothrock. Rothrock came to prominence not in kung fu comedies, but in the "girls with guns" cop genre of the late 1980s, in particular *Yes, Madam!* (dir. Corey Yuen, 1985), where she starred alongside Michelle Yeoh. Although these films were not primarily comedies, the genre mixed comic and action elements, and Rothrock's performances in particular are very much in the carnivalesque tradition described in this book: Logan, in *Hong Kong Action Cinema,* 142, lists her twice in his "Ten Best Hong Kong Comedy Fights," and Meaghan Morris has understood her ongoing popularity in Hong Kong (and relative critical failure in America) as due in large part to the ways that her performances fit into a broad tradition of Cantonese popular comedy. (Morris, "What Can a *Gwei Por* Do?" 570). While *Yes, Madam!* rejects the formula that places a male star at the core of the movie, it is clearly still in many ways about masculine gender anxiety, as Lo argues in *Excess and Masculinity,* esp. 97–103. It thus seems significant that Yeoh, too, also

emerged as an action star (comic and otherwise) initially through this "girl-cop" genre, and that Kara Hui also found a means within this genre to reinvent herself.

24. See, for example, bell hooks, "Is Paris Burning?," in *Black Looks,* 145–156.

25. See, for example, Butler, *Gender Trouble,* 24–25.

26. Micale, "Charcot," 372.

27. Micale, "Charcot," 406.

28. Micale, "Charcot," 377–378. Of course, as Micale notes, there are a number of reasons we should be careful about taking Charcot's case notes as evidence for a particular preponderance of hysteria among working class men.

29. Borossa, *Hysteria,* 57–59.

30. The kung fu film is, after all, not only a matter of race or nation but also emphatically classed. The relation of martial arts to working class masculinity is complex and revolves around a complication of gender that differs from more familiar Western models. In China, as Kam Louie and Louise Edwards have noted, masculinity is not articulated only around the poles of yin (female) and yang (male). Chinese culture includes two ideals of masculinity—the *wu* (martial) and the *wen* (scholarly). See Louie and Edwards, "Chinese Masculinity," 135–148. Over the last millennium, *wen* has been the more privileged term, allied as it is to the values of the elite "scholar" class, which took a leading role in the administration of Imperial China. The *wu,* or martial, was increasingly a preserve of people from lower classes, and was furthermore tainted by association with the "yin" forces of disruption, violence, and chaos. To identify one's masculinity with such "yin" forces thus involved a relation of "excess" to the yang of masculinity. Questions of class, masculinity, and the martial arts in contemporary China have been further explored in Boretz's *Gods, Ghosts, and Gangsters.*

31. The films in the Miracle Fighters series are *Miracle Fighters* (dir. Yuen Woo-ping, 1982), *Shaolin Drunkard* (dir. Yuen Woo-ping, 1983), *Taoism Drunkard* (dir. Yuen Cheung-yan, 1984), and *Young Taoism Fighter* (dir. Chen Chi-hwa, 1986).

32. Gunning, "Cinema of Attractions," 56–60.

33. In fact, cinematically, the Miracle Fighters series anticipates the stylistics of the 1990s swordplay films that Sarkar, as discussed above, identified as hysterical. Camera angles become more dramatic and skewed than in the drunken master films, and lighting often serves to create a dramatic chiaroscuro effect, perhaps drawn from the noirish Shaw Brothers swordplay films of Chor Yuen and Sun Chung, which were currently popular. The Miracle Fighters films also anticipate the genre and gender confusion that typified 1990s Hong Kong swordplays.

34. Drawing a further intertextual relationship to the drunken master films, when the dead master is offered his favorite wine, through camera superimposition the painting is made to roll its eyes and move its lips, and a red flush descends across its face. In this regard, a film about legacies and inheritance reflexively sets out a claim to its own "inheritance" of the Drunken Master's legacy and pays tribute to Simon Yuen as an ancestor of the tight-knit family group who made it.

35. *Mr. Vampire* was not the first such supernatural kung fu comedy focused around the figure of the hopping corpse. However, its success seems to have been the factor that sparked a multitude of imitations. Precursors include Sammo Hung's *Encounters of the Spooky Kind* (1980) and *The Dead and the Deadly* (1982), in the latter of which Lam Ching-ying, who would go on to star in *Mr. Vampire,* first took on the role of the Daoist exorcist master with which he would become so synonymous in Hong Kong culture. Hung's forays into supernatural kung fu were themselves foreshadowed in Lau Kar-leung's *Spiritual Boxer II* (1979), which provides a

strong link in terms of genre to the drunken master cycle. Lau's first *Spiritual Boxer* film (1975) had anticipated the figure of a disreputable, alcoholic kung fu master who would be key to the drunken master cycle. *Spiritual Boxer II* was not so much a sequel as a reworking of some of its themes. In it Wong Yue plays the apprentice to a drunken kung fu master and "corpse herder." When the master (Lau Kar-wing) gets into a drunken argument about gambling and breaks a leg, he leaves his bumbling apprentice to complete the job of returning the corpses to their ancestral homes—a job that is complicated by an escaped dissident (Gordon Liu) who has disguised himself among the corpses to return to his hometown to exact his vengeance on corrupt officials. While the film draws on the then-current motif of the drunken master, it also established a number of the visual tropes of the "corpse herder" and the travelling *geongsi* in Mandarin garb. For more on this genre, see Logan, *Hong Kong Action Cinema*, 100–113.

36. See Lam, "Hop on Pop," 46–51.
37. McNally, *Monsters of the Market*.
38. See, for example, Lam, "Hop on Pop," 47.
39. Marx and Engels, *Manifesto*, chap. 1.
40. Marx, *Eighteenth Brumaire*, chap. 2.
41. Tony Rayns, "Hard Boiled," 20.
42. Bordwell, *Minding Movies*, 25.
43. Stringer, "Problems," 45.
44. Stringer, "Problems," 46–49.
45. Sarkar, "Hong Kong Hysteria," 170.
46. Sarkar, "Hong Kong Hysteria," 166, 170.
47. In this book more generally, I have emphasized performance over the kind of narrative readings I have offered in the current chapter, and it is precisely in this aspect of the performed that the kind of narrative reading I have been primarily offering in this chapter—and that remains very much the bread and butter of film studies—is shown to be limited in its explanatory function. In this respect the popular film text displays something of the "resistance" to interpretation that is famous in the hysteric, with the critic or theorist perhaps always placed in the position of the "master" who attempts to impose a reading and to speak the truth of and for an other.

Chapter 6: Legacies

Epigraph. Foucault, "Nietzsche, Genealogy, History," 82.

1. See Duncan, "The Traditional Thing," 353–367.
2. Chow has even been called "the Hong Kong Jim Carrey." Kraicer, "Stephen Chow."
3. Wong, "Scholarism," 47–48.
4. For more on the founding of Scholarism and the opposition to the "Moral and National Education" program, see Wong, "Scholarism," 44–45.
5. Ngo, "Who Are Hong Kong Indigenous?"
6. Jenkins and Iyengar, "Hong Kong."
7. Hsieh, "In Hong Kong."
8. Lam, "Why Did Hongkongers Join?"
9. SCMP Reporters, "As It Happened."
10. Nicolas Atkin, "Hong Kong Protests."
11. Chow, "Hong Kong's Film Industry."
12. Chow, "Hong Kong's Film Industry."

13. Kraicer, "Stephen Chow."

14. Derrida, *Specters of Marx,* 63.

15. In its very subtitle—"The State of the Debt, the Work of Mourning and the New International"—Derrida's book, bringing up the problems of "debt" and "mourning" with which his discussion of Marx faces us, insists on this fact.

16. Tsui's *Butterfly Murders* (1979) might be counted as a kind of nihilistic anti-*wuxia* film (part science fiction and part mystery story) in which butterflies seem at first to be a new martial arts weapon behind a series of killings, before the secret weapon of mass destruction is revealed to be something like a machine gun. Tsui followed this up with *We're Going to Eat You* (1980), in which anxieties about the relation to the mainland were allegorized in the form of a village of inbred cannibals. *Dangerous Encounter—First Kind* (1980) envisioned a group of youths on a bombing spree and was heavily censored by the colonial government as being politically inflammatory.

17. *Swordsman* was officially directed by King Hu, but after he walked out in the early stages of filming over differences with Tsui in his role as producer, the film was completed by a combination of Tsui Hark, Ann Hui, Andrew Kam, and Ching Siu-tung, all uncredited.

18. Teo, *Chinese Martial Arts Cinema,* 148.

19. Dai, "Order/Anti-order," 81.

20. Sarkar, "Hong Kong Hysteria," 159–176.

21. Teo, *Chinese Martial Arts Cinema,* 161.

22. See, for example, Chan, "Figures of Hope," 486–514; Li, "Kung Fu," 537.

23. See the comprehensive Wong Fei-hung filmography compiled by Yau Lam in Po and Yau, *Mastering Virtue,* 136.

24. There were five sequels, and the series ran from 1991 to 1997. Tsui Hark directed the first three and the fifth of the series.

25. See the listing for the film on hkmdb.com.

26. According to the statistics offered on hkmdb.com, *Once Upon a Time in China II,* grossed HK$30,399,676, outperforming even the first instalment of the series. However, *Justice My Foot* grossed HK$49,884,734; *Royal Tramp* made HK$40,862,831; and *Royal Tramp II* brought in a further HK$36,583,964. *King of Beggars* would go on to take HK$31,514,995.

27. See Po, "Makers of the Wong Fei-hung Legend," 100–101. The idea of the young So Chan was also taken up in *The Young Vagabond* (dir. Lau Sze-yu, 1985).

28. Chan, "Rags to Riches."

29. In one scene, for example, the antidote to poison gas is a urine-soaked handkerchief tied around the mouth and nose; when one character complains of not being able to urinate, another tells her not to worry—he's got plenty for both.

30. Liu, *Stateless Subjects,* 11–12.

31. Louie and Edwards "Chinese Masculinity," 139.

32. Perhaps most famously it is there in *Enter the Dragon* (dir. Robert Clouse, 1973), in which the villain, Han, is secretly running a drug-manufacturing plant in a base hidden under his island fortress. In the bowels of this are imprisoned a small army of (presumably Chinese) prisoners, zombified through drugs, whom Bruce Lee frees at the end of the film to rise up against their oppressor. Opium is again, for example, a concern in the Angela Mao vehicle *Deadly China Doll* (dir. Huang Feng, 1973), in which the Japanese are smuggling opium into China as part of their plan to invade it. Similarly, *Opium and the Kung Fu Master* (Tang Chia, 1984) tells of a militia leader made weak by his addiction.

33. The working relation between Lau and Chan seems to have been somewhat tense, with Lau eventually leaving the production after artistic differences between the two, in particular regarding the fight choreography. Lau remains the credited director, but, by all accounts, the final fight at least was entirely put together by Chan. See Chan, *I Am Jackie Chan,* 354; Logan, *Hong Kong Action Cinema,* 81–82.

34. For an account of the development of Huo's literary and filmic depictions, see Po, "Wong Fei-hung," 7–11.

35. The *lei tai* was a raised platform on which sanctioned public fights between martial artists were held. Unlike the boxing ring, there were generally no ropes or barriers, and being thrown from the stage was one way to lose the match. Matches were either armed or unarmed and, with few rules, were sometimes fought to the death.

36. Makinen, "With Two Kung Fu Films, HBO Cautiously Tests the Waters."

37. Kay, "Exclusive."

38. According to internet film industry data site the-numbers.com, *Skiptrace* was the first-placed film at the Chinese box office on release, grossing CN¥870 million—the equivalent of around US$62 million—and made a global total of $134,675,459.

39. The film brought in US$138.8 million in the PRC in the first week of its release alone. Srinivas, "*Kung Fu Yoga.*"

40. Srinivas, "*Kung Fu Yoga.*"

41. Vetticad, "*Kung Fu Yoga.*"

42. Srinivas, "*Kung Fu Yoga.*"

Conclusion

Epigraph. Derrida, *Specters of Marx,* 45.

1. Kato, *From Kung Fu to Hip Hop,* 2–4.

2. Derrida, in *Specters of Marx,* 63, emphasizes the role of the media, which constitute something "neither living nor dead, present nor absent," in exacerbating the "spectralizing" logic of modernity. It is, in fact, precisely in relation to the media that Derrida coins the term "hauntology."

3. Debord, *Society of the Spectacle.*

4. Abbas, *Hong Kong,* 1–2.

5. Fanon, *Wretched of the Earth.*

6. Kato, *From Kung Fu to Hip Hop,* 3.

7. Gilroy, *Black Atlantic,* esp. 220–223.

8. Žižek, *Mapping Ideology,* 1.

9. Kirby, "The Death of Postmodernism."

10. Abbas, *Hong Kong,* 5.

11. Burt, "Shakespeare," 17–20.

12. Bordwell, *Planet Hong Kong,* esp. 1–11.

13. Clark, *The Painting of Modern Life,* 205–258.

14. See Po, "Wong Fei-hung," 7, 10–11; Wong, "Triumph," 17–24.

15. In martial mythology, Fong Sai-yuk was a comrade of Hung Hei-gun, founder of the Hung Gar style practiced by Wong Fei-hung. For more on the differences between the archetypes of Wong and Fong, and the ways that literary and cinematic depictions of the two have influenced each other, see, Po, "Wong Fei-hung," 11–14. Fong first appears in the 1893 novel *Evergreen.* Wong, "Triumph," 19.

16. Meulenbeld, *Demonic Warfare.*

17. I have also developed this argument in White, "Lau Kar-leung," 5–6.

18. Prashad, *Everybody Was Kung Fu Fighting*, 126–149.

19. Kelley, "People in Me," cited in Prashad, *Everybody Was Kung Fu Fighting*, 65. Kelley's capitalization.

20. Prashad, *Everybody Was Kung Fu Fighting*, 71.

21. Benjamin, *Illuminations*, 246. Benjamin's emphasis. It is Benjamin's "Theses"—and its conception of messianism—that Derrida has been discussing in the quote that forms this chapter's epigraph.

22. Benjamin, *Illuminations*, 248.

23. Benjamin, *Illuminations*, 246–248.

24. Benjamin, *Illuminations*, 90.

Bibliography

Abbas, Ackbar. *Hong Kong: Culture and the Politics of Disappearance.* Minneapolis: University of Minnesota Press, 1997.

Abraham, Nicolas, and Maria Torok. *The Shell and the Kernel.* Vol. 1. Chicago: University of Chicago Press, 1994.

Adorno, Theodor, and Max Horkheimer. *Dialectic of Enlightenment.* New York: Herder, 1969.

Anderson, Aaron D. "Asian Martial Arts Cinema, Dance, and the Cultural Languages of Gender." In *Chinese Connections: Critical Perspectives on Film, Identity and Diaspora,* edited by Tan See-Kam, Peter X. Feng and Gina Marchetti, 190–202. Philadelphia: Temple University Press, 2009.

Anderson, Benedict. *Imagined Communities: Reflections on the Origin and Spread of Nationalism.* Rev. ed. London: Verso, 1991.

Assayas, Olivier, and Charles Tesson, "Interview with Lau Kar-leung: The Last Shaolin," translated by Yves Gendron and Steve Feldman, in *Chang Cheh: The Godfather of Kung Fu,* http://changcheh.0catch.com/lau-int.htm. First published in French in *Cahiers du cinéma* 362–363 (1984): 26–30.

Atkin, Nicolas. "Hong Kong Protests Embrace Bruce Lee but Reject Jackie Chan in Tale of Two Martial Arts Heroes." *South China Morning Post,* June 29, 2019. https://www.scmp.com/sport/martial-arts/kung-fu/article/3016609/hong-kong-protests-embrace-bruce-lee-reject-jackie-chan.

Bakhtin, Mikhail. *Rabelais and His World.* Translated by Hélène Iswolsky. Bloomington: Indiana University Press, 1984.

Battersby, Christine. *The Sublime, Terror and Human Difference.* Abingdon: Routledge, 2007.

Baudrillard, Jean. "The Ecstasy of Communication." In *The Anti-Aesthetic: Essays on Postmodern Culture,* edited by Hal Foster, 126–134. Seattle: Bay Press, 1983.

Benjamin, Walter. "Experience and Poverty." In *Walter Benjamin: Selected Writings,* edited by Michael Jennings, Howard Eiland and Gary Smith, vol. 2, part 2, *1931–1934,* 731–736. Cambridge, MA: Harvard University Press, 1999.

———. *Gesammelte Schriften.* Edited by Rolf Tiedemann and Hermann Schweppenhauser. Frankfurt: Suhrkamp, 1985.

———. *Illuminations.* Edited by Hannah Arendt. Translated by Harry Zohn. London: Fontana, 1992.

———. "On Mickey Mouse." In *The Promise of Cinema: German Film Theory, 1907–1933,* edited by Anton Kaes, Nicholas Baer and Michael Cowan, 403. Oakland: University of California Press, 2016.

———. "These Surfaces for Rent." In *The Work of Art in the Age of Its Technological Reproducibility and Other Writing on Media,* edited by Michael W. Jennings, Brigid Doherty, and Thomas Y. Levin, translated by Edmund Jephcott, Rodney Livingstone, Howard Eiland, and Others, 173–174. Cambridge, MA: Harvard University Press, 2008.

———. "The Work of Art in the Age of Its Technical Reproducibility [First Version]." *Grey Room* 39 (2010): 11–37.

———. "The Work of Art in the Age of Its Technological Reproducibility [Second Version]." In *The Work of Art in the Age of Its Technological Reproducibility and Other Writings on Media,* edited by Michael W. Jennings, Brigid Doherty, and Thomas Y. Levin, translated by Edmund Jephcott, Rodney Livingstone, Howard Eiland, and Others, 19–55. Cambridge, MA: Harvard University Press, 2008.

Bersani, Leo. *The Freudian Body: Psychoanalysis and Art.* New York: Columbia University Press, 1986.

Bloom, Michael. "Chopsocky Slapstick: Violence as Humorous Excess in the Kung-Fu Comedy: From Jackie Chan to Stephen Chiau." *Off-Screen* 16, nos. 11–12 (2012), http://offscreen.com/view/chopsocky_slapstick.

Bollas, Christopher. *Hysteria.* London: Routledge, 2000.

Bordwell, David. "Aesthetics in Action: Kungfu, Gunplay, and Cinematic Expressivity." In *At Full Speed: Hong Kong Cinema in a Borderless World,* edited by Esther C. M. Yau, 73–94. Minneapolis: University of Minnesota Press, 2001.

———. *Minding Movies: Observations on the Art, Craft, and Business of Filmmaking.* Chicago: University of Chicago Press, 2011.

———. *Planet Hong Kong: Popular Cinema and the Art of Entertainment.* 2nd ed. Madison, WI: Irvington Way Institute Press, 2011.

Bordwell, David and Noël Carroll. *Post-Theory: Reconstructing Film Studies.* Madison: University of Wisconsin Press, 1996.

Boretz, Avron. *Gods, Ghosts, and Gangsters: Ritual Violence, Martial Arts, and Masculinity on the Margins of Chinese Society.* Honolulu: University of Hawaiʻi Press, 2010.

Borossa, Julia. *Hysteria.* Ideas in Psychoanalysis. Cambridge: Icon Books, 2001.

Bowman, Paul. *Beyond Bruce Lee: Chasing the Dragon through Film, Philosophy and Popular Culture.* New York: Columbia University Press, 2013.

———. *Martial Arts Studies: Disrupting Disciplinary Boundaries.* London: Rowman and Littlefield, 2015.

———. *Theorizing Bruce Lee: Film-Fantasy-Fighting-Philosophy.* Amsterdam: Rodopi, 2009.

Bronfen, Elisabeth. *The Knotted Subject: Hysteria and Its Discontents.* Princeton, NJ: Princeton University Press, 1998.

Burr, Martha. "The Kungfu Genius Behind *The Matrix:* Yuen Woo Ping Works his Magic on Laurence Fishburne and Keanu Reeves." *Kung Fu Magazine,* May 1999. Online edition. http://www.kungfumagazine.com/magazine/article.php?article=96.

Burt, Richard. "Shakespeare, Glo-Cali-zation, Race and the Small Screens of Post-Popular Culture." In *Shakespeare the Movie II: Popularizing the Plays on Film, TV, Video and DVD,* edited by Richard Burt and Lynda E. Boose, 14–36. London: Routledge, 2004.

Butler, Judith. *Gender Trouble: Feminism and the Subversion of Identity.* New York: Routledge, 1990.

Byrne, Eleanor, and Martin McQuillan. *Deconstrucing Disney.* London: Pluto Press, 1999.

Caygill, Howard. "Also Sprach Zapata." *Radical Philosophy* 171 (2011): 19–26.

Cha, Louis. *The Deer and the Cauldron,* trans. John Minford. 3 vols. Oxford: Oxford University Press, 1997–2003.

Chan, Gordon. "Rags to Riches: An Interview with Director Gordon Chan." *King of Beggars.* DVD. Directed by Gordon Chan. Hitchin: Hong Kong Legends, 2006.

Chan, Jachinson. "Bruce Lee's Fictional Modes of Masculinity." *Men and Masculinity* 2, no. 4 (2000): 371–387.

Chan, Jackie. *I Am Jackie Chan: My Life in Action.* London: Pan, 1998.

Chan, Stephen Ching-kiu. "Figures of Hope and the Filmic Imaginary of Jianghu in Contemporary Hong Kong Cinema." *Cultural Studies* 15, nos. 3–4 (2001): 486–514.

Chan, Ting-ching. "The 'Knockabout' Comic Kung-fu Films of Sammo Hung." In *A Study of the Hong Kong Martial Arts Film,* edited by Lau Shing-hon, 149–150. Hong Kong: HKIFF/Urban Council, 1980.

Chang, Cheh. *Chang Cheh: A Memoir.* Hong Kong: Hong Kong Film Archive, 2004.

———. "Creating the Martial Arts Film and the Hong Kong Cinema Style." In *The Making of Martial Arts Films: As Told by Filmmakers and Stars,* 16–24. Hong Kong: Hong Kong Film Archive, 1999.

Chen, Kuan-hsing. *Asia as Method: Toward Deimperialization.* Durham, NC: Duke University Press, 2010.

Cheung, Gary Ka-Wei. *Hong Kong's Watershed: The 1967 Riots.* Hong Kong: Hong Kong University Press, 2009.

Chow, Rey. *The Protestant Ethnic and the Spirit of Capitalism.* New York: Columbia University Press, 2002.

Chow, Vivienne. "Hong Kong's Film Industry Struggling to Regain the Fame as China Enters the Limelight." *South China Morning Post,* February 6, 2016. http://www.scmp.com/news/hong-kong/economy/article/1910072/hong-kongs-film-industry-struggling-regain-fame-china-enters.

Clark, T. J. *The Painting of Modern Life: Paris in the Art of Manet and His Followers.* Rev. ed. Princeton: Princeton University Press, 1999.

Clayton, Alex. *The Body in Hollywood Slapstick.* Jefferson, NC: McFarland, 2007.

Corcoran, John. *The Unauthorized Jackie Chan Encyclopedia: From "Project A" to "Shanghai Noon" and Beyond.* New York: McGraw Hill, 2002.

Corliss, Richard. "Go West, Hong Kong: John Woo and Jackie Chan Meet Hollywood." *Time,* February 26, 1996, 67.

Dai, Jinhua. "Order/Anti-order: Representation of Identity in Hong Kong Action Movies." In *Hong Kong Connections: Transnational Imagination in Action Cinema,* edited by Meaghan Morris, Siu Leung Li and Stephen Chan Ching-kiu, 81–94. Durham, NC: Duke University Press, 2005.

Dannen, Fredric and Barry Long. *Hong Kong Babylon: An Insider's Guide to the Hollywood of the East*. London: Faber and Faber, 1997.

DaMatta, Roberto. *Carnivals, Rogues and Heroes: An Interpretation of the Brazilian Dilemma*. Translated by John Drury. Notre Dame, IN: University of Notre Dame Press, 1991.

Debord, Guy. *The Society of the Spectacle*. Translated by Donald Nicholson-Smith. New York: Zone Books, 1994.

Deleuze, Gilles. "Postscript on the Societies of Control." *October* 59 (1992): 3–7.

Deleuze, Gilles, and Félix Guattari. *A Thousand Plateaus: Capitalism and Schizophrenia*. Translated by Brian Massumi. London: Athlone Press, 1988.

Derrida, Jacques. *Specters of Marx: The State of the Debt, the Work of Mourning and the New International*. Translated by Peggy Kamuf. New York: Routledge, 2006.

Desser, David. "The Kung Fu Craze: Hong Kong Cinema's First American Reception." In *The Cinema of Hong Kong: History, Arts, Identity*, edited by David Desser and Poshek Fu, 19–43. Cambridge: Cambridge University Press, 2000.

Didi-Huberman, Georges. *The Invention of Hysteria: Charcot and the Photographic Iconography of Salpêtrière*. Translated by Alisa Hartz. Cambridge, MA: MIT Press, 2003.

Duncan, Sydney. "The Traditional Thing in the Modern Age: Contextual Perspectives on Buster Keaton and Jackie Chan." *New Review of Film and Television Studies* 5, no. 3 (2007): 353–367.

Eagleton, Terry. *Walter Benjamin: Towards a Revolutionary Criticism*. London: Verso, 1981.

Esherick, Joseph. *The Origins of the Boxer Uprising*. Berkeley: University of California Press, 1987.

Fang, Karen. *Arresting Cinema: Surveillance in Hong Kong Film*. Stanford, CA: Stanford University Press, 2017.

Fanon, Frantz. *The Wretched of the Earth*. Translated by Constance Farrington. London: Penguin 2001.

Farrer, D. S., and John Whalen-Bridge, eds. *Martial Arts as Embodied Knowledge: Asian Traditions in a Transnational World*. New York: SUNY Press, 2011.

Fiske, John. *Reading Popular Culture*. Boston, MA: Unwin Hyman, 1989.

Foucault, Michel. *The Birth of Biopolitics: Lectures at the Collège de France, 1978–1979*. London: Palgrave, 2008.

———. *Discipline and Punish: The Birth of the Prison*. London: Penguin, 1991.

———. *The History of Sexuality*. 3 vols. London: Penguin, 1990.

———. "Nietzsche, Genealogy, History." In *The Foucault Reader*, edited by Paul Rabinow, 76–100. London: Penguin, 1991.

———. *Security, Territory, Population: Lectures at the Collège de France, 1977–1978*. London: Palgrave, 2009.

Fu, Poshek. "The 1960s: Modernity, Youth Culture and Hong Kong Cinema." In *The Cinema of Hong Kong: History, Arts, Identity*, edited by Poshek Fu and David Desser, 73–74. Cambridge: Cambridge University Press, 2000.

Fu, Poshek, ed. *China Forever: The Shaw Brothers and Diasporic Cinema*. Urbana: University of Illinois Press, 2008.

Gallagher, Mark. “Masculinity in Translation: Jackie Chan’s Transcultural Star Text,” *Velvet Light Trap* 39 (1997): 23–41.

Gallop, Jane. *The Daughter’s Seduction: Feminism and Psychoanalysis.* Ithaca, NY: Cornell University Press, 1982.

Gateward, Frances. “Wong Fei Hung in da House: Kung Fu Cinema and Hip Hop Culture.” In *Chinese Connections: Critical Perspectives on Film, Identity, and Diaspora,* edited by Gina Marchetti, Peter X. Feng, and Tan See-Kam, 51–67. New York: Temple University Press, 2006.

Gentry, Clyde. *Jackie Chan: Inside the Dragon.* Dallas, TX: Taylor Trade, 1997.

Gilroy, Paul. *The Black Atlantic: Modernity and Double Consciousness.* London: Verso, 1993.

Gunning, Tom. “The Cinema of Attractions: Early Film, its Spectator, and the Avant-Garde.” In *Early Cinema: Space, Frame, Narrative,* edited by Thomas Elsaesser, 56–63. London: British Film Institute, 1990.

Halberstam, Judith. *Female Masculinity.* New York: Duke University Press, 1998.

Hall, Stuart. “Notes on Deconstructing the ‘Popular.’” In *Cultural Theory and Popular Culture: A Reader,* edited by John Storey, 442–453. 2nd. ed. London: Prentice Hall, 1998.

Hammond, Stefan and Mike Wilkins. *Sex and Zen & a Bullet in the Head.* New York: Simon and Schuster, 1996.

Hansen, Miriam. “Benjamin and Cinema: Not a One-Way Street.” In *Benjamin’s Ghosts: Interventions in Contemporary Literary and Cultural Theory,* edited by Gerhard Richter, 41–73. Stanford: Stanford University Press, 2002.

Heath, Stephen. “Film and System: Terms of Analysis.” *Screen,* 16, no. 1 (1975): 7–77.

Hirschkop, Ken. “Introduction: Bakhtin and Cultural Theory.” In *Bakhtin and Cultural Theory,* edited by Ken Hirschkop and David Shepherd, 1–38. Manchester: Manchester University Press, 1989.

Holquist, Michael. *Dialogism: Bakhtin and His World.* 2nd ed. London: Routledge, 2002.

Hong Kong Film Archive, *Golden Harvest: Leading Change in Changing Times.* Hong Kong: Hong Kong Film Archive, 2013.

———. *The Shaw Screen: A Preliminary Study.* Hong Kong: Hong Kong Film Archive, 2003.

hooks, bell. *Black Looks: Race and Representation.* Boston, MA: South End Press, 1992.

Hsieh, Stephen. “In Hong Kong, a Young Generation of Protesters Fights for the Future.” *Vice News,* October 14, 2014. https://news.vice.com/article/in-hong-kong-a-young-generation-of-protesters-fights-for-the-future.

Hung, Ho-fung. “Uncertainty in the Enclave.” *New Left Review* 66 (2010): 55–77.

Hunt, Leon. *Kung Fu Cult Masters: From Bruce Lee to Crouching Tiger.* London: Wallflower, 2003.

Jameson, Fredric. *Postmodernism, or, the Cultural Logic of Late Capitalism.* London: Verso, 1991.

Jayamanne, Laleen. “Let’s Miscegenate: Jackie Chan and His African-American Connection.” In *Hong Kong Connections: Transnational Imagination in Action Cinema,* edited by Meaghan Morris, Siu Leung Li and Stephen Chan Ching-kiu, 151–162. New York: Duke University Press, 2005.

Jenkins, Nash, and Rishi Iyengar. "Hong Kong Sees Violent Start to Chinese New Year as Protesters Clash with Police." *Time,* February 8, 2016. http://time.com/4213191/hong-kong-riot-protest/.

Kaes, Anton, Nicholas Baer and Michael Cowan, eds. *The Promise of Cinema: German Film Theory, 1907–1933.* Oakland: University of California Press, 2016.

Kaminsky, Stuart. "Italian Westerns and Kung Fu Films: Genres of Violence." In *Graphic Violence on the Screen,* edited by Thomas Atkins, 47–68. New York: Monarch, 1976.

Kato, M. T. *From Kung Fu to Hip Hop: Globalization, Revolution, and Popular Culture.* New York: SUNY Press, 2007.

Kay, Jeremy. "Exclusive Takes *Skiptrace* to Cannes." *Screen Daily,* May 6, 2013. http://www.screendaily.com/news/distribution/exclusive-takes-skiptrace-to-cannes/5054627.article.

Kelley, Robin. "People in Me." *ColorLines* 1, no. 3 (1999): 5–7.

Kendrick, James. *Film Violence: History, Ideology, Genre.* London: Wallflower, 2009.

Kennedy, Brian, and Elizabeth Guo. *Chinese Martial Arts Training Manuals: A Historical Survey.* Berkeley: Blue Snake Books, 2005.

———. *Jingwu: The School that Transformed Kung Fu.* Berkeley: North Atlantic Books, 2010.

Kirby, Alan. "The Death of Postmodernism and Beyond." *Philosophy Now* 58 (2006). https://philosophynow.org/issues/58/The_Death_of_Postmodernism_And_Beyond.

Klein, Melanie. *Envy and Gratitude and Other Works, 1946–1963.* London: Vintage, 1997.

Kraicer, Shelly. "Stephen Chow: A Guide for the Perplexed." *Cinema Scope* 10 (2002). Archived on *Cinema Scope Online* at http://cinema-scope.com/cinema-scope-online/11043/.

Lacoue-Labarthe, Philippe. *Heidegger, Art and Politics.* Translated by Chris Turner. Oxford: Blackwell, 1990.

Lai, Linda Chiu-han. "Film and Enigmatization: Nostalgia, Nonsense and Remembering." In *At Full Speed: Hong Kong Cinema in a Borderless World,* edited by Esther Yau, 231–250. Minneapolis: University of Minnesota Press, 2001.

Lam, Jeffie. "Why Did Hongkongers Join Million-strong March to Protest Extradition Bill? It's about Protecting Freedom, and It's in their DNA." *South China Morning Post,* June 10, 2019. Online edition. https://www.scmp.com/news/hong-kong/politics/article/3013758/why-did-hundreds-thousands-hongkongers-take-streets-protest.

Lam, Stephanie. "Hop on Pop: *Jiangshi* Films in a Transnational Context." *CineAction* 78 (2009): 46–51.

Lau, Jenny. "Besides Fists and Blood: Michael Hui and Cantonese Comedy." In *The Cinema of Hong Kong: History, Arts, Identity,* edited by Poshek Fu and David Desser, 158–175. Cambridge: Cambridge University Press, 2000.

Lau, Tai-muk. "Conflict and Desire: Dialogues between the Hong Kong Martial Arts Genre and Social Issues in the Past 40 Years." In *The Making of Martial Arts Films: As Told By Filmmakers and Stars,* 30–34. Hong Kong: HKFA / Urban Council, 1999.

Le Blanc, Michelle, and Colin Odell. *Jackie Chan.* Harpendon, UK: Pocket Essentials, 2000.

Leslie, Esther. *Hollywood Flatlands: Animation, Critical Theory and the Avant-garde.* London: Verso, 2002.

Li, Siu Leung. "Kung Fu: Negotiating Nationalism and Modernity." *Cultural Studies* 15, nos. 3/4 (2001): 515–542.

Liu, Petrus. *Stateless Subjects: Chinese Martial Arts Literature and Postcolonial History.* Honolulu: University of Hawai'i Press: 2011.

Lo, Kwai-Cheung. *Chinese Face/Off: The Transnational Culture of Hong Kong.* Champaign: University of Illinois Press, 2005.

———. *Excess and Masculinity in Asian Cultural Productions.* New York: SUNY Press, 2010.

———. "Muscles and Subjectivity: A Short History of the Masculine Body in Hong Kong Popular Culture." *Camera Obscura* 39 (1996): 105–125

Logan, Bey. *Hong Kong Action Cinema.* London: Titan Books, 1995.

Louie, Kam, and Louise Edwards. "Chinese Masculinity: Theorizing '*Wen*' and '*Wu.*'" *East Asian History* 8 (1994): 135–148.

Mackerras, Colin, and Elizabeth Wichmann. "Introduction." In *Chinese Theater: From its Origins to the Present Day,* edited by Colin Mackerras, 1–6. Honolulu: University of Hawai'i Press, 1983.

Makinen, Julie. "With Two Kung Fu Films, HBO Cautiously Tests the Waters in China." *LA Times,* August 22, 2016. Online edition. http://www.latimes.com/entertainment/envelope/cotown/la-et-ct-hbo-china-20160818-snap-story.html

Mandle, Chris. "Jackie Chan in Second Place in Forbes' Highest Paid Actors List after Magazine Includes Actors Working outside US Movie Industry." *Independent,* August 4, 2015. Online edition. http://www.independent.co.uk/news/people/jackie-chan-climbs-to-second-place-in-forbes-highest-paid-actors-list-after-magazine-includes-actors-10438319.html.

Marx, Karl. *Capital.* Volume 1. [1867] Translated by Samuel Moore and Edward Aveling. Available online from the Marxists Internet Archive, 2015, https://www.marxists.org/archive/marx/works/download/pdf/Capital-Volume-I.pdf.

———. *The Eighteenth Brumaire of Louis Bonaparte* [1852]. Available online from Marxists Internet Archive, 1999, https://www.marxists.org/archive/marx/works/1852/18th-brumaire/index.htm.

Marx, Karl and Friedrich Engels. *Manifesto of the Communist Party.* [1848] Translated by Samuel Moore. Available online from the Marxists Internet Archive, 2000, https://www.marxists.org/archive/marx/works/1848/communist-manifesto/.

Maslin, Janet. "Kicks, Swivels and Wisecracks on Hollywood Boulevard." *New York Times,* September 18, 1998. Online edition. http://www.nytimes.com/1998/09/18/movies/film-review-kicks-swivels-and-wisecracks-on-hollywood-boulevard.html.

Massumi, Brian. *A User's Guide to Capitalism and Schizophrenia: Deviations from Deleuze and Guattar*i. Cambridge, MA: MIT Press, 1992.

McNally, David. *Monsters of the Market: Zombies, Vampires and Global Capitalism.* Chicago, IL: Haymarket Books, 2012.

Meulenbeld, Mark. *Demonic Warfare: Daoism, Territorial Networks, and the History of a Ming Novel.* Honolulu: University of Hawai'i Press, 2015.

Micale, Mark. *Approaching Hysteria: Disease and Its Interpretations.* Princeton, NJ: Princeton University Press, 1995.

———. "Charcot and the Idea of Hysteria in the Male: Gender, Mental Science, and Medical Diagnosis in Late Nineteenth-century France." *Medical History* 34 (1990): 363–411.

Mitchell, Juliet. *Mad Men and Medusas.* London: Allen Lane, 2000.

Morris, Andrew D. *Marrow of the Nation: A History of Sport and Physical Culture in Republican China.* Berkeley: University of California Press, 2004.

Morris, Meaghan. "What Can a *Gwei Por* Do? Cynthia Rothrock's Hong Kong Career," *Inter-Asia Cultural Studies* 13, no. 4 (2012): 559–575.

———. "A Question of Legacy: What is the Use of Kung Fu?" *Journal of the Moving Image* 12 (2014): 59–75.

Mulvey, Laura. "Visual Pleasure and Narrative Cinema." *Screen* 16, no. 4 (1975): 6–18.

Neocleous, Mark. "Resisting Resilience." *Radical Philosophy* 178 (2013): 2–7.

Ng, Ho. "Kung Fu Comedies: Tradition, Structure, Character." In *A Study of the Hong Kong Swordplay Film, 1945–1980,* edited by Lau Shing-hon, 42–46. Hong Kong: HKIFF/Urban Council, 1980.

Ngo, Jennifer. "Explained: Who Are Hong Kong Indigenous and What Was Their Role in the Mong Kok Protest and Riot?" *South China Morning Post,* February 9, 2016. Online edition. http://www.scmp.com/news/hong-kong/politics/article/1910850/explained-who-are-hong-kong-indigenous-and-what-was-their.

Ninth Hong Kong International Film Festival. *Tradition of Hong Kong Comedy.* Hong Kong: Hong Kong Urban Council, 1986.

Nitta, Keiko. "An Equivocal Space for the Protestant Ethnic: US Popular Culture and Martial Arts Fantasia." *Social Semiotics* 20, no. 4 (2010): 377–392.

Phillips, Scott Park. *Possible Origins: A Cultural History of Chinese Martial Arts, Theater and Religion.* Kindle ed. San Francisco: Angry Baby Books, 2016.

Pluth, Ed. *Badiou: A Philosophy of the New.* London: Polity, 2010.

Po, Fung. "Makers of the Wong Fei-hung Legend." In *Mastering Virtue: The Cinematic Legend of a Martial Artist,* edited by Po Fung and Lau Yam, 96–112. Hong Kong: Hong Kong Film Archive, 2012.

———. "Wong Fei-hung and His Three Companions." In *Mastering Virtue: The Cinematic Legend of a Martial Artist,* edited by Po Fung and Lau Yam, 7–16. Hong Kong: Hong Kong Film Archive, 2012.

Po, Fung and Lau Yam, eds. *Mastering Virtue: The Cinematic Legend of a Martial Artist.* Hong Kong: Hong Kong Film Archive, 2012.

Prashad, Vijay. *Everybody Was Kung Fu Fighting: Afro-Asian Connections and the Myth of Cultural Purity.* Boston, MA: Beacon Press, 2001.

Rayns, Tony. "Hard Boiled." *Sight and Sound* 12, no. 4 (1992): 20–23.

Rediff India Abroad. "What Scares Jackie the Most." September 1, 2006. http://www.rediff.com/movies/2006/sep/01jackie.htm.

Rovin, Jeff and Kathy Tracy. *The Essential Jackie Chan Sourcebook: A Fan's Unauthorized Guide to the Ultimate Action-Film Star!* New York: Simon and Schuster, 1997.

Russo, Charles. *Striking Distance: Bruce Lee and the Dawn of Martial Arts in America.* Lincoln: University of Nebraska Press, 2016.

Sarkar, Bhaskar. "Hong Kong Hysteria: Martial Arts Tales from a Mutating World." In *At Full Speed: Hong Kong Cinema in a Borderless World,* edited by Esther C. M. Yau, 159–176. Minneapolis: University of Minnesota Press, 2001.

SCMP Reporters. "As It Happened: A Historic Day in Hong Kong Concludes Peacefully as Organisers Claim almost 2 Million People Came Out in Protest against the Fugitive Bill." *South China Morning Post,* June 16, 2019. Online edition. https://www.scmp.com/news/hong-kong/politics/article/3014695/sea-black-hong-kong-will-march-against-suspended.

Shaviro, Steven. *The Cinematic Body.* Minneapolis: University of Minnesota Press, 1993.

Shi, Nai'an and Luo Guanzhong. *Outlaws of the Marsh.* Translated and abridged by Sidney Shapiro. Hong Kong: Commercial Press, 1986.

Showalter, Elaine. *Hystories: Hysterical Epidemics and Modern Culture.* London: Picador, 1998.

Shu, Yuan. "Reading the Kung Fu Film in the American Context: From Bruce Lee to Jackie Chan." *Journal of Popular Film and Television* 31, no. 2 (2003): 50–59.

Smith, Paul. *Clint Eastwood: A Cultural Production.* Minneapolis: University of Minnesota Press, 1993.

Smith-Rosenberg, Carroll. *Disorderly Conduct: Visions of Gender in Victorian America.* Oxford: Oxford University Press, 1985.

Srinivas, S. V. "*Kung Fu Yoga:* Why Indian Film Industry Can't Forget Jackie Chan-Starrer in a Hurry." *First Post,* February 5, 2017. http://www.firstpost.com/entertainment/kung-fu-yoga-why-indian-film-industry-cant-forget-jackie-chan-starrer-in-a-hurry-3267330.html.

Stallybrass, Peter, and Allon White. *The Politics and Poetics of Transgression.* London: Methuen, 1986.

Stam, Robert. *Subversive Pleasures: Bakhtin, Cultural Criticism, and Film.* Baltimore: Johns Hopkins University Press, 1989.

Stokes, Lisa, and Michael Hoover. *City on Fire: Hong Kong Cinema.* London: Verso, 2001.

Storey, John. *Cultural Theory and Popular Culture: An Introduction,* 3rd. ed. Harlow: Pearson, 2001.

Strauss, Neil. "Faster Than a Speeding Bullet, But Also Humanly Fallible." *New York Times,* January 30, 1995. Online edition. http://www.nytimes.com/1995/01/30/movies/faster-than-a-speeding-bullet-but-also-humanly-fallible.html.

Stringer, Julian. "Problems with the Treatment of Hong Kong Cinema as Camp." *Asian Cinema* 8, no. 2 (1996/7): 44–65.

Tasker, Yvonne. *Spectacular Bodies: Gender, Genre and the Action Cinema.* London: Routledge, 1993.

Teo, Stephen. "The 1970s: Movement and Transition." In *The Cinema of Hong Kong: History, Arts, Identity,* edited by Poshek Fu and David Desser, 90–110. Cambridge: Cambridge University Press, 2000.

———. *Chinese Martial Arts Cinema: The Wuxia Tradition.* Edinburgh: Edinburgh University Press, 2009.

———. *Hong Kong Cinema: The Extra Dimension.* London: British Film Institute, 1997.

Thompson, Kristin. "The Concept of Cinematic Excess." *Ciné-Tracts* 1, no. 2 (1977): 54–63.

Thorpe, Ashley. *The Role of the* Chou *("Clown") in Traditional Chinese Drama: Comedy, Criticism and Cosmology on the Chinese Stage.* Lewiston, NY: Edwin Mellen Press, 2007.

Vetticad, Anna M. M. "*Kung Fu Yoga* Movie Review: Jackie Chan, Sonu Sood are Squandered in this Dated Tosh." *First Post,* February 4, 2017. Online edition. http://www.firstpost.com/entertainment/bollywood/kung-fu-yoga-movie-review-jackie-chan-sonu-sood-are-squandered-in-this-dated-tosh-3264128.html.

Vojković, Sasha. *Yuen Woo Ping's Wing Chun.* Hong Kong: Hong Kong University Press, 2009.

Wajeman, Gérard. "The Hysteric's Discourse." In "Hystoria," edited by Helena Schulz-Keil. Special issue, *Lacan Study Notes* 6–9 (1988): 1–22.

Ward, Annalee. *Mouse Morality: The Rhetoric of Disney Animated Film.* Austin: University of Texas Press, 2002.

Wasko, Janet. *Understanding Disney: The Manufacture of Fantasy.* Cambridge: Polity Press, 2001.

White, Allon. *Carnival, Hysteria, and Writing: Collected Essays and Autobiography.* Oxford: Clarendon, 1993.

———. "Hysteria and the End of Carnival: Festivity in Bourgeois Neurosis." In *The Violence of Representation: Literature and the History of Violence,* edited by Nancy Armstrong and Leonard Tennenhouse, 157–170. London: Routledge, 1989.

White, Luke. "Lau Kar-leung with Walter Benjamin: Storytelling, Authenticity, Film Performance and Martial Arts Pedagogy." *Journalism Media and Cultural Studies* 5 (2014). http://www.cardiff.ac.uk/jomec/jomecjournal/5-june2014/White_Authenticity.pdf.

———. "A 'Narrow World, Strewn with Prohibitions': Chang Cheh's *The Assassin* and the 1967 Hong Kong Riots." *Asian Cinema* 26, no. 1 (2015): 79–98.

———. "Toward an Aesthetic of Weightlessness: *Qinggong* and Wire-fu." In *RoCH Fans and Legends,* edited by susan pui san lok, 60. [ePub.] Derby/Manchester: Derby Quad and the Centre for Contemporary Chinese Art, 2016.

Williams, Linda. "Film Bodies: Gender, Genre and Excess." In *Film Genre Reader II,* edited by Barry Keith Grant, 140–157. Austin: University of Texas Press, 1995.

Wills, Claire. "Upsetting the Public: Carnival, Hysteria and Women's Texts." In *Bakhtin and Cultural Theory,* edited by Ken Hirschkop and David Shepherd, 130–151. Manchester: Manchester University Press, 1989.

Wong, Chung-ming. "Triumph of the Martial Spirit: The Rise and Fall of Guangdong–Hong Kong Combat Novels." In *Mastering Virtue: The Cinematic Legend of a Martial Artist,* edited by Po Fung and Lau Yam, 17–24. Hong Kong: Hong Kong Film Archive, 2012.

Wong, Joshua. "Scholarism on the March." [Interview.] *New Left Review* 92 (2015): 43–52.

Wu, Ch'eng-en. *Monkey.* Translated by Arthur Waley. Harmondsworth: Penguin, 1961.

Yip, Man-Fung, *Martial Arts Cinema and Hong Kong Modernity: Aesthetics, Representation, Circulation.* Hong Kong: Hong Kong University Press, 2017.

Yung, Sai-shing. "Moving Body: The Interactions Between Chinese Opera and Action Cinema." In *Hong Kong Connections: Transnational Imagination in Action Cinema*, edited by Meaghan Morris, Siu Leung Li and Stephen Chan Ching-kiu, 21–34. Hong Kong: Hong Kong University Press, 2005.

Žižek, Slavoj. *Mapping Ideology*. London: Verso, 1994.

——. "Symptom." In *Feminism and Psychoanalysis: A Critical Dictionary*, edited by Elizabeth Wright, 423–427. Oxford: Blackwell, 1992.

Selected Filmography

Back Alley Princess (*Malu xiao yingxiong*), dir. Lo Wei, Golden Harvest, 1973.

City Hunter (*Chengshi lieren*), dir. Wong Jing, Golden Harvest / Paragon Films, 1993.

Crippled Avengers (*Can que*), dir. Chang Cheh, Shaw Bros., 1978.

Dance of the Drunk Mantis (*Nanbei zui quan*), dir. Yuen Woo-ping, Seasonal Film Corporation, 1979.

Deep Thrust (US) aka. *Lady Whirlwind* (HK) (*Tiezhang xuanfengtui*), dir. Huang Feng, Golden Harvest, 1972.

Dirty Ho (*Lantou He*), dir. Lau Kar-leung, Shaw Bros., 1979.

Dirty Tiger, Crazy Frog! (*Laohu tianji*), dir. Karl Maka, Gar Bo Films, 1978.

The Dead and the Deadly (*Ren xia ren*), dir. Wu Ma, Golden Harvest, 1982.

Dreadnaught (*Yongzhe wuju*), dir. Yuen Woo-ping, Golden Harvest, 1981.

Drunken Arts and Crippled Fist (*Guai quan xiaozi*), dir. Tong Dik, Dragon Film, 1979.

Drunken Master (*Zui quan*), dir. Yuen Woo-ping, Seasonal Film Corporation, 1978.

Drunken Master II (*Zui quan II*), dir. Lau Kar-leung, Golden Harvest, 1994.

Encounter of the Spooky Kind (*Gui da gui*), dir. Sammo Hung Kam-bo, Bo Ho Films, 1980.

Enter the Dragon (*Longzheng hudou*), dir. Robert Clouse, Golden Harvest / Warner Bros. / Concord Productions, 1973.

Fearless (*Huo Yuanjia*), dir. Ronny Yu Yan-tai, Beijing Film Studio of China Film Group / Singhe Co., 2006.

The Fearless Hyena (*Xiao quan guaizhao*), dir. Jackie Chan, Goodyear Movie Company, 1979.

Fist of Fury (HK) aka. *The Chinese Connection* (US) (*Jingwu men*), dir. Lo Wei, Golden Harvest, 1972.

Games Gamblers Play (*Guima shuangxing*), dir. Michael Hui, Golden Harvest, 1974.

God of Cookery (*Shi shen*), dir. Stephen Chow / Lee Lik-chee, Star Overseas, 1996.

Heroes among Heroes (*Su Qi'er*), dir. Yuen Woo-ping / Chan Chin-chung, Art Sea Films / Golden Film, 1993.

House of 72 Tenants (*Qishi'er jia fangke*), dir. Chor Yuen, Shaw Bros., 1973.

The Iron-fisted Monk (*Sande Heshang yu Zhuangmi Liu*), dir. Sammo Hung Kam-bo, Golden Harvest, 1977.

King of Beggars (*Wu zhangyuan Su Qi'er*), dir. Gordon Chan Kar-shan, Win's Movie Production Co., 1992.

Knockabout (*Zajia xiaozi*), dir. Sammo Hung Kam-bo, Golden Harvest, 1979.

Kung Fu Hustle (*Gongfu*), dir. Stephen Chow, Beijing Film Studio / Columbia Pictures Film Production Asia / Huayi Bros. / Taihe Film Investment, 2004.

Kung Fu Yoga (*Gongfu yujia*), dir. Stanley Tong Gwai-lai, Sparkle Roll Media / Taihe Entertainment / Shinework / Well Go, 2017.

Lady Is the Boss (*Zhangmenren*), dir. Lau Kar-leung, Shaw Bros., 1983.

The Last Message (*Tiancai yu baichi*), dir. Michael Hui, Golden Harvest, 1975.

Legendary Weapons of China (*Shiba ban wuyi*), dir. Lau Kar-leung, Shaw Bros., 1982.

Mad Monkey Kung Fu (*Feng hou*), dir. Lau Kar-leung, Shaw Bros., 1979.

The Magnificent Butcher (*Lin Shirong*), dir. Yuen Woo-ping, Golden Harvest, 1979.

Master of the Drunken Fist: Beggar So, dir. Guo Jianying, 2016, HBO Asia, 2017.

The Miracle Fighters (*Qimen dunjia*), dir. Yuen Woo-ping, Golden Harvest, 1982.

Mr. Vampire (*Jiangshi xiansheng*), dir. Ricky Lau Koon-wai, Bo Ho Films, 1985.

My Young Auntie (*Zhangbei*), dir. Lau Kar-leung, Shaw Bros., 1981.

The Mystery of Chessboxing (*Shuang ma lianhuan*), dir. Joseph Kuo Nan-hong, Hong Hwa International Films, 1979.

Odd Couple (*Boming dandao duoming qiang*), dir. Lau Kar-wing, Gar Bo Films, 1979.

Once a Cop (*Chaoji jihua*), dir. Stanley Tong Gwai-lai, Golden Harvest, 1993.

Once upon a Time in China (*Huang Feihong*), dir. Tsui Hark, Golden Harvest, 1991.

The Pilferer's Progress aka. *Money Crazy* (*Faqianhan*), dir. John Woo, Golden Harvest, 1977.

Police Story (*Jingcha gushi*), dir. Jackie Chan, Golden Way / Paragon Films, 1985.

Police Story II (*Jingcha gushi xuji*), dir. Jackie Chan / Chen Chih-hwa, Golden Way Films, 1988.

Police Story III: Supercop (*Jingcha gushi III: chaoji jingcha*), dir. Stanley Tong Gwai-lai, Golden Harvest, 1992.

Police Story IV: First Strike (*Jingcha gushi IV: zhi jiandan renwu*), dir. Stanley Tong Gwai-lai, Golden Harvest, 1996.

The Private Eyes (*Banjin baliang*), dir. Michael Hui, Golden Harvest, 1976.

The Prodigal Son (*Baijiazi*), dir. Sammo Hung, Golden Harvest, 1981.

Project A (*"A" jihua*), dir. Jackie Chan, Golden Harvest, 1983.

Project A II (*"A" jihua xuji*), dir. Jackie Chan, Golden Harvest, 1987.

Return to the 36th Chamber (*Shaolin dapeng dashi*), dir. Lau Kar-leung, Shaw Bros., 1980.

Royal Tramp (*Luding ji*), dir. Wong Jing, Win's Movie Productions, 1992.

Royal Tramp II (*Luding ji II: zhi shenlong jiao*), dir. Wong Jing, Win's Movie Productions, 1992.

Rumble in the Bronx (*Hongfan qu*), dir. Stanley Tong Gwai-lai, Golden Harvest, 1995.

Rush Hour, dir. Brett Ratner, New Line Cinema / Roger Birnbaum Productions, 1998.

Shanghai Noon, dir. Tom Dey, Touchstone Pictures / Spyglass Entertainment / Roger Birnbaum Productions / Jackie Chan Films, 2000.

Shaolin Drunkard (*Tianshi zhuangxie*), dir. Yuen Woo-ping, First Films Organisation, 1983.

Shaolin Soccer (*Shaolin zuqiu*), dir. Stephen Chow, Universe Entertainment / Star Overseas, 2001.

Skiptrace (*Juedi tao wang*), dir. Renny Harlin, Exclusive Media / Talent International, 2016.

Sleeping Fist (*Shui quan guaizhao*), dir. Teddy Yip, East Asia Film Co., 1979.

Snake in the Eagle's Shadow (*Shexing diaoshou*), dir. Yuen Woo-ping, Seasonal Film Corporation, 1978.

The Spiritual Boxer (*Shenda*), dir. Lau Kar-leung, Shaw Bros., 1975.

Spiritual Boxer II (*Maoshan Jiangshi quan*), dir. Lau Kar-leung, Shaw Bros., 1979.

The Story of Drunken Master (*Zui xia Su Qi'er*), dir. Ngai Ho-fung / Wu Pang, Golden Tripod Film Co., 1979.

Taoism Drunkard (*Guima tianshi*), dir. Yuen Cheung-yan, Lo Wei Motion Picture Co., 1984.

The Thundering Mantis (*Dian tanglang*), dir. Teddy Yip, East Asia Film Co., 1980.

True Legend (*Su Qi'er*), dir. Yuen Woo-ping, China Film Group / Beijing Forbidden City Film Co. / Edko, 2010.

Way of the Dragon (*Menglong guojiang*), dir. Bruce Lee, Concord Productions, 1972.

Who Am I? (*Wo shi shei*), dir. Benny Chan / Jackie Chan, Golden Harvest, 1998.

Wing Chun (*Yongchun*), dir. Yuen Woo-ping, Wo Ping Films, 1994.

Winners & Sinners (*Qimou miaoji wu fuxing*), dir. Sammo Hung, Golden Harvest, 1983.

Yes, Madam! (*Huangjia shijie*), dir. Corey Yuen, D&B Films, 1985.

The Young Master (*Shidi Chuma*), dir. Jackie Chan, Golden Harvest, 1980.

The Young Taoism Fighter (*Yinyang qibing*), dir. Chen Chi-hwa, Lo Wei Motion Picture Co., 1986.

Index

Page numbers in boldface type refer to illustrations

About the Author

Luke White is senior lecturer in visual culture and fine art at Middlesex University, London.